THE
EASTERN
EUROPE
COLLECTION

Title -# LETTERS
FROM THE LEVANT
DURING THE EMBASSY
TO CONSTANTINOPLE 1716-18

(Pierrepont)

Lady Mary Wortley Montagu

ARNO PRESS & THE NEW YORK TIMES
New York - 1971

Reprint Edition 1971 by Arno Press Inc.

Reprinted from a copy in
The Harvard University Library

LC# 71-135825

ISBN 0-405-02767-2

The Eastern Europe Collection
ISBN for complete set: 0-405-02730-3

Manufactured in the United States of America

LETTERS FROM THE LEVANT,

DURING THE

EMBASSY TO CONSTANTINOPLE,

1716—18.

BY

LADY MARY WORTLEY MONTAGU.

WITH

A Preliminary Discourse and Notes,

CONTAINING

A Sketch of her Ladyship's Character, Moral and Literary,

BY

J. A. ST. JOHN, ESQ.

LONDON:

JOSEPH RICKERBY, SHERBOURN LANE,

KING WILLIAM STREET, CITY.

1838.

LONDON:

JOSEPH RICKERBY, PRINTER,
SHERBOURN LANE.

CONTENTS.

𝔓𝔯𝔢𝔩𝔦𝔪𝔦𝔫𝔞𝔯𝔭 𝔇𝔦𝔰𝔠𝔬𝔲𝔯𝔰𝔢.

𝔓𝔯𝔢𝔣𝔞𝔠𝔢, 𝔟𝔭 𝔞 𝔏𝔞𝔡𝔭.

𝔏𝔢𝔱𝔱𝔢𝔯𝔰.

Letters.

8 CONTENTS.

PAGE

Letters.

PRELIMINARY

DISCOURSE.

PRELIMINARY DISCOURSE.

It is by no means my intention to convert these prefatory remarks into a formal memoir. All I here aim at is to convey, by a brief sketch, a correct idea of Lady Montagu's character, moral and literary, which may possibly be rendered somewhat more intelligible by occasional glances at the spirit and manners of her age. Circumstances, partly perhaps accidental, led me several years ago to bestow more than ordinary attention on the writings of this very charming author. Some of her manuscript poetry came into my hands; I included her in the list of " Celebrated Travellers," (¹) whose lives I had undertaken to narrate; she had described, with much vivacity and elegance, a part of the world over which my fancy had always hung enamoured; and her opinions, though not free from prejudice, coincided, I found, with my own, on the nature of that seclusion in which women have always lived in the East.— These were reasons sufficient for my regarding, with more than ordinary interest, the too scanty

---

(¹) Vol. II. pp. 72—102.

relics of her genius, of which I could not intimate a more flattering criticism than by class-
ing them, as I have, among the masterpieces of
English prose composition. Others, too,—and those
no bad judges in literature,—entertain, on the subject of her ladyship's letters, convictions no less
favourable than my own. In fact, they are not
merely read extensively, which is sometimes the
fortune of very bad books, but admiration of them
is generally commensurate with the taste and
talents of their reader.

In addition to these circumstances, may be mentioned the factitious interest excited by the recent
publication of several original letters of her ladyship, which, coming forth at length from the obscurity of desks and escritoires, where they had for
years been buried, have almost the air of things
risen from the dead. But these, it must be confessed, have nothing to do with the present collection. Not a single letter from Constantinople, or
any other part of the Ottoman empire, has been
discovered ; no new anecdotes, no additional information, nothing, in short, has come to light
which at all enlarges our knowledge of what her
ladyship saw or experienced during her brief,
but amusing Oriental peregrinations. Whatever
novelty is found in Lord Wharncliffe's work has
reference solely to Lady Mary's own personal history, before the period of her Eastern travels, or
after her return. She had, in fact, made the most
of everything she possessed relative to the Turks ;
so that we may be satisfied the present volume

contains not only all she ever designed to publish, but all she ever wrote on the subject, with the exception of that private journal which the Countess of Bute thought it necessary to destroy. Therefore, though it may be matter of regret that her observations do not embrace a wider field, we can indulge none on the score that any portion of the picture has perished. It is a bird's-eye view, indeed, but we possess it complete, as it issued from the artist's hands.

It will perhaps be thought, however, that time has diminished the value of Lady Montagu's remarks, which some may suppose to have been superseded by the researches of later and profounder travellers. But this view of the matter would be erroneous. A hundred foreigners might in her own day have passed over the same ground, have beheld the same sights, conversed with the same persons ; and yet not one of the whole number have been able to compose letters like hers. The merit is not in the stuff, but in the workmanship ; or, rather, in the rare union of good fortune and skill, which brought under her eye things worth painting, and enabled her to paint them with matchless felicity. There is a strange fatality in literature. Too often the rude, ignorant incapable, who estimate humanity, as the Turks do beauty, by the ton, are conducted by what is called *luck* over scenes the most interesting upon earth, which they describe *tant bien que mal*, but to the great entertainment of those who know nothing better. On the other hand, it falls, perhaps, to

b 2

the lot of the ablest minds to be confined within
the circle of their own country, where, it is possible,
they have nothing very remarkable to depict; but,
nevertheless, experiencing the lust of making pictures of nature and manners, they pour forth the
riches of their genius upon the things within their
reach, and thus sometimes embalm and give perpe-
tuity to combinations of matter and mental habits,
deserving in themselves of little notice. In Lady
Montagu's case, however, the scene was worthy of
the artist, and the artist of the scene. The portions of Turkey she visited, next to Greece proper,
may be regarded as the most classic spots in
Europe or Asia,—the spots peopled with noblest
associations, rendered illustrious and beautiful to
the imagination by the spells of poetry hitherto
unequalled, and hallowed by regrets for the past
which the experience of every step awakens in the
mind.

The moral and political state of things which
she witnessed has also its charms. It was her lot
to contemplate society in the Ottoman capital at
a period that may almost be considered one of
transition. The magnificence and power of the
Mohammeds and the Suleymans had passed away,
—so likewise, in great measure, had the peculiar
pride and haughty fierceness of the nation, which
had already in part begun to affect that softness
and refined tolerance of manners which, in the
progress of all warlike tribes, replace the rude
self-sufficiency of victorious soldiers. Lady Montagu's friend Ahmed Bey, who would willingly

have initiated her in the mysteries of the Koran, and many other mysteries, at Adrianople, was the prototype of all those Turkish gentlemen, mere reflections of European gentility, whom one now finds in the great cities of the East. Other, though less marked, specimens of the same brood fell in her ladyship's way ; altogether sufficed to show that the Ottomans were no longer what they had been. Indeed, vestiges could even then be discovered of that spirit of innovation and change which has since produced an Abdoul Hamid, a Mahmood, and a Mohammed Ali, though it would be too much to expect to find in Lady Montagu anything distinctly indicative of the advent of these moral revolutionists.

At the period of her visit there was also another peculiarity in Turkish manners, which, though undergoing great and rapid modifications, will no doubt long continue to be characteristic of the nation : I mean the striking contrast presented by the rough, uncouth, turbulent, uncertain existence of the men, and the life of tranquil enjoyment led by the women in the harems. Her ladyship does not, in so many words, point out this very peculiar feature in the ethical economy of the Ottomans ; but her work suggests it, and furnishes many curious illustrations of the way in which it practically works. At the first blush this part of their customs appears to possess advantages over our own. It unquestionably preserves among women a degree of simplicity and softness of manner unknown in those countries where the sexes

jostle rudely against each other, and in studies,
habits, tone, and outward bearing are scarcely dis-
tinguishable. A woman in the East has a woman's
mind, and is not a sort of man in petticoats. Her
experience of the world is limited in the extreme.
She walks abroad, indeed, and can see what is
going on around her, but only as one sees a thea-
trical representation, without approaching nearly,
sometimes without comprehending it. Her children, her husband, her near relations, a small
circle of female friends;—these constitute for her
all that we term society. She does not mingle
with men till she forgets which is which. She does
not dine, sup, drink wine, dance with strangers,
until husband, home and all that it contains become indifferent to her. She is ignorant, indeed,
if you will; but her husband does not discover it;
and for this plain reason,—that he is no wiser himself. Our ladies, of course, are superior, because
they are ours; but if they are more knowing, they
are less women ; and the wight who should hope,
in England, to escape from the din of politics,
and the other exciting topics which disturb him
out of doors, by retiring to the apartments of his
wife, might perhaps find her in conclave with a
troop of attorneys, arranging a plan of operations
for the ensuing election.

But these remarks are merely thrown out by the
way : I proceed with Lady Mary. It will at once
be perceived that if, in communicating her experience to friends in England, she had failed to work
out a series of interesting pictures, it could only

have arisen from lack of power to make a proper use of the materials before her. But in this respect she was not wanting. Nature had endued her mind with singular acuteness, vivacity, quickness, versatility. She could seize at once upon the salient points of most subjects, give the whole a place in her imagination, and reflect it fresh and brilliant, and in all the vividness of truth, upon the minds of others. She could at least do this for the things she generally chose to handle; for, aware that it was not for her to fathom the depths of questions of abstruse learning or recondite philosophy, she felt no inclination to attempt it, and was thus spared the mortification of defeat and failure.

There is, nevertheless, much useful philosophy in Lady Montagu's Letters. Not formal, indeed, or appearing in set dissertations ; but scattered up and down, amid descriptions of the gayest objects, scandalous anecdotes, or lively disquisitions on dress. But this is chiefly true of her early letters, those, for example, from the East, and the several places she visited on the way to it : for her philosophy was the fruit of temperament. So long as she was herself happy in the possession of high health and animal spirits, the physical satisfaction she enjoyed overflowed abundantly into her style, and gave it life, gave it buoyancy, gave it all those nameless graces which cluster round the creation of a mind perfectly at ease, on good terms with itself, and with the world also, and seeking nothing so eagerly as opportunities for giving vent to the pent-up waters of delight. Hence the indefinable charm of

these compositions. It is like walking in the morning over sunlit hills, while every leaf is dewy, and
every copse ringing with the matin anthems of the
birds. There are breezes about us impregnated
with perfume, and as we breathe them our fancy
puts forth its wings, and bears us away to scenes
glowing with all the warmth of the south.

But she outlived all this. Like most other vo-
taries of fashion and pleasure, she soon learned to
look with a cynical eye upon the world ; and her
style and manner immediately partook of the chill
communicated to her feelings. Once passed the
meridian of life, she grew morose and misanthro-
pical. Her old friends,—in many cases become enemies,—were overwhelmed with ridicule, which, if
there existed no positive breach, was poured on them
in secret, and, if a quarrel had taken place, was
converted into the fiercest sarcasm and most un-
sparing hatred. If truth would furnish weapons
for carrying on the warfare, she would accept of
its alliance, and fight beneath its banner; if not,
she had recourse to falsehood ; for her object was
revenge, and, so that could be obtained, it mattered
little how. The fault, no doubt, was shared by
most persons of rank and fashion in her time. Pro-
fligacy of every kind was the order of the day. Few
persons of any pretensions to distinction knew, or
apparently cared to know, whose children their
wives laid at their door. From the king, who
counted every courtier's wife as an inmate of his harem, down to the most insignificant lord in waiting,
there prevailed an utter contempt for morals and

decency; virtue, there was none; and, as truth never lags behind the other celestial visitants of the breast, it was not to be expected that any one, and least of all a wit like Lady Montagu, should pay the slightest regard to the justice or verity of what the tongue uttered.

This consideration constitutes, it must be confessed, a drawback from the pleasure which her writings afford. She stands before us like Envy, brandishing her sting, wounding right and left, every person who falls in her way, but more especially the young and beautiful, whom she detested for having supplanted her. But this happened somewhat late in life, when grey hairs, and the lassitude attendant on constant intrigue, had driven her abroad, an exile from those spots,

> Where round and round the ghosts of beauty glide,
> And haunt the places where their honour died;

and led the faded favourite of a court to conceal her own spectral features from herself beneath a mask. Comparatively little of this spirit will be discovered in the present volume; and what little is visible refers less to any imperfections in phy-, sical form, than to the moral character. The latter, she knew, was her own weak point. It was therefore painful to her to cherish the belief in sublime female ethics, of which she could not, without considerable self-reproach, admit the existence. But with respect to beauty the case was different. She possessed in a very high degree those graces of figure, blandishments of mien, and alluring charac-

teristics of feature, which, if they be not the τὸ
καλὸν, are very closely allied to it, and often, even
among good judges, pass muster in its stead. Hence
another and a peculiar charm in her earlier correspondence.   It is full of pictures of feminine loveli-
ness, dashed off with strokes of fire, infinitely too glowing to be supposed to have proceeded from one woman speaking of another. Look, for example, at
her full-length likeness of the Empress of Austria,
of Fatima, and the girls, who, like the daughters of
Herodias, danced before her. Can anything be less
feminine, and yet more chaste and beautiful than
her splendid raptures, cast into the composition to
supply the place of description, when the language
sunk under the accumulation of her surprise and
admiration ?

Contemplating these I can never be at a loss to
account for the extraordinary popularity of these
letters. We are all affected through the medium
of the imagination, and their ministers, the senses ;
and what they both concur to recommend, can need
no other passport. Besides, in addition to those
longer passages where she employs all the resources
of art to fascinate the reader, there are a thousand
others, where, as if without design, hurried glimpses
of beauty, are snatched Actæon-like, but without
Actæon's danger, amid the marble baths, cool kiosks,
and odoriferous gardens of the East. Among these,
the scene in the Hammams of Sophia may be enu-
merated. Nothing could be more admirably managed. An inferior writer, or one more a slave to
the senses than to fame, would infallibly have

spoiled it. We should have been offended with grossness, or with the affectation of mystery; there would have been hints, abrupt pauses, asterisks; a great show of reluctance to achieve a picture designedly begun; much simpering, and many blushes. Lady Montagu takes refuge in simplicity and truth; and a vision of fairies sporting on the moonlit margin of the ocean, unconscious of the existence of mankind, could not be more chaste or more poetical than her picture of those Turkish ladies, placed before us in the costume of Eve, and with all Eve's modesty. This is high merit, and would that I could attribute it to her on all occasions! Lord Wharncliffe, with praiseworthy tenderness for the reputation of his ancestress, seeks to palliate her too frequent want of delicacy, by tracing it to the taste and habits of the times in which she lived. "With regard to that correspondence" (with Lady Mar,) he observes, "it cannot be denied that parts are written with a freedom of expression which would not be tolerated in the present day; and those parts may, perhaps, be deemed sometimes to trespass beyond the bounds of strict delicacy. The reader must, however, bear in mind, that these letters were written as confidential communications *from one sister to another*, at a period when the feeling upon such subjects was by no means so nice as it is at present; and that expressions with which we now find great fault, might then be used by persons of the greatest propriety of conduct, and would only be considered as painting freely, and more keenly ridiculing, the vices and

follies of the society in which the writer found herself, and not as used for the purpose of indulging
in grossness of language. So considered, it is hoped
that the publishing of these letters as they were
written will not be objected to ; while, on the other
hand, they abound in the wit and talent so peculiar
to Lady Mary, and it would have been very difficult to alter or curtail them without injury to their
spirit."

Should the reader not be convinced by these arguments, I confess he will be exactly in the same predicament with me. Both wit and satire may, in my
humble opinion, flourish extremely well without
grossness of language ; and the propensities of her
contemporaries for grossness had much less influence,
I fear, on Lady Mary than her own. Still, they no
doubt served to keep her dereliction of delicacy in
countenance ; for, when the majority do wrong, we
can always shelter our own frailties under the broad
projection of general example. But, however this
may be, we need not reject what is good because
something of inferior quality is mingled with it.
Most writers of former ages have erred on this very
point. To Shakspeare, to Spenser, to Chaucer,
nay, even to Milton, the noblest of them all, more
or less of coarseness may be objected ; and if intel-
lects like these, filled with a world of thought
worthy of the purest dwellings among the golden
spheres of the firmament, could not wholly, in the
elaboration of their works, escape the taint of earth,
who could hope to find Lady Montagu resist the
infection : more especially as her character, taste,

and temperament powerfully seconded the influence of external circumstances ?

To understand, however, the nature of that influence, and the channels through which it operated on her mind, we must consider a little in detail the elements of her education, and the peculiar position she occupied in the world. There is a vast fund of charity in human nature. When people discover anything amiss in an individual respecting whose merits they are required to come to some decision, their first impulse is to look about for some other person, or persons, upon whom they may shift a portion, at least, of the blame; and if they do not readily find such, then they have recourse to the combination óf events, to that fatal chain of causes and effects which encircles every human creature, and is often supposed irresistibly to determine the very form and colour of our lives. In Lady Montagu's case, some, because she read Latin, have traced to that her masculine tastes, and the grossness into which they sometimes degenerated. They conclude, apparently, that the learned languages enjoy a monopoly of this kind of ware, and that all who obtain the key which admits into those ancient sanctuaries must infallibly be polluted by the rich, mysterious, but somewhat luxurious imagery which there meets the eye in every dusky chamber and mouldering recess. But in learning as in travelling different eyes dwell on very different things. Imagine a knot of visitors descending into the subterranean palaces of Thebes, called the Tombs of the Kings, and observe how they will distribute and employ

themselves. The poetical, the imaginative, they
who yearn after immortality, and traverse with flut-
tering hearts, and aspiring desires the vestibule of
death, flock instinctively about the mystic groups
which seem to open up vistas into the realms of
Hades, and all those shadowy transactions that people the regions beyond the grave. All, however,
will not be attracted by the same objects. To the
worldly-minded, gross, sensual gnome, those portions
of the paintings which belong to the rites of Athor,
will prove far more interesting than the recondite
symbols connected with the loftier dogmas of religion. On these he will dwell, to these he will again
and again return ; and he will perhaps issue from
the tombs with a mind more depraved than he entered with.

It is just so with learning. " To the pure, all
things are pure ;" and *vice versa ;* so that nothing
can be more absurd than to trace to a source external to the mind, habits of thought and peculiarities
of feeling evidently intransmissible, depending probably for their complete developement on accident,
but referrible originally to the native bent and complexion of the character. With regard to Lady
Montagu's Latin, I should say that its influence,
little or great, was good as far as it went. It furnished her faculties with employment, and fostered
habits of application ; and thus, by calling into
activity the powers of the understanding, weakened
those more dangerous ones of the imagination,
which, in a fiery temperament like hers, require
some strong curb.

If any circumstance in her education is to be particularly lamented, it is, that, by the early death of her mother, she was deprived of her best guide, and abandoned to the direction of almost the worst she could have had; since her father, a mere man of pleasure, comprehended no more than one of his horses, the nature or design of female intellectual training, and the more he had meddled with it, would only have spoiled it the more. From all the evidence now remaining on the subject it appears that, though, when somewhat older, his children were sources of anything but gratification to the Earl, afterwards Duke of Kingston, yet Lady Mary, at least, was at first quite a favourite. In proof of this Lord Wharncliffe tells a good story, with which the reader cannot fail to be amused:—"A trifling incident, which Lady Mary loved to recall, will prove how much she was the object of Lord Kingston's pride and fondness in her childhood. As a leader of the fashionable world, and a strenuous Whig in party, he of course belonged to the Kit-cat Club. One day, at a meeting to choose toasts for the year, a whim seized him to nominate her, then not eight years old, a candidate; alleging that she was far prettier than any lady on the list. The other members demurred, because the rules of the club forbade them to elect a beauty whom they had never seen. 'Then you shall see her,' cried he; and in the gaiety of the moment, sent orders home to have her finely dressed, and brought to him at the tavern; where she was received with acclamations, her claim unanimously allowed, her health drunk by every one present, and her name engraved in due form upon a drinking glass. The company consisted of some of the most eminent men in England : she went from the lap of one poet, or patriot, or statesman, to the arms of another ; was feasted with sweetmeats, overwhelmed with caresses, and, what perhaps already pleased her better than either, heard her wit and beauty loudly extolled on every side. Pleasure, she said, was too poor a word to express her sensations ; they amounted to ecstacy : never again throughout her whole future life, did she pass so happy a day. Nor, indeed, could she ; for the love of admiration which this scene was calculated to excite or increase, could never again be so fully gratified : there is always some alloying ingredient in the cup, some drawback upon the triumphs of grown people. Her father carried on the frolic, and, we may conclude, confirmed the taste, by having her picture painted for the club-room, that she might be enrolled a regular toast."

This anecdote at once lets us into the secret of the man's character, and, at the same time, shows how unnecessary it is to have recourse to the roundabout way of Latin, in order to account for the introduction and prevalence of certain trains of thought in her mind. Initiated in the mysteries of a tavern-club, enrolled a member of it, her name engraved on a drinking-glass, and her imagination familiarized with the orgies celebrated in those days by aristocratic Bacchanals, she could have nothing to learn from Ovid or Catullus, from Horace or Lucretius, from Persius or Juvenal. But whatever she learned, her labours were voluntary. Nothing was forced upon her; for there appears to be no foundation for the supposition that she was bred up with her brother, and taught the learned languages by the same tutor. In fact, from every part of her works, it is abundantly clear that she understood nothing of Greek; and even in Roman literature had never proceeded much beyond the threshold. But by this I mean no reproach. In an age when women in general studied scarcely at all, and received no instruction beyond what is now bestowed on cooks and housemaids, it was no little merit to step voluntarily beyond the circle, and acquire even the slightest tincture of classical knowledge.

Mr. Dallaway, however, takes a different view of her ladyship's acquirements. He is satisfied with nothing less than superiority in scholarship over Lady Jane Grey, the Duchess of Norfolk, and Lady Lumley. There is, indeed, something like ambiguity in his decision,—for, while claiming *more* learning for her ladyship, he admits that she had *less*, which is very ingenuous;—but then, in order to have the advantage over his adversaries somewhere, he contends that, if her knowledge was more limited, she nevertheless made a much better use of what she did know. "A comparison with her ladyship's predecessors of her own sex and quality will redound to her superiority. Lady Jane Grey read Plato in Greek, and the two daughters of the last Fitzalan, Earl of Arundel, the Duchess of Norfolk, and Lady Lumley, translated and published books from that language; but this

c

was the learning of the cloister, and not that of
the world. Nearer her own time, the Duchess of
Newcastle composed folios of romances, but her
imaginary personages are strangers to this lower
sphere, and are disgusting by their pedantry
and unnatural manners. Lady Mary Wortley
Montagu applied her learning to improve her
knowledge of the world. She read mankind as she
had read her books, with sagacity and discrimina-
tion. The influence of a classical education over
her mind was apparent in the purity of her style,
rather than in the ambition of displaying her acquirements, whilst it enabled her to give grace of
expression and novelty to maxims of morality or
prudence, which would have lost much of their usefulness, had they been communicated in a less
agreeable manner."

Lord Wharncliffe takes a much abler view of the
matter, and, I am persuaded, a far truer one. He
describes her ladyship's studies as undertaken
spontaneously, and irregularly sketched out ; but,
pursued with a vehemence and passion, never experienced save where the mind is grasping at what
it loves. An enlightened guide, whose advice
should have been esteemed and acted on, might no
doubt have proved of considerable service ; but as the
flesh of tame animals, which feed in prescribed pastures, and within certain fixed limits, is less sweet
than that of the wild and free, which roam and graze
over the unconfined domains of nature, so the knowledge we ourselves gather, while following the
promptings of appetite, is generally of a superior

quality to that which is crammed into our memories
by masters and tutors. The one, preferred from
some concealed affinity to the character of the mind,
blends happily with its experience, of which it
seems to form a part; the other remains for ever
distinct, a jewelled patch, perchance, on a tattered
robe,—glittering, gorgeous, but egregiously out of
place.

It has by some been conjectured that Lady Mary
was fortunate enough to possess such a guide
as I have hinted at above; nay, two; which,
perhaps, she found less advantageous than half
that degree of good fortune might have proved.
"She probably had some assistance from Mr.
William Fielding, her mother's brother, a man of
parts, who perceived her capacity, corresponded
with her, and encouraged her pursuit of information.
And she herself acknowledges her obligations to
Bishop Burnet for 'condescending to direct the
studies of a girl.' Nevertheless, though labouring
to acquire what may be termed masculine knowledge, and translating under the Bishop's eye, the
Latin version of Epictetus, she was by no means
disposed to neglect works of fancy and fiction, but
got by heart all the poetry that came in her way,
and indulged herself in the luxury of reading every
romance as yet invented. For she possessed, and
left after her, the whole library of Mrs. Lennox's
Female Quixote,—Cleopatra, Cassandra, Clelia,
Cyrus, Pharamond, Ibrahim, &c. &c.—all like the
Lady Arabella's collection, ' Englished,' mostly by
' persons of honour.' The chief favourite appeared

to have been a translation of Monsieur Honoré
d'Urfe's Astrea, once the delight of Henri Quatre
and his court, and still admired and quoted by the
savans who flourished under Louis XIV.   In a
blank page of this massive volume, (which might
have counterbalanced a pig of lead of the same
size,) Lady Mary had written in her fairest youth-
ful hand the names and characteristic qualities of
the chief personages thus : 'The beautiful Diana,
the volatile Climene, the melancholy Doris, Cela-
don the faithful, Adamas the wise,' and so on ;
forming two long columns."

Among her ladyship's favourite books([2]) there was

([2]) The names of several are given by Lord Wharncliffe.—
" From the books Lady Mary died possessed of, which were but
few, she appears to have been particularly fond of that ancient English drama lately revived among us ; for she had several volumes
of differently sized, and wretchedly printed plays bound up together,
such as the Duke of Roxburghe would have bought at any price,
the works of Shirley, Ford, Marston, Heywood, Webster and
the rest, as far back as Gammer Gurton's Needle, and coming
down to the trash of Durfey.   But Lillo's domestic tragedies
were what she most admired ; for ' My lady used to declare,'
said the old servant so often quoted, ' that whoever did not cry at
George Barnwell must deserve to be hanged.'   And she passed
the same sentence on people who could see unmoved the fine scene
between Dorax and Sebastian, in Dryden, who was also one of
her favourite authors.   She had his plays, his fables, and his
Virgil, in folio, as they were first published ; Theobald's edition
of Shakspeare, manifestly much read ; and Tonson's quarto Milton.   Besides Cowley, Waller, Denham, &c., there were some
less known poets, some of an earlier age, such as Suckling and
Drayton.   Nothing further can be called to mind, except the outward shape of three ultra-sized volumes, the works of Margaret,
Duchess of Newcastle."

one which held the same place in my own boyish estimation : the " History of Hiempsal, King of Numidia," which, though she had read many a long-winded romance, appeared to her, " beautiful beyond them all." To her latest hour she used to regret having lost sight of this book; but without cause, for, had she found what she sought, it would only have been to discover how extravagantly her young judgment had erred. Rousseau entertained a similar admiration for some rude village lay he had often heard in his boyhood, scraps of which,— halves or quarters of verses,—dwelt all his life long upon his memory, suggesting beautiful thoughts by the power of association. But he was too wise ever to procure a complete copy of the ballad, which might probably have dissipated at once and for ever one of the few illusions that rendered life sweet to him.

From her own letters something may be learned, though not enough, of the society in which it was at first her lot to exhibit her extraordinary accomplishments ; and few will deny that it was casting pearls before swine. For rude in every respect our ancestors were; gross in their feeding, grosser in their thoughts. Women held a low rank among them. They had not within many degrees approached the point we ourselves have in this respect attained. Among the rich and noble a fine woman was reckoned an agreeable courtezan, among the poor an useful beast of burden. Few, very few, even among wits and philosophers, had elevated their imaginations to the true point of view, in which woman, where all her mental and moral qualities are brought into play, is regarded as the highest culminating point of humanity, the most beautiful thing in an universe of beauty, the nearest approach we know to that perfect state of existence to be enjoyed in a better world.

From studying the poets and the philosophers, old or new, Lady Mary, like every other lady of those days, was compelled to pass to the study of carving a joint; an useful accomplishment to the mother of a family where assistance is not to be obtained; but absurd in persons who could have kept a practical anatomist of this kind expressly for the purpose. Lord Wharncliffe shows up the ridicule of the practice with much effect :—

" Some particulars, in themselves too insignificant to be worth recording, may yet interest the curious, by setting before them the manners of their ancestors.—Lord Dorchester having no wife to do the honours of his table at Thoresby, imposed that task upon his eldest daughter, as soon as she had bodily strength for the office : which in those days required no small share. For the mistress of a country mansion was not only to invite—that is, urge and tease—her company to eat more than human throats could conveniently swallow, but to carve every dish, when chosen, with her own hands,—the greater the lady, the more indispensable the duty. Each joint was carried up in its turn, to be operated upon by her, and by her alone ;—since the peers and knights on either hand were so far from being bound to offer their assistance, that the very master of the house, posted opposite to her, might not operate as her croupier; his department was to push the bottle after dinner. As for the crowd of guests, the most inconsiderable among them,—the curate, the subaltern, or squire's younger brother,—if suffered by her neglect to help himself to a slice of the mutton placed before him, would have chewed it in bitterness, and gone home an affronted man, half inclined to give a wrong vote at the next election. There were then professed carving-masters, who taught young ladies the art scientifically; from one of whom Lady Mary said she took lessons three times a week, that she might be perfect on her father's public days; when, in order to perform her functions without interruption, she was forced to eat her own dinner alone an hour or two beforehand."

The fate of these ignorant ladies was generally to be made the prey of the other sex. With minds unfurnished, and passions undisciplined, they went forth into the world, relying, when they possessed any, on their personal attractions, which were to stand them instead of knowledge and principle, and commonly concluded by filling the scandalous chronicles of the times with their disreputable adventures and melancholy end. Most of the ladies who figure in the pages of Lady Mary belonged to the class which in a virtuous community would be condemned to wear a badge of distinction. The court overflowed with creatures of this ambiguous genus; that is, with women who, without the slightest pretensions to character, occupied situations where respectability should be

looked for. Courts in general are anything but
schools of morality. For princes usually consider
themselves elevated by their position above the
necessity of practising the duties which other men
are required to fulfil, and accordingly set those
around them an example too readily followed.
To converse with them, in most cases, a woman
must place her modesty in abeyance. To inhabit
their palaces is to be polluted. Even the man
whom our political church enrolls among its mar-
tyrs was in conversation so lewd and depraved
that no woman of delicacy could be in his company without pain.

This being the general rule, therefore, we are
not surprised at the extreme laxity of morals that
prevailed at the court of George I., of which Lady
Montagu has drawn an interesting and animated,
if not a very edifying picture. In fact, this royal
coterie, consisting of the " king's playfellows, *male*
and female," could not have fallen into better
hands. She possessed all the acuteness and sagacity necessary for penetrating into their characters,
together with the talent to describe them in their
true colours, from which she was not at all deterred
by any foolish qualms of good nature. On the
contrary, it evidently afforded her pleasure to hold
them up to the contempt of posterity. She loved
the employment, and, when many others offered
themselves, selected it in preference, as one more
congenial to her feelings, and better suited to her
powers. And, in truth, there is considerable amusement in such sketches of what is enacted in the
green-room, and behind the scenes, by the actors

in that pompous and expensive drama by which
the old and vicious communities of Europe have
been for so many generations amused.

Her ladyship, writing with her usual freedom,
and careful not to attribute to any man more good
qualities than she could help, observes, that " when
King George ascended the throne, he was surrounded by all his German ministers and playfellows male and female. Baron Goritz was the
most considerable among them both for birth and
fortune. He had managed the king's treasury for
thirty years, with the utmost fidelity and economy;
and had the true German honesty, being a plain,
sincere, and unambitious man. Bernstoff, the secretary, was of a different turn. He was avaricious,
artful, and designing; and had got his share in
the king's councils by bribing his women. Robo-
tun was employed in these matters, and had the
sanguine ambition of a Frenchman. He resolved
there should be an English ministry of his choosing; and, knowing none of them personally but
Townshend, he had not failed to recommend him
to his master, and his master to the king, as the
only proper person for the important post of
secretary of state; and he entered upon that office
with universal applause, having at that time a
very popular character, which he might probably
have retained for ever if he had not been entirely
governed by his wife and her brother, Robert Walpole, whom he immediately advanced to be pay-
master, esteemed a post of exceeding profit, and
very necessary for his indebted estate.

" But he had yet higher views, or rather he found it necessary to move higher, lest he should not be able to keep that. The Earl of Wharton, now marquis, both hated and despised him. His large estate, the whole income of which was spent in the service of the party, and his own parts, made him considerable ; though his profligate life lessened that weight that a more regular conduct would have given him.

" Lord Halifax, who was now advanced to the dignity of earl, and graced with the garter, and first commissioner of the treasury, treated him with contempt. The Earl of Nottingham, who had the real merit of having renounced the ministry in Queen Anne's reign, when he thought they were going to alter the succession, was not to be reconciled to Walpole, whom he looked upon as stigmatized for corruption.

" The Duke of Marlborough, who in his old age was making the same figure at court that he did when he first came into it,—I mean, bowing and smiling in the antechamber while Townshend was in the closet,—was not, however, pleased with Walpole, who began to behave to him with the insolence of new favour; and his duchess, who never restrained her tongue in her life, used to make public jokes of the beggary she first knew him in, when her caprice gave him a considerable place, against the opinion of Lord Godolphin and the Duke of Marlborough.

" To balance these, he had introduced some

friends of his own, by his recommendation to Lord
Townshend (who did nothing but by his instiga-
tion.)   Colonel Stanhope was made the other
secretary of state.   He had been unfortunate in
Spain, and there did not want those who attributed it to ill conduct; but he was called generous,
brave, true to his friends, and had an an air of probity
which prejudiced the world in his favour."

The king's own character she paints with peculiar felicity, and from intimate knowledge and experience.   She had, moreover, no theory to make
out.   Her object was simply literary ambition;
for she designed her pictures for the press; and,
from what had happened to other persons who, in
other reigns, had left papers behind them, foresaw
clearly what would come to pass in her own case.
We may therefore place the firmer reliance on
what is said, and it requires no extraordinary
sagacity to reflect how great must be the happiness
of a people whose government is directed by indi-
viduals of the calibre and principles of George I.;
and how much religion and morality must be
benefited by the example of so very upright and
pious, and decorous a prince. " The king's character may be comprised in very few words.   In
private life he would have been called an honest
blockhead ; and Fortune, that made him a king,
added nothing to his happiness, only prejudiced
his honesty, and shortened his days.   No man was
ever more free from ambition; he loved money, but
loved to keep his own, without being rapacious
of other men's.   He would have grown rich by

saving, but was incapable of laying schemes for
getting; he was more properly dull than lazy,
and would have been so well contented to have
remained in his little town of Hanover, that if the
ambition of those about him had not been greater
than his own, we should never have seen him in
England; and the natural honesty of his temper,
joined with the narrow notions of a low education,
made him look upon his acceptance of the crown
as an act of usurpation, which was always uneasy
to him. But he was carried by the stream of the
people about him, in that, as in every action of
his life. He could speak no English, and was past
the age of learning it. Our customs and laws
were all mysteries to him, which he neither tried
to understand, nor was capable of understanding
if he had endeavoured it. He was passively good-
natured, and wished all mankind enjoyed quiet,
if they would let him do so. The mistress that
followed him hither was so much of his own
temper, that I do not wonder at the engagement
between them. She was duller than himself, and
consequently did not find out that he was so; and
had lived in that figure at Hanover almost forty
years, (for she came hither at threescore,) without
meddling in any affairs of the electorate; content
with the small pension he allowed her, and the
honour of his visits when he had nothing else to
do, which happened very often. She even refused
coming hither at first, fearing that the people of
England, who, she thought, were accustomed to
use their kings barbarously, might chop off his

head in the first fortnight; and had not love or
gratitude enough to venture being involved in his
ruin.   And the poor man was in peril of coming
hither without knowing where to pass his even-
ings; which he was accustomed to do in the apartments of women, free from business.   But Madame
Kilmansegg saved him from this misfortune.   She
was told that Mademoiselle Schulenberg scrupled
at this terrible journey ; and took the opportunity
of offering her service to his Majesty, who willingly
accepted of it; though he did not offer to facilitate
it to her by the payment of her debts, which made
it very difficult for her to leave Hanover without
the permission of her creditors.   But she was a
woman of wit and spirit, and knew very well of
what importance this step was to her fortune.   She
got out of the town in disguise, and made the best
of her way in a post-chaise to Holland, from
whence she embarked with the king, and arrived
at the same time with him in England; which
was enough to make her called his mistress, or
at least so great a favourite that the whole court
began to pay her uncommon respect."

Next in importance is the character of that adventurous old courtezan, Madame Kilmansegg,
which forms a very proper pendante to that of
his most gracious Majesty.   We have seen above
that, although he accepted very readily of her
services, the praiseworthy devotion to his pleasures
which she displayed could make no impression on
his purse, so that, to enjoy the honour of accompa-
nying him, she was compelled to make use of all her

ingenuity in cheating her creditors. What George I.
might have been, had fortune confined him to a
private station, it would of course be difficult to
decide : a blockhead, possibly, but I much question
whether he would have been an honest one ; for if
the being a prince could not protect him from
becoming accessary to what, in vulgar English,
would be denominated swindling, it is not easy to
believe that he would have escaped the influence
of still greater temptations.

To proceed, however, with Madame Kilmansegg :—" This lady deserves I should be a little particular in her character, there being something in
it worth speaking of. She was past forty : she
had never been a beauty, but certainly very agreeable in her person when adorned by youth ; and
had once appeared so charming to the King, that it
was said the divorce and ruin of the beautiful Princess, the Duke of Zell's daughter, was owing to the
hopes her mother (who was declared mistress to
the King's father, and all-powerful in his court,)
had of setting her daughter in her place ; and that
the project did not succeed by the passion which
Madame Kilmansegg took for M. Kilmansegg, who
was son of a merchant of Hamburg, and after having a child by him, there was nothing left for her
but to marry him. Her ambitious mother ran mad
with the disappointment, and died in that deplorable
manner, leaving forty thousand pounds, which she
had heaped by the favour of the Elector, to this
daughter ; which was very easily squandered by one
of her temper. She was both luxurious and generous,

devoted to her pleasures, and seemed to have taken
Lord Rochester's resolution of avoiding all sorts of
self-denial.   She had a greater vivacity in conversation than ever I knew in a German of either sex.
She loved reading and had a taste of all polite
learning.   Her humour was easy and sociable.
Her constitution inclined her to gallantry.   She
was well-bred and amusing in company.   She
knew both how to please and be pleased, and had
experience enough to know it was hard to do either
without money.   Her unlimited expenses had left
her with very little remaining, and she made what
haste she could to make advantage of the opinion
the English had of her power with the King, by
receiving the presents that were made her from all
quarters; and which she knew very well must
cease when it was known that the King's idleness
carried him to her lodgings without either regard for her advice, or affection for her person,
which time and very bad paint had left without
any of the charms which had once attracted
him.   His best-beloved mistress remained still at
Hanover, which was the beautiful Countess of
Platen."

Before we complete the picture of the king's
harem, it may be worth while to expose a palpable
fallacy which occurs in the passage immediately
ensuing.   Speaking of the Countess of Platen,
" perhaps," says Lady Mary, " *it will be thought* a
digression in this place to tell the story of his
amour with her ; but, *as I write only for myself*, I
shall always think I am at liberty to make what

digressions I think fit, *proper or improper ;* besides
that, in my opinion, nothing can set the king's
character in a clearer light." Now it demands no
particular sagacity to detect the absurdity of sophis-
try like this. Palpable contradiction lies on the
very surface of it. Pretending to write only *for
herself,* she says, " it will perhaps *be thought,"* &c.
But, if others besides herself were not to see what
she wrote, how were they to think any thing about
the matter ? Besides, people do not write for
themselves, whatever they may say ; and, if they
did so, would most unquestionably never pause to
consider whether what flowed from the pen would
fall under the denomination of a digression, or not.
It is clear, therefore, that Lady Montagu designed
her Memoir for the public, as, indeed, she did
every thing else that she wrote; and only coquetted
with the reader, or sought to excuse her unfeminine freedom of language, when she pretended to
be labouring solely for her own amusement.

I now proceed with the king's " playthings," two
of whom had the advantage of being very nearly
related to each other. For the Countess of Platen,
we are informed, " was married to Madame Kilmansegg's brother, the most considerable man in
Hanover for birth and fortune ; and her beauty
was as far beyond that of any of the other women
that appeared. However, the king saw her every
day without taking notice of it, and contented
himself with his habitual commerce with Made-
Schulenberg.

" In those little courts there is no distinction of

much value but what arises from the favour of the
prince; and Madame Platen saw with great indignation that all her charms were passed over un-
regarded; and she took a method to get over this
misfortune which would never have entered into
the head of a woman of sense, and yet which met
with wonderful success. She asked an audience
of his Highness, who granted it without guessing
what she meant by it; and she told him that as
nobody could refuse her the first rank in that
place, it was very mortifying to see his Highness
not show her any mark of favour; and, as no
person could be more attached to his person than
herself, she begged with tears in her fine eyes that
he would alter his behaviour to her. The Elector,
very much astonished at this complaint, answered
that he did not know any reason he had given her
to believe he was wanting in respect for her, and
that he thought her not only the greatest lady, but
the greatest beauty of the court. ' If that be true,
sire,' replied she, sobbing, ' why do you pass all
your time with Mademoiselle Schulenberg, while I
hardly receive the honour of a visit from you?'
His Higness promised to mend his manners, and
from that time was very assiduous in waiting upon
her. This ended in a fondness, which her husband disliked so much that he parted with her; and
she had the glory of possessing the heart and person of her master, and to turn the whole stream of
courtiers that used to attend Mademoiselle Schulenberg to her side. However, he did not break with
his first love, and often went to her apartment to

d

cut paper, which was his chief employment there; which the Countess of Platen easily permitted him, having often occasion for his absence. She was naturally gallant; and, after having thus satisfied her ambition, pursued her warmer inclinations."

Great people, as we learn from history, are always mixed up at court with very little people, who perform for them their dirty work, and commonly contrive to rise by it. In fact, the way to fortune in all monarchies lies through subservience and meanness. Every courtier is more or less a Cleon, whose Indian-rubber conscience will stretch to any dimensions, and recover its elasticity, in a moment. We read the history of the majority of the breed in that of Mr. Craggs, whose father exercised in those immaculate regions the office of pimp and procurer, first for royalty itself, and afterwards for the Duke of Marlborough, [3] or any one who could

---

[3] Lord Wharncliffe has several very characteristic anecdotes of the Duchess, whom Pope has immortalized under the name of Atossa, and whose correspondence is just now brought before the public:—

"She was extremely communicative, and it need not be added, proportionably entertaining; thus far, too, very fair and candid,—she laboured at no self-vindication, but told facts just as they were, or as she believed them to be, with an openness and honesty that almost redeemed her faults; though this might partly proceed from never thinking herself in the wrong, or caring what was thought of her by others. She had still, at great age, considerable remains of beauty, most expressive eyes, and the finest fair hair imaginable, the colour of which she said she had preserved unchanged by the constant use of honey-water, —hardly snch as perfumers now sell, for that has an unlucky aptitude to turn the hair grey. By this superb head of hair hung a tale, an instance of her waywardness and violence, which

pay. By these means, with "a very uncommon genius, a head well turned for calculation, and great industry," he contrived to work himself upward from the rank of footman to a courtezan of quality, to a situation of no small distinction, from whence his son by similar arts ascended until he became secretary of state.

Madame Kilmansegg, who possessed more power

(strange to say) she took particular pleasure in telling. None of her charms, when they were at the proudest height, had been so fondly prized by the poor duke her husband. Therefore, one day, upon his offending her by some act of disobedience to her '*strong sovereign will*,'* the bright thought occurred, as she sat considering how she could plague him most, that it would be a hearty vexation to see his favourite tresses cut off. Instantly the deed was done; she cropped them short, and laid them in an antechamber he must pass through to enter her apartment. But, to her cruel disappointment, he passed, enterred, and repassed, calm enough to provoke a saint; neither angry nor sorrowful; seemingly quite unconscious both of his crime and his punishment. Concluding he must have overlooked the hair, she ran to secure it. Lo! it had vanished; and she remained in great perplexity the rest of the day. The next, as he continued silent, and her looking-glass spoke the change a rueful one, she began for once to think she had done rather a foolish thing. Nothing more ever transpired upon the subject until after the duke's death, when she found her beautiful ringlets carefully laid by in a cabinet where he kept whatever he held most precious: and at this point of the story she regularly fell a-crying."

"She laid claim to a portion of her late husband's personal estate, and the affair could only be settled by what is called an amicable suit : but for a suit with her to go on *amicably* was a thing about as likely as for an oil-shop set on fire to be slow in burning; so the flame no sooner kindled than she insisted upon giving it full vent, and amused the world by pleading her own

* ———————— ' Highly crested pride,
Strong sovereign will, and some desire to chide.'—
Parnell's Rise of Woman.

and stood higher through her vices than any honest woman in the kingdom, carried on a flourishing trade in places. Speaking of the republic of Venice, Lady Montagu observes in her letters that in such forms of government women are all powerful; and she means virtuous women. Their influence, however, whatever be their character, is generally mischievous in politics; but, as in the court of

---

cause in the court of Chancery. Among the property disputed was the famous diamond-hilted sword. ' That sword,' said she to the court emphatically, ' that sword *my* lord would have carried to the gates of Paris. Am I to live to see the diamonds picked off one by one, and lodged at the pawnbroker's ?' The new duke's habits of squandering and running in debt gave force to the sarcasm ; yet people smiled when they recollected that his younger brother, Jack Spencer, who, besides equalling him in these respects, * made the town ring with some wild frolic every day, kept a fast hold of the old lady's favour all the while, and in her eyes could do nothing wrong.

"One more of her descendants must be named,—Lady Anne Egerton, the deceased Lady Bridgewater's only daughter, married first to Wriothesly, Duke of Bedford, and secondly to Lord Jersey. This lady inherited such a share of her grandmother's imperial spirit, as to match her pretty fairly, and insure daggers' drawing as soon as it should find time and opportunity to display itself. But, ere the stormy season set in, the granddame had acquired her picture ; which she afterwards made a monument of vengeance, in no vulgar or ordinary mode. She did not give it away ; nor sell it to a broker ; nor send it up to a lumber-garret ; nor even turn its front to the wall. She had the face blackened over, and this sentence, *She is much blacker within,* inscribed in large letters on the frame. And thus, placed in her usual sitting-room, it was exhibited to all beholders."

* " It was a rule with both brothers ' *never to dirty their fingers with silver ;*' and as they, like all other gentlemen at that time, went about in hackney-chairs, the chairmen used to fight for the honour of carrying them, in hopes of picking up the guinea sure to be flung instead of a shilling when they were set down."

George I., it was the most profligate of the sex that bore sway, the consequence to the public must have been infinitely more disastrous.   Madame Kilman-segg's proceedings are an excellent illustration of this point.   She looked, Lady Montagu informs us, to the one thing needful, "getting what money she could by the sale of places, and the credulity of those who thought themselves very politic in securing her favour."   And among those who wriggled their way to office through this dirty track, many of our principal nobility stood fore-most.   Lord Halifax, for example, besides contri-buting to her treasury, condescended to place him-self on a level with footman Craggs, and to forward his ambitious schemes by ministering to her de-praved passions.

While this venerable old sinner was thus amus-ing herself, and feathering her nest, another mem-ber of his majesty's establishment of " playfellows" arrived from the Continent, bringing along with her a neice, who was designed to occupy the same post in the harem of the Prince of Wales.   For some short time, indeed, the damsel had enjoyed that high honour in Germany ; but the arrange-ment not being according to the Princess's taste, which appears always to have been consulted in such matters, was soon broken up.   This young man, whose character exposed him to the scorn of historians, is thus felicitously disposed by the Lady Mary :—

" The fire of his temper appeared in every look and gesture ; which, being unhappily under the di-

rection of a small understanding, was every day
throwing him upon some indiscretion. He was
naturally sincere, and his pride told him that he
was placed above constraint; not reflecting that a
high rank carries along with it a necessity of a
more decent and regular behaviour than is expected from those who are not set in so conspicuous
a light. He was so far from being of that opinion,
that he looked on all the men and women he saw
as creatures he might kick or kiss for his diversion;
and, whenever he met with any opposition in those
designs, he thought his opposers insolent rebels to
the will of God, who created them for his use, and
judged of the merit of all people by their ready
submission to his orders, or the relation they had
to his power. And in this view he looked upon
the princess as the most meritorious of her sex;
and she took care to keep him in that sentiment by
all the arts she was mistress of. He had married
her by inclination; his good-natured father had
been so complaisant as to let him choose a wife for
himself. She was of the house of Anspach, and
brought him no great addition either of money or
alliance; but was at that time esteemed a German
beauty, and had that genius which qualified her
for the government of a fool, and made her despicable in the eyes of men of sense; I mean a low
cunning, which gave her an inclination to cheat all
the people she conversed with, and often cheated
herself in the first place, by showing her the wrong
side of her interest, not having understanding
enough to observe that falsehood in conversation,

like red on the face, should be used very seldom and very sparingly, or they destroy that interest and beauty which they are designed to heighten.

" Her first thought on her marriage was to secure to herself the sole and whole direction of her spouse ; and to that purpose she counterfeited the most extravagant fondness for his person ; yet, at the same time, so devoted to his pleasures, (which she often told him were the rule of all her thoughts and actions,) that whenever he thought proper to find them with other women, she even loved whoever was instrumental to his entertainment, and never resented anything but what appeared to her a want of respect for him; and in this light she really could not help taking notice that the presents made to her on her wedding were not worthy of his bride, and at least she ought to have had all his mother's jewels.   This was enough to make him lose all respect for his indulgent father.   He downright abused his ministers, and talked impertinently to his old grandmother the Princess Sophia ; which ended in such a coldness towards all his family as left him entirely under the government of his wife."

" But my pen wanders, I demand it back !"

From these court sketches, by which Lady Montagu has charmed us away from the consideration of her own career and character, let us go back to the period of her first acquaintance with Mr. Wortley, which took its rise in a way by no means uncommon.   His sister, Anne Wortley, with whom

Lady Mary was on terms of friendship and correspondence, formed the first link in the chain which bound together two persons admirably unsuited to each other, and whose happiness could scarcely have been more effectually marred than by their union. Lord Wharncliffe is at some pains to rescue Mr. Wortley from the charge of having been an unintellectual and insipid person. He is quite right. Mr. Wortley was a clever man, a man of business, and a scholar, but possessed no claims, I apprehend, to be considered a man of genius, which is probably all that was meant by those persons who considered his " parts more solid than brilliant." His connexion with the wits of his time, and his friendship for Addison, independently of other considerations, would, however, prove nothing ; for he possessed what many of those wits wanted, wealth ; and it is well known that the highest minds, minds far superior to those of Steele, Garth, or Mannering, often find it convenient to associate with opulent dunces. Besides, men love to relax sometimes, and this they can do better by far with persons of inferior powers, than in company where a feeling of rivalry maintains a feverish excitement agreeable for the moment, but not to be constantly endured.

However this may be, Mr. Wortley, on becoming acquainted with Lady Mary, paid the penalty of his ignorance of the female sex. His inexperience was caught at once. Her powers of mind and charms of person, indeed, render his thraldom excuseable, but it was not the less unfortunate, for, from that day to his death, her glaring imperfections constituted the principal source of all his infelicity. But let us suffer Lord Wharncliffe to describe their first meeting.

" His society was principally male; the wits and politicians of that day forming a class quite distinct from the ' white gloved beaus' attendant upon ladies. Indeed, as the education of women had then reached its lowest ebb, and if not coquettes, or gossips, or diligent card-players, their best praise was to be notable housewives, Mr. Wortley, however fond of his sister, could have no particular motive to seek the acquaintance of her companions. His surprise and delight were the greater, when one afternoon, having by chance loitered in her apartment till visitors arrived, he saw Lady Mary Pierrepont for the first time, and on entering into conversation with her, found, in addition to beauty which charmed him, not only brilliant wit, but a thinking and cultivated mind. He was especially struck with the discovery that she understood Latin, and could relish his beloved classics. Something that passed, led to the mention of Quintus Curtius, which she said she had never read. This was a fair handle for a piece of gallantry; in a few days, she received a superb edition of the author, with these lines facing the title page :—

' Beauty like this, had vanquish'd Persia shown,
The Macedon had laid his empire down,
And polished Greece obey'd a barb'rous throne.
Had wit so bright adorned a Grecian dame,

The am'rous youth had lost his thirst for fame,
Nor distant India sought through Syria's plain ;
But to the muses' stream with her had run,
And thought her lover more than Ammon's son.'"

Having taken this first decisive step, Mr. Wortley, against his better judgment, continued the
siege of her ladyship's heart, and his erotic tactics
were very peculiar. He wrote letters which his sister Anne forwarded in her own name, though their
warmth and animation were such that to the classic
Lady Mary, they might well have appeared to proceed from a second Sappho. As their love-plot
thickened, Mr. Wortley betrayed considerable
weakness. He saw very distinctly that she did not
love him, and that probably she never would ; yet
he continued dangling about her, irresolute, dis-
pleased with himself and her, and waiting, apparently, for chance to deliver him from a misfortune
from which he wanted the courage to deliver himself. But chance declined the ungrateful task.
One event after another brought them closer and
closer together, and at length the very circumstances
which threatened to be propitious to him,—her
father's displeasure,—proved decisive of his fate :
to cut the matter short, she offered him her hand
against her father's consent, and partly from love,
partly to torment the old man, he accepted it.

The system upon which matrimonial alliances
were formed in those days is explained in a few
words by Lord Wharncliffe.

" A man who is about to sell an estate, seldom
thinks it necessary to enquire whether it will please

or displease his tenantry to be transferred to a new landlord; and just as little then did parents in disposing of a daughter conceive it necessary to consult her will and pleasure. For a young lady to interpose, or claim the right of choice, was almost thought, as it is in France, a species of indelicacy."

It had already for years been her ladyship's practice to keep a diary, to which in part may be attributed the ease and fluency of her style; and, though the earlier portions of it had, from excess of prudence, been consumed by her sister, she again immediately after her marriage resumed the habit, noting down daily what she did, saw, or heard. Her propensity to record and circulate scandal was inveterate. Everything she has left behind her bears the mark of this failing, and her journal we may be sure, in which the faults and failings of her friends were probably embalmed for their better preservation, would have afforded a rich treat to the lovers of secret history. But Lady Bute, to whom the deposit had descended, destroyed this monument of her mother's passion for defamation. She possessed a cooler head, and apparently a more generous heart; her relationship to the writer could not blind her reason; and the arguments by which it was sometimes attempted, by the younger branches of the family, to prevail on her to spare the manuscript, were met by a reply so honourable to her feelings, that I cannot resist the temptation of introducing it here.

" When pressed on this head," observes Lord

Wharncliffe, "she would ask whether, supposing the
case one's own, one could bear the thought of having every crude opinion, every transient wish, every
angry feeling that had flitted across one's mind,
exposed to the world after one was no more? And
though she always spoke of Lady Mary with great
respect, yet it might be perceived that she knew it
had been too much her custom to note down and
enlarge upon all the scandalous rumours of the
day, without weighing their truth, or even their
probability ; to record as certain facts stories that
perhaps sprang up like mushrooms from the dirt,
and had as brief an existence, but tended to defame
persons of the most spotless character." A speci-
men of the manner in which it was written has
been preserved ; and from its tone the reader will
be satisfied that " were such details made public,
they would neither edify the world, nor do honour
to her memory."

" What passed every day was set down ; often
only in a line, or half a line, as thus : ' stayed at
home alone—went to such a place—saw such a
person ;' so that frequently three or four weeks
took up but a single page. Sometimes, again, an
occurrence or a conversation would be given at very
great length ; sometimes dispatched with one sharp
sentence, like the following humorous application of
a speech in Dryden's Spanish Friar ; ' Lady Hin-
chinbroke has a dead daughter—it were unchristian
not to be sorry for my cousin's misfortune ; but if
she has no live son, Mr. Wortley is heir—so there
is comfort for a Christian."

Most persons acquainted with the literature of Lady Montagu's age will probably have been struck by the absence which it almost everywhere exhibits of that admiration of whatever belongs to the beauties of external nature, now felt or affected by all. But tastes of this kind depend entirely on fashion. No distinguished writer having, at that period, chosen to transfer his sympathies from mankind to inanimate things, it was not considered a mark of genius to be exclusively in love with forests, or mountains, or lakes; and accordingly men thought it unnecessary, whatever they might feel, to entertain their readers with studies of the picturesque. In many cases the reason of this might no doubt be traced to the artificial manners and townish habits of literary men. They could not speak of the country, which for the most part they never saw; or, if they chanced to catch a glimpse of it on the way to or from their patron's villa, their ideas were too much occupied with their Epithalamium, or birth-day ode, or with the reception they had met, or were to meet with, to allow things so insignificant as fields and trees to intrude upon their associations. And this is equally the case now. But *nature* has become fashionable, and every one, including the man who has nothing to eat, must feign, whenever it is mentioned, to be in raptures; though in his eyes, peradventure, the most sublime thing it contains may be a beef-steak.

Lord Wharncliffe, however, goes too far when he infers, as in the " Introductory Anecdotes" he does, that the pleasure we derive from beholding the green earth, with all its varied features, are artificial, and berhymed into us by the poets. On the contrary, they are the offspring of a healthy state of the mind, and came back to us when we escaped from that artificial numbness of fancy and all the creative powers, which had seized upon the national intellect in the reign of Anne and the first three Georges. The ability to judge in the case of the picturesque will certainly be commensurate, in general, with the pains and assiduity with which it is cultivated; and therefore we may be better critics in scenery than the great majority of our ancestors, though no poets that ever lived have left so many evidences of intense admiration for everything beautiful in the external world, or so many admirably finished landscapes, as Chaucer, Spenser, Shakspear, and Milton. Burnet, too, of the Charter-house, whom Lord Wharncliffe adduces as an admirer of flat surfaces, entertained magnificent conceptions of the earth's grandeur in its present state; and few writers from his time to ours have shadowed forth its sublime features more in the style of a great landscape-painter. I might perhaps say—*none*, for I know of none in any language who has placed before the imagination a nobler scene than Burnet has delineated in describing a view he once enjoyed from a promontory of the Maritime Alps.

I subjoin the passages to which my attention was first directed by Mr. Wordsworth, (Works, V. 395. f.) but shall not attempt to translate it, as no

language I could employ would do justice to
Burnet.—

"Si quod verò Natura nobis dedit spectaculum,
in hâc tellure, verè gratum, et philosopho dignum,
id semel mihi contigisse arbitror; cùm ex celsis-
simâ rupe speculabundus ad oram maris Mediter-
ranei hinc æquor cæruleum, illine tractus Alpinos
prospexi; nihil quidem magìs dispar aut dissi-
mile, nec in suo genere magìs egregium et singu-
lare. Hoc theatrum ego facilè prætulerim Roma-
nis cunctis, Gr æcisve ; atque id quod natura hîc
spectandum exhibet, scenicis ludis omnibus, aut
amphitheatri certaminibus. Nihil hîc elegans, aut
venustum, sed ingens et magnificum, et quod placet
magnitudine suâ et quâdam specie immensitatis.
Hinc intuebar maris æquabilem superficiem, usque
et usque diffusam, quantum maximùm oculorum
acies ferri potuit; illinc disruptissimam terræ
faciem, et vastas moles variè elevatas aut depressas,
erectas, propendentes, reclinatas, coacervatas, om-
ni situ inæquali et turbido. Placuit ex hâc parte,
Naturæ unitas et simplicitas, et inexhausta quæ-
dam planities; ex altera, multiformis confusio
magnorum corporum, et insanæ rerum strages :
quas cùm intuebar, non urbis alicujus aut oppidi,
sed confracti mundi rudera, ante oculos habere
mihi visus sum. In singulis ferè montibus erat ali-
quid insolens et mirabile, sed præ cæteris mihi
placebat illa, quâ sedebam, rupes; erat maxima et
altissima, et quâ terram respiciebat molliori ascensu
altitudinem suam dissimulabat; quâ verò mare,
horrendum præceps, et quasi ad perpendiculum

facta, instar parietis. Prætereà facies illa marina
adeò erat laevis ac uniformis (quod in rupibus ali-
quando observare licet) ac si scissa fuisset à summo
ad imum, in illo plano ; vel terræ motu aliquo, aut
fulmine, divulsa. Ima pars rupis erat cava,
recessusque habuit ; et saxeos specus, euntes in
vacuum montem ; sive naturâ pridem factos,
sive exesos mari, et undarum crebris ictibus : in
hos enim cum impetu ruebant et fragore, æstuan-
tis maris fluctus ; quos iterum spumantes reddidit
antrum, et quasi ab imo ventre evomuit. Dextrum
latus montis erat præruptum, aspero saxo et
nudâ caute ; sinistrum non adeò neglexerat Natura, arboribus ut pote ornatum : et prope pedem
montis rivus limpidæ aquæ prorupit ; qui cùm
vicinam vallem irrigaverat, lento motu serpens, et
per varios mæandros, quasi ad protrahendam vitam,
in magno mari absorptus subito periit. Denique in
summo vertice promontorii commodè eminebat
saxum, cui insidebam contemplabundus. Vale
augusta sedes, Rege digna : Augusta rupes, semper
mihi memoranda !" P. 89. *Telluris Theoria Sacra
&c. Editio secunda.*

Of Wharncliffe Lodge, since I have not seen
it, I will not pretend to speak ; but, whatever may
be its beauty, we can feel little surprise it should
have excited nothing like "transport" in the mind of
Lady Mary, who could pass almost unmoved over
the loveliest portions of the East. Her editor's remarks, however, though unfounded in the case of
Burnet, are not altogether unworthy of attention.

"The first mention of Wharncliffe in Lady Mary's

journal, after calling there to visit her father-in-law
when on her road to some other place, was very
remarkable; considering that she had hitherto
known only the midland counties and the environs
of London, and probably had never before seen any
thing like picturesque or romantic scenery.   One
would have supposed the sight of so wild and
beautiful a prospect as that eagle's nest commands,
very sure to occasion surprise, if not excite transport, in a mind gifted with the least imagination.
But no; nothing could be colder or more slight
than the notice she took of it, almost making an
excuse for saying thus much in its favour—' that
it was a sequestered rural spot, quite of a rude nature; yet had something in it that she owned she
did not dislike, odd as her fancy might appear.'
In after-days, her letters to Mr. Wortley do it
more justice; possibly to please him; but the
journal gave the original impression, and how may
that be accounted for ?   Can it be, that the tastes
and pleasures which we now esteem most peculiarly natural are, in fact, artificial.   What we
have merely read, and talked, and rhymed and
sketched ourselves into ? plants that require ma-
nure and culture, instead of sprouting freely from
the soil ?   Certainly, our forefathers were little
more alive to them than the American settler, who
sees in a wood a nuisance he must clear away, and in
a waterfall only the means of turning a mill.   Burnet, of the Charterhouse, lived and wrote but a few
years before Lady Mary Wortley : it may be remembered that his theory of the antediluvian

e

globe supposes it to have had a surface perfectly flat, smooth and level; and for this reason amongst others, because the earth in its goodly pristine state, the fair work of an Almighty Creator, could not have been deformed by such unsightly protuberances as rocks and mountains. These were the tokens of Divine wrath, vestiges of that awful convulsion which tore the old world to pieces; therefore he naturally regarded them with horror. His hypothesis might have been the same, how contrary soever the opinion of his contemporaries; but he never would have brought this argument to support it, if the majority of postdiluvians he was writing to, had, like ourselves, considered Earth's protuberances as her finest features. How far were they from suspecting that a future generation would delight in viewing the lakes and climbing the fells of Cumberland!"

It has been seen from what I have already said, that the women of Lady Montagu's age were not overburdened with knowledge of any kind, but the men, it is quite clear, condescended in most cases to keep them in countenance, for even an acquaintance with the French language now common in all but the lowest ranks, was then thought to be an accomplishment qualifying a man for the highest office of the state.

" Upon the death of Queen Anne, Mr. Wortley's friends coming into power he was appointed a lord of the treasury. He had long been an active, efficient member of parliament, and when he first obtained this office, people expected that he would

have a considerable sway in the new King's coun-
sels : for a reason which will seem rather surprising,—he was the only man at the board (excepting perhaps Lord Halifax) who could converse
with his majesty, because the only one who spoke
French ; consequently much of the business must
have gone through his hands, if the sovereign, like
his predecessors, William and Anne, had assisted
in person at the meetings of the commissioners.
But George the First leaving finance-affairs and
others to be managed as his ministers pleased,
Mr. Wortley had no more personal intercourse
with him than the rest. Lady Mary frequently
attracted his notice, and likewise that of the Prince
of Wales (George the Second.) By her journal
indeed, it might have been imagined that the
latter admired her rather more than the Princess
(though usually far from jealous) could quite ap-
prove. For once, in a rapture, he called her royal
highness from the card-table to look how becomingly Lady Mary was dressed ! ' Lady Mary always dresses well,' said the princess drily, and returned to her cards. However, his favour was soon
withdrawn, and hers regained. The father and son
were already almost at their first setting out, upon
such hostile terms, that, the moment the prince heard
of Lady Mary's having been at one of the king's
select parties, he grew not only cool but resentful,
taunting her as a deserter gone over to the enemy's
camp ; and thenceforward she dressed becomingly
in vain. An increase of graciousness on the part
of the princess made her amends."

Here we find ourselves brought back again, by the waywardness of our subject, to the court of George the First. A former editor of Lady Mary's works observes, that the court of this prince was "modelled upon that of Louis the Fifteenth." He may possibly have meant, for he has expressed himself very ill,—that it bore a strong resemblance to that court; which, if grossness and sensuality be any thing like vice, it certainly did. It in fact consisted of nothing but a knot of courtezans and profligates, of which the ridiculous old king and his unprincipled son formed the central point. The hatred of the prince for his father has been noticed in the passage above quoted from Lord Wharncliffe, and will of itself be sufficient to determine the light in which he must be held by the reader: the rest of them figure, in his lordship's pages, as follows:—

" George the First went to the play or opera in a sedan-chair, and sate, like another gentleman, in the corner of a lady's (a German lady's) box, with a couple of Turks in waiting instead of lords and grooms of the bedchamber. In one respect his court, if court it could be called, bore some resemblance to the old establishment of Versailles. There was a Madame de Maintenon. Of the three favourite ladies who had accompanied him from Hanover, viz. Mademoiselle de Schulenberg, the Countess Platen, and Madame Kilmansegg, the first alone, whom he created Duchess of Kendal, was lodged in St. James's Palace, and had such respect paid her as very much confirmed the rumour of a left-hand marriage. She presided at the king's

evening parties, consisting of the Germans who
formed his familiar society, a few English ladies,
and fewer English men : among them Mr. Craggs,
the secretary of state, who had been at Hanover
in the queen's time, and by thus having the *entrée*
in private, passed for a sort of favourite."

The practice of calling things by their right
names would very much conduce to the rendering
of literature a real benefit to the public. In the
present instance, for example, it would wonderfully facilitate our search after right notions, if
fashion would permit of our applying the proper
epithets to the class of females who filled the palace, and constituted the only companions of the
king. But virtue, as Montesquieu rightly observes, is not the principle of monarchy ; and generally has nothing to do at court, at least at such
courts as that of George the First, where no man
who valued his wife's or daughter's reputation at a
straw, could permit her to be introduced. We
find, however, and we may draw what inference we
please from the discovery,—that the wives of the
nobility were forward to associate with the king's
women, the Laises and Phrynes, and Ninons of
their day. Virtue was nothing, character was
nothing ; adultery, and every other excess of moral
turpitude, assumed a charming appearance when
practised and patronized by royalty ; when every
law human and divine was broken and trampled
under foot and openly laughed at by a king " by
the grace of God !" Lord Wharncliffe may, well
say that " the motto on all palace-gates is *Hush !*"

But, if the world be content to laugh at those things, let it do so. I cannot join in the merriment. In my opinion vice in all shapes is a " *triste plaisir*," and most of all so when it is indulged to the detriment of a whole people. Lord Wharncliffe, however will relieve us from this dilemma, by describing the manner in which his great grandame dissipated the ennui of the king and his harem.

" Lady Mary's journal related a ridiculous adventure of her own at one of these royal parties; which, by the bye, stood in great need of some laughing matter to enliven them; for they seem to have been even more dull than it was reasonable to expect they should be. She had on one evening a particular engagement that made her wish to be dismissed unusually early; she explained her reasons to the Duchess of Kendal, and the Duchess informed the King, who, after a few complimentary remonstrances, appeared to acquiesce. But when he saw her about to take her leave, he began battling the point afresh, declaring it was unfair and perfidious to cheat him in such a manner, and saying many other fine things, in spite of which she at last contrived to escape. At the foot of the great stairs she ran against Secretary Craggs just coming in, who stopped her to inquire what was the matter ? were the company put off ? She told him why she went away, and how urgently the king had pressed her to stay longer; possibly dwelling on that head with some small complacency. Mr. Craggs made no remark; but, when he had heard

all, snatching her up in his arms as a nurse carries a child, he ran full speed with her up stairs,
deposited her within the ante-chamber, kissed both
her hands respectfully, (still not saying a word,)
and vanished. The pages seeing her returned,
they knew not how, hastily threw open the inner
doors, and, before she had recovered her breath, she
found herself again in the kings presence. " *Ah !
la re-voilà !*" cried he and the Duchess, extremely
pleased, and began thanking her for her obliging
change of mind. The motto on all palace gates is
' *Hush !*' as Lady Mary very well knew. She had
not to learn that mystery and caution ever spread
their awful wings over the precincts of a court;
where nobody knows what dire mischief may ensue
from one unlucky syllable blabbed about anything,
or about *nothing*, at a wrong time. But she was be-
wildered, fluttered, and entirely off her guard; so,
beginning giddily with ' Oh Lord, sir! I have been
so frightened !' she told his majesty the whole
story exactly as she would have told it to any one
else. He had not done exclaiming, nor his Germans wondering, when again the door flew open,
and the attendants announced Mr. Secretary Craggs,
who, but that moment arrived, it should seem, entered with the usual obeisance, and as composed an
air as if nothing had happened. ' *Mais comment
donc, Monsieur Craggs,*' said the king, going up to
him, ' *est-ce que c'est l'usage de ce pays de porter des
belles dames comme un sac de froment ?* ' ' Is it the
custom of this country to carry about fair ladies
like a sack of wheat ?' The minister, struck dumb

by this unexpected attack, stood a minute or two not knowing which way to look; then, recovering his self-possession, answered with a low bow, ' There is nothing I would not do for your majesty's satisfaction.' This was coming off tolerably well; but he did not forgive the tell-tale culprit, in whose ear, watching his opportunity when the king turned from them, he muttered a bitter reproach, with a round oath to enforce it; ' which I durst not resent,' continued she, ' for I had drawn it upon myself; and indeed I was heartily vexed at my own imprudence.'"

Lord Wharncliffe, who tells several very good anecdotes, has a particularly amusing story about the Princess Sophia, mother of George the First. To relish all the details of it, however, two or three circumstances should be considered: in the first place, the old lady, who is represented as so quick-witted and frisky, must have been upwards of eighty years old; secondly, if the portrait of the Pretender was of the usual size and hung in the usual way, it would have required the stature of a giantess to conceal it. But anecdotes are made, not to be sifted, but enjoyed; we will therefore suffer his lordship to relate the matter in his own way:—

" The name of George the First recals a remarkable anecdote of his mother, the Princess Sophia, which Mr. Wortley and Lady Mary heard from Lord Halifax. When he and Lord Dorset were dispatched by the whig administration npon the welcome errand of announcing to her the act of parliament that secured the Hanover succession, at the same time carrying the garter to the electoral prince, her grandson, they were received, as may be supposed, with every mark of distinction. At their first formal audience, as they commenced a set speech, after delivering their credentials, the old electress, who was standing, gave a kind of start, and almost *ran* to one corner of the room, where, fixing her back against the wall, she remained stiff and erect as if glued to it, till the ceremony ended, and they withdrew. Her behaviour being in all other respects very dignified and decorous, they were at a loss to divine what could have occasioned this extraordinary *move,* and very curious to discover the meaning of it; a secret which Lord Halifax at length got at, by dint of sifting and cross-questioning her courtiers. She had suddenly recollected that there hung in that room a picture of her cousin, the PRETENDER, and, in a fright lest it should catch their eyes, could hit upon no expedient to hide it but by screening it with her own person. The good princess, however, was not in the least disloyal to herself; she harboured no dislike to the prospect of a crown, nor any scruples about accepting it; but, nevertheless, valuing her Stuart descent, she had a family feeling for the young man, whom she firmly believed to be as much James the Second's son as George the First was her own. That is to say, she was what at the time all England would have styled ' *a rank Jacobite.'* "

I shall not enter here into many details on the subject of *inoculation,* which Lady Montagu had the merit of introducing into England. It had attracted her attention during the stay of the embassy at Adrianople, and she had the hardihood to make the experiment on her own children. The practice would appear to have prevailed from time immemorial among the Turks, who, as might have been expected, entrusted it entirely to the management of a number of old women, the same, probably, with the *protegées* of Eilithyia. Upon Lady Mary's return to England, Mr. Maitland, the surgeon of the embassy, endeavoured to introduce the practice in London; and, in 1721, the public attention having been strongly directed to the subject, and the curiosity of professional men awakened, an experiment, sanctioned by government and the College of Physicians, was made upon five condemned criminals. With four of these wretches it perfectly succeeded; and the fifth, a woman, in whose case it failed, afterwards confessed that she had taken the infection in the natural way during her infancy. (⁴) The merit of Lady Montague in this matter can scarcely be overrated, particularly when we consider the obloquy and insult she endured in the course of the undertaking. " The clamours raised against the practice, and consequently against her, were beyond belief. The faculty all rose in arms *to a man,* (this is a figure of speech; I have already named an exception,) foretelling failure and the most disastrous consequences; the *clergy* descanted from their *pulpits* on the impiety of thus seeking to

(⁴) Lives of Celebrated Travellers, II. 9.

take events out of the hand of Providence; the common people were *taught* (by the clergy!) to hoot at her as an unnatural mother, who had risked the lives of her own children" to preserve theirs!

The Mohammedan muftis used at one time to enlarge with great unction on the *impiety* of drinking coffee; and here we find our enlightened Oxford and Cambridge *clergy* declaiming against the impiety of *taking physic;* for admitting a milder virus into the constitution to keep out a more pestilential one, is nothing more. I do not feel so well satisfied of the correctness of his lordship's account of the *faculty's* proceedings; and can by no means re-echo the atrocious accusation implied in the close of the following passage. But let the profession answer it. " We now read in grave medical biography that the discovery was instantly hailed, and the method adopted, by the principal members of that profession. Very likely they left this recorded; for, whenever an invention or a project,— and the same may be said of persons,—has made its way so well by itself as to establish a certain reputation, most people are sure to find out that they always patronized it from the beginning; and a happy gift of forgetfulness enables many to believe their own assertion. But what said Lady Mary of the actual fact, and actual time ? Why, that the four great physicians deputed by government to watch the progress of her daughter's inoculation betrayed, not only such incredulity as to its success, but such an unwillingness to have it succeed, such an evident spirit of rancour and malignity, that she never cared to leave the child alone with them one second, lest it should in some secret way suffer from their interference."

It has already been observed that Lady Mary delighted in sarcasm; and persons afflicted with this propensity seldom preserve a friend long. But something more than the indulgence of satirical habits must be imagined to account for her lady-ship's rupture with Pope, and the mutual rancour with which they ever after regarded each other. Dallaway enters into the quarrel with the spirit of a toad-eater to her ladyship's family, and labours to cast all the blame on the poet. Lord Wharn-cliffe is more generous; but still naturally, and perhaps excusably leans towards the lady's side :—
" The next point of much consequence in Lady Mary Wortley's history is her quarrel with Pope. If this had made less noise, and been less canvassed, it would be desirable to pass it by unnoticed; for, when two persons of distinguished abilities misemploy their talents, and degrade themselves by striving to vilify each other, the honest part of their admirers must feel more inclination to avert their eyes from the conflict than to engage in it as partizan of either. Her own statement, however, was this: that at some ill-chosen time, when she least expected what romances call a *declaration*, he made such passionate love to her as, in spite of her utmost endeavours to be angry and look grave, provoked an immediate fit of laughter; from which moment he became her implacable enemy."

Nothing very favourable to her ladyship appears, however, to have been discovered in her papers, or it would have been brought forward; so that on this point we are left to infer what we can from the evidence of a few facts. For my own part, I imagine the quarrel arose as follows: in the earlier part of her life she was a strong admirer of genius, and encouraged and returned the passion of literary men, of Pope among the rest. As her years increased, the admiration for intellect diminished; a new class of lovers obtained the preference; the reign of the physical succeeded to the sentimental, Lord Harvey, ([5]) &c. to Pope and Congreve; and a quarrel with the discarded swains became a necessary consequence. Lord Wharncliffe might not choose to give this obvious explanation of the matter, but her ladyship's character is too legibly traced in her works to leave the point at all doubtful. Still this by no means justifies the virulence of Pope's attacks. He should have left such paltry vengeance to the lords and ladies who borrowed their philosophy, as they did their morals, from the court.

But though none, I believe, experienced so much severity as Pope at her ladyship's hands,— and he almost deserved it for persuading her she

---

([5]) Of this *inamorato* of her ladyship, Lord Wharncliffe says: "It has been handed down as a proof of the extreme to which Lord Harvey carried his effeminate nicety, that, when asked at dinner whether he would have some beef, he answered, ' Beef? —Oh, no!—Faugh! Don't you know I never eat beef, nor *horse*, nor any of those things?'—Could any mortal have said this in earnest?"

could write poetry,—few that ever became acquainted with her escaped. Many, anticipating
what would happen, declined the honour ; but
Lord Wharncliffe informs us that of the scurrilous
ballads and slanderous aspersions on private character attributed to Lady Mary, a great number
were written by other persons. However, having
once acquired a reputation in this department of
literature, it stuck to her, and the effects sometimes showed themselves in the following manner.
" The impression these unjust imputations made
upon her mind will now be shown. When Lady
Bute was nearly grown up, some of her young
friends wanted to bring about an acquaintance
between her and Miss Furnese, (⁶) an heiress of
their own age. Miss Wortley had no objection ;
but Miss Furnese held off, and so resolutely, that
they insisted upon knowing the reason. 'Why,
then,' said she, at last, ' I will honestly own, your
praises of Miss Wortley make me sure I shall dislike her. You tell me she is lively and clever, now
I know I am very dull ; so, of course, she will
despise me, and turn me into ridicule, and I am
resolved to keep out of her way.' The young set
laughed most heartily at this avowal ; and Lady
Bute, laughing too when told of it, ran to divert
her mother with the story. But, instead of amusing Lady Mary, it made her unusually serious.
' Now, child,' she began, after a moment's reflec-

(⁶) Married to Lewis, Earl of Rockingham, and afterwards
the third wife of Francis, Earl of Guildford.

tion, ' you see nothing in this but a good joke, an absurdity to laugh at ; and are not aware what an important lesson you have received ; one which you ought to remember as long as you live. What that poor girl in her simplicity has uttered aloud, is no more than what passes in the mind of every dull person you will meet with. Those who cannot but feel that they are deficient in ability, always look with a mixture of fear and aversion on people cleverer than themselves ; regarding them as born their natural enemies. If ever, then, you feel yourself flattered by the reputation of superiority, remember that, to be the object of suspicion, jealousy, and a secret dislike, is the sure price you must pay for it.' "

With these few intimations respecting the character and habits of the author, which appeared necessary to the proper understanding of many parts of the ensuing correspondence, we leave the reader to enter on the letters themselves.

J. A. ST. JOHN.

Hampsted, March, 1838.

LETTERS FROM THE LEVANT.

1716—18.

PREFACE.

BY A LADY, — 1724.

I was going, like common editors, to advertise the reader of the beauties and excellencies of the work laid before him : to tell him, that the illustrious author had opportunities that other travellers, whatever their quality or curiosity may have been, cannot obtain ; and a genius capable of making the best improvement of every opportunity. But if the reader, after perusing *one* letter only, has not discernment to distinguish that natural elegance, that delicacy of sentiment and observation, that easy gracefulness and lovely simplicity (which is the perfection of writing,) in which these *Letters* exceed all that has appeared in this kind, or almost in any other, let him lay the book down and leave it to those who have.

The noble author had the goodness to lend me her MS. to satisfy my curiosity in some inquiries I had made concerning her travels ; and when I had it in my hands, how was it possible to part with it ? I once had the vanity to hope I might acquaint the public that it owed this invaluable treasure to my importunities. But, alas ! the most ingenious author has condemned it to obscurity during her life ; and conviction, as well as deference, obliges me to yield to her reasons. However, if these Letters appear hereafter, when I am in my grave, let this attend them, in testimony to posterity, that among her contemporaries, *one* woman, at least, was just to her merit.

There is not any thing so excellent but some will carp at it, and the rather because of its excellency. But to such hyper-critics I shall not say . . . .

B 2

I confess I am malicious enough to desire that the world should see to how much better purpose the ladies travel than their lords ; and that, whilst it is surfeited with *male* travels, all in the same tone, and stuffed with the same trifles, a lady has the skill to strike out a new path, and to embellish a worn-out subject with variety of fresh and elegant entertainment. For, besides the vivacity and spirit which enliven every part, and that inimitable beauty which spreads through the whole ; besides the purity of the style, for which it may justly be accounted the standard of the English tongue ; the reader will find a more true and accurate account of the customs and manners of the several nations with whom this lady conversed, than he can in any other author. But, as her ladyship's penetration discovers the inmost follies of the heart, so the candour of her temper passed over them with an air of pity, rather than reproach ; treating with the politeness of a court and the gentleness of a lady, what the severity of her judgment could not but condemn.

In short, let her own sex, at least, do her justice ; lay aside diabolical Envy, and its *brother* Malice,(¹) with all their accursed company, sly whispering, cruel backbiting, spiteful detraction, and the rest of that hideous crew, which I hope are very falsely said to attend the *tea-table*, being more apt to think they frequent those public places where virtuous women never come. Let the men malign one another, if they think fit, and strive to pull down merit when they cannot equal it. Let us be better natured than to give way to any unkind or disrespectful thought of so bright an ornament of our sex merely because she has better sense ; for I doubt not but our hearts will tell us, that this is the real and unpardonable offence, whatever may be pretended. Let us be better Christians than to look upon her with an evil eye, only because the Giver of all good gifts has intrusted and adorned her with the most excellent talents. Rather let us freely own the superiority of this sublime genius, as I do,

---

(¹) This fair and elegant prefacer has resolved that malice should be of the masculine gender : I believe it is both masculine and feminine, and I heartily wish it were neuter.

in the sincerity of my soul ; pleased that a *woman* triumphs, and proud to follow in her train.   Let us offer her the palm which is so justly her due ; and if we pretend to any laurels, lay them willingly at her feet.

MARY ASTON.

December 18, 1724.

> Charm'd into love of what obscures my fame,
> If I had wit, I'd celebrate her name,
> And all the beauties of her mind proclaim ;
> Till Malice, deafen'd with the mighty sound,
> Its ill-concerted calumnies confound :
> Let fall the mask, and with pale Envy meet,
> To ask, and find, their pardon at her feet.

You see, madam, how I lay every thing at your feet. As the tautology shows the poverty of my genius, it likewise shows the extent of your empire over my imagination.

May 31, 1725.

LETTERS.

I.

TO THE COUNTESS OF MAR. (^{2})

Rotterdam, Aug. 3, O. S. 1716.

I FLATTER myself, dear sister, that I shall give you some pleasure in letting you know that I have safely passed the sea, though we had the ill fortune of a storm. We were persuaded by the captain of the yacht to set out in a calm, and he pretended there was nothing so easy as to tide it over : but, after two days slowly moving, the wind blew so hard, that none of the sailors could keep their feet, and we were all Sunday night tossed very handsomely. I never saw a man more frightened than the captain.

For my part, I have been so lucky, neither to suffer from fear nor sea-sickness ; though I confess

---

(^{2}) Lady Frances Pierrepont, second daughter of Evelyn, first Duke of Kingston, married John Erskine, Earl of Mar, who was secretary of state for Scotland in 1705, joined the Pretender in 1715, was attainted in 1716, and died at Aix-la-Chapelle in 1732. George I. confirmed to Lady Mar the jointure on Lord Mar's forfeited estate, to which she was entitled by her marriage-settlement, with remainder to her daughter, Lady Frances Erskine. She resided many years at Paris.

I was so impatient to see myself once more upon dry land, that I would not stay till the yacht could get to Rotterdam, but went in the long-boat to Helvoet-sluys, where we had voitures to carry us to the Brill.

I was charmed with the neatness of that little town ; but my arrival at Rotterdam presented me a new scene of pleasure. All the streets are paved with broad stones, and before many of the meanest artificers' doors are placed seats of various coloured marbles, (³) so neatly kept, that, I assure you, I walked almost all over the town yesterday *incognita,* in my slippers, without receiving one spot of dirt ; (⁴) and you may see the Dutch maids washing the pavement of the street with more application than ours do our bedchambers. The town seems so full of people, with such busy faces, all in motion, that I can hardly fancy it is not some celebrated fair ; but I see it is every day the same. It is certain no town can be more advantageously situated for commerce. Here are seven large canals, on which the merchants' ships come up to the very doors of their houses. The shops and warehouses are of a surprising neatness and magnificence, filled with an incredible quantity of fine merchandize, and so much cheaper than what we see in England, that I have much ado to per-

---

(³) A similar fashion still prevails in the East ; and is noticed by the very earliest writers of antiquity. In Greece these marble seats were rubbed with odoriferous oils.—ED.

(⁴) Here, from the inartificial construction of the sentence, her ladyship would appear to insinuate that she walked over the marble seats. But the pavement, of course, is meant.—ED.

suade myself I am still so near it. Here is neither
dirt nor beggary to be seen. One is not shocked
with those loathsome cripples, so common in London, nor teased with the importunity of idle fellows
and wenches that choose to be nasty and lazy.
The common servants, and little shopwomen here,
are more nicely clean than most of our ladies; and
the great variety of neat dresses (every woman
dressing her head after her own fashion) is an
additional pleasure in seeing the town.

You see, hitherto, dear sister, I make no complaints; and, if I continue to like travelling as
well as I do at present, I shall not repent my
project. It will go a great way in making me
satisfied with it, if it affords me an opportunity of
entertaining you. But it is not from Holland that
you may expect a disinterested offer. I can write
enough in the style of Rotterdam, to tell you
plainly, in one word, that I expect returns of all
the London news. You see I have already learnt
to make a good bargain; and that it is not for
nothing I will so much as tell you I am your affec-
tionate sister.

II.

TO MRS. SKERRET.([5])

Hague, Aug. 5, 1716.

I MAKE haste to tell you, dear madam, that, after
all the dreadful fatigues you threatened me with, I

([5]) Afterward the second wife of Robert, first Earl of Orford.

am hitherto very well pleased with my journey.
We take care to make such short stages every day,
that I rather fancy myself upon parties of pleasure
than upon the road ; and sure nothing can be
more agreeable than travelling in Holland. The
whole country appears a large garden ; the roads
are well paved, shaded on each side with rows of
trees, and bordered with large canals, full of boats,
passing and repassing. Every twenty paces gives
you the prospect of some villa, and every four
hours that of a large town, so surprisingly neat, I
am sure you would be charmed with them. The
place I am now at is certainly one of the finest
villages in the world. Here are several squares
finely built, and (what I think a particular beauty)
the whole set with thick large trees. The *Vor-hout*
is, at the same time, the Hyde Park and Mall of the
people of quality ; for they take the air in it both
on foot and in coaches. There are shops for wafers,
cool liquors, &c.

I have been to see several of the most celebrated
gardens, but I will not tease you with their descriptions. I dare say you think my letter already long
enough. But I must not conclude without begging
your pardon for not obeying your commands, in
sending the lace you ordered me. Upon my word,
I can yet find none that is not dearer than you
may buy it at London. If you want any India
goods, here are great variety of pennyworths ; and
I shall follow your orders with great pleasure and
exactness, being,

Dear madam, &c. &c.

III.

TO MRS. S. C.

Nimeguen, Aug. 13, 1716.

I AM extremely sorry, my dear S., that your fears of disobliging your relations, and their fears for your health and safety, have hindered me from enjoying the happiness of your company, and you the pleasure of a diverting journey. I receive some degree of mortification from every agreeable novelty or pleasing prospect, by the reflection of your having so unluckily missed the delight which I know it would have given you.

If you were with me in this town, you would be ready to expect to receive visits from your Nottingham friends. No two places were ever more resembling; one has but to give the Maese the name of the Trent, and there is no distinguishing the prospect. The houses, like those of Nottingham, are built one above another, and are intermixed in the same manner with trees and gardens. The tower they call Julius Cæsar's has the same situation with Nottingham castle; and I cannot help fancying, I see from it the Trentfield, Adboulton, &c., places so well known to us. It is true, the fortifications make a considerable difference. All the learned in the art of war bestow great commendations on them; for my part, that know nothing of the matter, I shall content myself with telling you, it is a very pretty walk on the ramparts, on which there is a tower, very deservedly called the Belvidere; where people go to drink coffee, tea, &c., and enjoy one of the finest prospects in the world. The public walks have no great beauty but the thick shade of the trees, which is solemnly delightful. But I must not forget to take notice of the bridge, which appeared very surprising to me ; it is large enough to hold hundreds of men, with horses and carriages. They give the value of an English twopence to get upon it, and then away they go, bridge and all, to the other side of the river, with so slow a motion, one is hardly sensible of any at all.

I was yesterday at the French church, and stared very much at their manner of service. The parson clapped on a broad brimmed hat in the first place, which gave him entirely the air of *what d'ye call him*, in Bartholomew fair, which he kept up by extraordinary antic gestures, and preaching much such stuff as the other talked to the puppets. However, the congregation seemed to receive it with great devotion ; and I was informed by some of his flock that he is a person of particular fame amongst them. I believe, by this time, you are as much tired with my account of him as I was with his sermon ; but I am sure your brother will excuse a digression in favour of the church of England. You know speaking disrespectfully of the Calvinists is the same thing as speaking honourably of the church. Adieu, my dear S., always remember me ; and be assured I can never forget you, &c., &c.

IV.

TO THE LADY RICH.(⁶)

Cologne, Aug. 16, 1716.

IF my Lady Rich could have any notion of the fatigues that I have suffered these two last days, I am sure she would own it a great proof of regard, that I now sit down to write to her. We hired horses from Nimeguen hither, not having the conveniency of the post, and found but very indifferent accommodations at Reinberg, our first stage ; but that was nothing to what I suffered yesterday. We were in hopes to reach Cologne; our horses tired at Stamel, three hours from it, where I was forced to pass the night in my clothes, in a room not at all better than a hovel; for, though I have my own bed with me, I had no mind to undress, where the wind came from a thousand places. We left this wretched lodging at daybreak, and about six this morning came safe here, where I got immediately into bed. I slept so well for three hours that I found myself perfectly recovered, and have had spirits enough to go and see all that is curious in the town, that is to say, the churches, for here is nothing else worth seeing.

(⁶) The wife of Sir Robert Rich, Bart., of London. She was a daughter of Colonel Griffin, and had an appointment about the person of the Princess of Wales, afterwards Queen Caroline.

This is a very large town, but the most part of it is old built. The Jesuits' church is the neatest, which was showed me, in a very complaisant manner, by a handsome young Jesuit ; who, not knowing who I was, took a liberty in his compliments and railleries which very much diverted me. Having never before seen anything of that nature, I could not enough admire the magnificence of the altars, the rich images of the saints, (all of massy silver,) and the *enchassures* of the relics; though I could not help murmuring in my heart, at the profusion of pearls, diamonds, and rubies, bestowed in the adornment of rotten teeth and dirty rags. I own that I had wickedness enough to covet St. Ursula's pearl necklaces ; though, perhaps, this was no wickedness at all, an image not being certainly one's neighbour ; but I went yet farther, and wished she herself converted into dressing-plate. I should also gladly see converted into silver, a great St. Christopher, which I imagine would look very well in a cistern.

These were my pious reflections ; though I was very well satisfied to see, piled up to the honour of our nation, the skulls of the eleven thousand virgins. I have seen some hundreds of relics here of no less consequence ; but I will not imitate the common style of travellers so far as to give you a list of them, being persuaded that you have no manner of curiosity for the titles given to jaw-bones and bits of worm-eaten wood.—Adieu, I am just going to supper, where I shall drink your health in an admirable sort of Lorrain wine, which

I am sure is the same you call Burgundy in London, &c., &c

V.

TO THE COUNTESS OF BRISTOL. ([7])

Nuremberg, Aug. 22, 1716.

AFTER five days travelling post, I could not sit down to write on any other occasion, than to tell my dear Lady Bristol that I have not forgotten her obliging command, of sending her some account of my travels.

I have already passed a large part of Germany, have seen all that is remarkable in Cologne, Frankfort, Wurtzburg, and this place. It is impossible not to observe the difference between the free towns ([8]) and those under the government of absolute princes, as all the little sovereigns of Germany are. In the first there appears an air of commerce and plenty : the streets are well built, and full of people, neatly and plainly dressed : the shops are loaded with merchandise, and the commonalty are clean and cheerful. In the other, you see a sort of shabby finery, a number of dirty people of

---

([7]) Elizabeth, daughter and heir of Sir Thomas Felton, Bart., of Playford, County of Suffolk, second wife of John Hervey, first Earl or Bristol. She died in 1741.

([8]) Excepting, perhaps, in Prussia, the same difference is still observable. Yet the Germans have made no serious efforts to better themselves.—ED.

quality, tawdered out; narrow nasty streets out of
repair, wretchedly thin of inhabitants, and above
half of the common sort asking alms. I cannot
help fancying one under the figure of a clean
Dutch citizen's wife, and the other like a poor
town lady of pleasure, painted and ribboned out
in her head-dress, with tarnished silver-laced shoes,
a ragged under-petticoat; a miserable mixture of
vice and poverty.

They have sumptuary laws in this town, which
distinguish their rank by their dress, prevent the
excess which ruins so many other cities, and has a
more agreeable effect to the eye of a stranger than
our fashions. I think, after the Archbishop of
Cambray having declared for them, I need not be
ashamed to own that I wish these laws were in
force in other parts of the world. When one considers impartially the merit of a rich suit of clothes
in most places, the respect and the smiles of favour
it procures, not to speak of the envy and the sighs
it occasions (which is very often the principal
charm to the wearer,) one is forced to confess that
there is need of an uncommon understanding to
resist the temptation of pleasing friends and mortifying rivals ; and that it is natural to young people to fall into a folly which betrays them to that
want of money which is the source of a thousand
basenesses. What numbers of men have begun
the world with generous inclinations, that have
afterwards been the instruments of bringing misery
on a whole people, being led by vain expense
into debts that they could clear no other way

but by the forfeit of their honour, and which
they never could have contracted, if the respect
the many pay to habits was fixed by law only
to a particular colour or cut of plain cloth !
These reflections draw after them others that are
too melancholy. I will make haste to put them
out of your head by the farce of relics, with
which I have been entertained in all the Romish
churches.

The Lutherans are not quite free from these
follies. I have seen here, in the principal church,
a large piece of the cross set in jewels, and the
point of the spear, which they told me, very
gravely, was the same that pierced the side of our
Saviour. But I was particularly diverted in a
little Roman Catholic church, which is permitted
here, where the professors of that religion are not
very rich, and consequently cannot adorn their
images in so rich a manner as their neighbours.
For, not to be quite destitute 'of all finery, they
have dressed up an image of our Saviour over the
altar, in a fair full-bottomed wig, very well powdered. I imagine I see your ladyship stare at this
article, of which you very much doubt the veracity;
but, upon my word, I have not yet made use of
the privilege of a traveller ; and my whole account
is written with the same plain sincerity of heart
with which I assure you that I am, dear madam,
yours, &c., &c.

VI.

TO MRS. THISTLETHWAYTE.

Ratisbon, Aug. 30, 1716.

I HAD the pleasure of receiving yours but the day before I left London. I give you a thousand thanks for your good wishes, and have such an opinion of their efficacy, that I am persuaded I owe in part to them the good luck of having proceeded so far on my long journey without any ill accident; for I do not reckon it any to have been stopped a few days in this town by a cold, since it has not only given me an opportunity of seeing all that is curious in it, but of making some acquaintance with the ladies, who have all been to see me with great civility, particularly Madame ——, the wife of our king's envoy from Hanover. She has carried me to all the assemblies, and I have been magnificently entertained at her house, which is one of the finest here.

You know that all the nobility of this place are envoys from different states. Here are a great number of them, and they might pass their time agreeably enough if they were less delicate on the point of ceremony. But, instead of joining in the design of making the town as pleasant to one another as they can, and improving their little societies, they amuse themselves no other way than with perpetual quarrels, which they take care to eternize, by leaving them to their successors; and an envoy to Ratisbon receives, regularly, half-a-dozen quarrels among the perquisites of his employment.

You may be sure the ladies are not wanting, on their side, in cherishing and improving these important *picques*, which divide the town almost into as many parties as there are families. They choose rather to suffer the mortification of sitting almost alone on their assembly nights, than to recede one jot from their pretensions. I have not been here above a week, and yet I have heard from almost every one of them the whole history of their wrongs, and dreadful complaints of the injustice of their neighbours, in hopes to draw me to their party. But I think it very prudent to remain neuter; though, if I were to stay among them, there would be no possibility of continuing so, their quarrels running so high that they will not be civil to those that visit their adversaries. The foundation of these everlasting disputes turns entirely upon rank, place, and the title of Excellency, which they all pretend to; and, what is very hard, will give it to nobody. For my part, I could not forbear advising them (for the public good) to give the title of Excellency to every body, which would include the receiving it from every body; but the very mention of such a dishonourable peace was received with as much indignation as Mrs. Black-aire did the motion of a reference : and, indeed, I began to think myself ill-natured, to offer to take from them, in a town where there are so few diversions, so entertaining an amusement. I know that

c. 2

my peaceable disposition already gives me a very
ill figure, and that it is *publicly* whispered, as a
piece of impertinent pride in me, that I have hitherto been saucily civil to every body, as if I thought
nobody good enough to quarrel with. I should be
obliged to change my behaviour, if I did not intend to pursue my journey in a few days.

I have been to see the churches here, and had
the permission of touching the relics, which was
never suffered in places where I was not known.
I had, by this privilege, the opportunity of making
an observation, which I doubt not might have been
made in all the other churches, that the emeralds
and rubies which they show round their relics and
images are most of them false; though they tell
you that many of the *crosses* and *Madonnas*, set
round with these stones, have been the gifts of the
emperors and other great princes. I do not doubt,
indeed, but they were at first jewels of value; but
the good fathers have found it convenient to apply
them to other uses, and the people are just as well
satisfied with bits of glass. Among these relics
they showed me a prodigious claw, set in gold,
which they called the claw of a griffin ; (⁹) and I
could not forbear asking the reverend priest that

(⁹) Her ladyship's "griffin's claw" is modest compared with
a relic shown in one of the continental churches to a recent
traveller. This was a small black bottle, which, to common
eyes, appeared to be quite empty. "Friend," said he to the
priest, "there is nothing in this bottle." "Nothing, sir!"
answered the good man, with much concern, "nothing! why,
it contains some of the darkness that overspread the land of
Egypt!"—ED.

showed it, Whether the griffin was a saint ? This
question almost put him beside his gravity; but
he answered, They only kept it as a curiosity.
I was very much scandalized at a large silver
image of the *Trinity*, where the *Father* is represented under the figure of a decrepit old man,
with a beard down to his knees, and a triple crown
on his head, holding in his arms the *Son*, fixed on
the cross, and the *Holy Ghost*, in the shape of a
dove, hovering over him.

Madam —— is come this minute to call me to
the assembly, and forces me to tell you, very
abruptly, that I am ever yours, &c., &c.

VII.

TO THE COUNTESS OF MAR.

Vienna, Sept. 8, 1716.

I AM now, my dear sister, safely arrived at Vienna;
and, I thank God, have not at all suffered in my
health, nor (what is dearer to me) in that of my
child, ([10]) by all our fatigues.

We travelled by water from Ratisbon, a journey
perfectly agreeable, down the Danube, in one of
those little vessels that they very properly call
wooden houses, having in them all the conveniences of a palace, stoves in the chambers, kit-

---

([10]) Edward Wortley Montagu, her only son, was born
1713.

chens, &c. They are rowed by twelve men each, and move with such incredible swiftness, that in the same day you have the pleasure of a vast variety of prospects; and within the space of a few hours, you have the pleasure of seeing a populous city adorned with magnificent palaces, and the most romantic solitudes which appear distant from the commerce of mankind, the banks of the Danube being charmingly diversified with woods, rocks, mountains covered with vines, fields of corn, large cities, and ruins of ancient castles. I saw the great towns of Passau and Lintz, famous for the retreat of the imperial court when Vienna was besieged.

This town, which has the honour of being the emperor's residence, did not at all answer my ideas of it, being much less than I expected to find it; the streets are very close, and so narrow one cannot observe the fine fronts of the palaces, though many of them very well deserve observation, being truly magnificent. They are built of fine white stone, and are excessively high. For, as the town is too little for the number of the people that desire to live in it, the builders seem to have projected to repair that misfortune by clapping one town on the top of another, most of the houses being of five, and some of them six stories. You may easily imagine that the streets being so narrow the rooms are extremely dark; and, what is an inconvenience much more intolerable, in my opinion, there is no house that has so few as five or six families in it. The apartments of the greatest ladies, and even of the ministers of state, are divided but by a partition from that of a tailor or shoemaker ; and I know nobody that has above two floors in any house, one for their own use, and one higher for their servants. Those that have houses of their own let out the rest of them to whoever will take them; and thus the great stairs (which are all of stone) are as common and as dirty as the street. ([11]) It is true, when you have once travelled through them, nothing can be more surprisingly magnificent than the apartments. They are commonly a *suite* of eight or ten large rooms, all inlaid, the doors and windows richly carved and gilt, and the furniture such as is seldom seen in the palaces of sovereign princes in other countries. Their apartments are adorned with hangings of the finest tapestry of Brussels, prodigious looking-glasses in silver frames, fine japan tables, beds, chairs, canopies, and window-curtains of the richest Genoa damask or velvet, almost covered with gold lace or embroidery. The whole is made gay by pictures, and vast jars of japan china, and in almost every room large lustres of rock crystal.

([11]) Since Lady Mary wrote, the English have become sufficiently familiar with continental lodging-houses, which are much alike in all great cities. Though the stairs, it must be confessed, are seldom over cleanly, the internal arrangements are superior to our own ; every floor having its separate kitchen, and every other convenience required in a house. This is more particularly the case in Paris, where the lower floors are magnificently furnished, while the upper ones are accommodated to the means of humbler lodgers.—ED.

I have already had the honour of being invited to dinner by several of the first people of quality ; and I must do them the justice to say, the good taste and magnificence of their tables very well answered to that of their furniture. I have been more than once entertained with fifty dishes of meat, all served in silver, and well dressed ; the dessert proportionable, served in the finest china, But the variety and richness of their wines is what appears the most surprising. The constant way is, to lay a list of their names upon the plates of the guests, along with the napkins, (¹²) and I have counted several times the number of eighteen different sorts, all exquisite in their kinds.

I was yesterday at Count Schönbrunn, (¹³) the vice-chancellor's garden, where I was invited to dinner. I must own I never saw a place so perfectly delightful as the fauxburg of Vienna. It is very large, and almost wholly composed of delicious palaces. If the emperor found it proper to permit the gates of the town to be laid open, that the fauxburg might be joined to it, he would have one of the largest and best built cities in Europe.

(¹²) A very similar practice prevailed at the tables of the ancients, where a list of the various dishes, &c., was placed before the guests, as at an ordinary, and every one chose what he liked best.—ED.

(¹³) The palace of Schönbrunn is distant about two miles from Vienna. It was designed by John Bernard Fischers, the Palladio of Germany, in 1696, and was afterwards used as a hunting-seat by the emperor and his court.

Count Schönbrunn's villa is one of the most magnificent; the furniture, all rich brocades, so well fancied and fitted up nothing can look more gay and splendid ; not to speak of a gallery full of rarities of coral, mother-of-pearl, &c., and throughout the whole house, a profusion of gilding, carving, fine paintings, the most beautiful porcelain, statues of alabaster and ivory, and vast orange and lemon-trees in gilt pots. The dinner was perfectly fine and well ordered, and made still more agreeable by the good humour of the count.

I have not yet been at court, being forced to stay for my gown, without which there is no waiting on the empress; though I am not without great impatience to see a beauty that has been the admiration of so many different nations. When I have had the honour, I will not fail to let you know my real thoughts, always taking a particular pleasure in communicating them to my dear sister.

VIII.

MR. POPE TO LADY MONTAGU.

MADAM,   Twickenham, Aug. 18, 1716.

I CAN say little to recommend the letters I am beginning to write to you, ([14]) but that they will

---

([14]) The reader, whether I point it out or not, will feel how

be the most impartial representations of a free
heart, and the truest copies you ever saw, though
of a very mean original. Not a feature will be
softened, or any advantageous light employed to
make the ugly thing a little less hideous, but you
shall find it in all respects most horribly like.
You will do me an injustice if you look upon any
thing I shall say from this instant, as a compliment
either to you or to myself: whatever I write will
be the real thought of that hour, and I know you
will no more expect it of me to persevere till death
in every sentiment or notion I now set down, than
you would imagine a man's face should never
change after his picture was once drawn.

The freedom I shall use in this manner of thinking aloud, (as somebody calls it,) or talking upon
paper, may, indeed, prove me a fool, but it will
prove me one of the best sort of fools, the honest
ones. And since what folly we have will infallibly
buoy up at one time or other, in spite of all our
art to keep it down, it is almost foolish to take any

---

inferior, in the epistolary style, Pope was to Lady Mary. We
observe him straining after effect, full of false conceits, extravagant expressions, and evidences of a passion he was too weak
to subdue, and too timid to confess. This circumstance renders
his letters peculiarly insipid. He strives to cloak his feelings
sometimes with a show of religion, sometimes with affected
admiration for his fair correspondent's talents, and anon with the
cold mask of friendly esteem ; but all the while his meaning is
clear, and was pre-eminently so to the lady herself. Nothing
that Pope has left behind him are so little calculated to recommend him to posterity, either as a man or as an author, as the
letters in this collection.—ED.

pains to conceal it at all, and almost knavish to do it from those that are our friends. If Momus's project had taken, of having windows in our breasts, I should be for carrying it further, and making those windows casements: that, while a man showed his heart to all the world, he might do something more for his friends, even take it out, and trust it to their handllng. I think I love you as well as king Herod could Herodias, (though I never had so much as one dance with you,) and would as freely give you my heart in a dish as he did another's head. But since Jupiter will not have it so, I must be content to show my taste in life as I do my taste in painting, by loving to have as little drapery as possible, because it is good to use people to what they must be acquainted with; and there will certainly come some day of judgment to uncover every soul of us. We shall then see how the prudes of this world owed all their fine figure only to their being a little straiter laced, and that they were naturally as arrant squabs as those that went more loose, nay, as those that never girded their loins at all.

But a particular reason to engage you to write your thoughts the more freely to me is, that I am confident no one knows you better. For I find, when others express their opinion of you, it falls very short of mine, and I am sure, at the same time, theirs is such as you would think sufficiently in your favour.

You may easily imagine how desirous I must be of a correspondence with a person who had taught

me long ago that it was as possible to esteem at
first sight as to love : and who has since ruined me
for all the conversation of one sex, and almost all
the friendship of the other.   I am but too sensible,
through your means, that the company of men
wants a certain softness to recommend it, and that
of women wants everything else.   How often have
I been quietly going to take possession of that
tranquillity and indolence I had so long found in
the country, when one evening of your conversation has spoiled me for a *solitaire* too !   Books
have lost their effect upon me ; and I was convinced since I saw you that there is something more
powerful than philosophy, and, since I heard you,
that there is one alive wiser than all the sages.
A plague of female wisdom ! it makes a man ten
times more uneasy than his own !   What is very
strange, Virtue herself, when you have the dressing
her, is too amiable for one's repose.   What a world
of good might you have done in your time, if you
had allowed half the fine gentlemen who have seen
you to have but conversed with you ?   They would
have been strangely caught, while they thought
only to fall in love with a fair face, and you had
bewitched them with reason and virtue ; two beauties that the very fops pretend to have no acquaintance with.

The unhappy distance at which we correspond
removes a great many of those punctilious restric-
tions and decorums that oftentimes in nearer conversation prejudice truth to save good breeding.   I
may now hear of my faults, and you of your good

qualities, without a blush on either side. We converse upon such unfortunate generous terms as exclude the regards of fear, shame, or design in either of us. And methinks it would be as ungenerous a part to impose even in a single thought upon each other, in this state of separation, as for spirits of a different sphere, who have so little intercourse with us, to employ that little, (as some would make us think they do,) in putting tricks and delusions upon poor mortals.

Let me begin, then, madam, by asking you a question, which may enable me to judge better of my own conduct than most instances of my life. In what manner did I behave the last hour I saw you ? What degree of concern did I discover when I felt a misfortune, which I hope you never will feel, that of parting from what one most esteems ? For if my parting looked but like that of your common acquaintance, I am the greatest of all the hypocrites that ever decency made

I never since pass by the house but with the same sort of melancholy that we feel upon seeing the tomb of a friend, which only serves to put us in mind of what we have lost. I reflect upon the circumstances of your departure, your behaviour in what I may call your last moments, and I indulge a gloomy kind of satisfaction in thinking you gave some of those last moments to me. I would fain imagine this was not accidental, but proceeded from a penetration which I know you have, in finding out the truth of people's sentiments, and that you were not unwilling the last

man that would have parted with you should be
the last that did. I really looked upon you then
as the friends of Curtius might have done upon
that hero in the instant he was devoting himself to
glory, and running to be lost, out of generosity. I
was obliged to admire your resolution in as great a
degree as I deplored it; and could only wish that
Heaven would reward so much merit as was to be
taken from us, with all the felicity it could enjoy
elsewhere. May that person for whom you have
left all the world be so just as to prefer you to all
the world. I believe his good understanding has
engaged him to do so hitherto, and I think his
gratitude must for the future. May you continue
to think him worthy of whatever you have done;
may you ever look upon him with the eyes of a
first lover, nay, if possible, with all the unreasonable happy fondness of an unexperienced one, surrounded with all the enchantments and ideas of
romance and poetry. In a word, may you receive
from him as many pleasures and gratifications as
even I think you can give. I wish this from my
heart, and while I examine what passes there in
regard to you, I cannot but glory in my own heart
that it is capable of so much generosity. I am,
with all unalterable esteem and sincerity,

Madam,

Your most faithful obedient

humble servant,

A. POPE.

IX.

TO MR. POPE. ([15])

Vienna, Sept. 14, 1716

PERHAPS you will laugh at me for thanking you very gravely for all the obliging concern you express for me.   It is certain that I may, if I please, take the fine things you say, to me for wit and raillery; and, it may be, it would be taking them right.   But I never, in my life, was half so well disposed to believe you in earnest as I am at present, and that distance, which makes the continuation of your friendship improbable, has very much increased my faith in it.

I find that I have, (as well as the rest of my sex,) whatever face I set on it, a strong disposition to believe in miracles.   Do not fancy, however, that I am infected by the air of these popish countries; I have, indeed, so far wandered from the discipline of the church of England as to have been last Sunday at the opera, which was performed in

---

([15]) In the eighth volume of Pope's Works, are first published thirteen of his letters to Lady Mary Wortley Montagu, communicated to Dr. Warton by the present primate of Ireland. These MSS. are in the possession of the Marquis of Bute.   As many are without date, the arrangement of them must be directed by circumstances; and, as most of them were written to Lady Mary during her first absence from England, we shall advert to them, as making a part of this correspondence.

The letter of Pope, to which this is an answer, is printed from the original MS.

the garden of the *Favorita;* ([16]) and I was so much
pleased with it, I have not yet repented my seeing
it. Nothing of that kind ever was more magnificent ; and I can easily believe what I am told, that
the decorations and habits cost the emperor thirty
thousand pounds sterling. The stage was built
over a very large canal, and, at the beginning of
the second act, divided into two parts, discovering
the water, on which there immediately came, from
different parts, two fleets of little gilded vessels,
that gave the representation of a naval fight. It is
not easy to imagine the beauty of this scene, which
I took particular notice of. But all the rest were
perfectly fine in their kind. The story of the
opera is the enchantment of Alcina, which gives
opportunities for a great variety of machines, and
changes of the scenes, which are performed with a
surprising swiftness. The theatre is so large that
it is hard to carry the eye to the end of it, and the

([16]) There are few things in which Protestantism differs more
from Catholicism than the spirit in which the Sunday is spent
by the professors of each.   Among Catholics it is nothing more
than a holiday, a periodical cessation from labour, which they
devote chiefly to amusement.   Protestants, on the other hand,
when they act up to the rules of their faith, convert it into a season of contrition, and strict religious exercise.   Both, I think,
run into extremes.   Harmless amusement must be harmless,
even on Sunday.   Fenelon had, perhaps, a right conception of
the matter ; for, when a priest of his diocese forbade the weekly
meetings of the peasantry, who used on that day to assemble and
dance on the village-green, the good bishop gently reprimanded
him, and said, " Let them dance as much as they please.   They
might be much worse employed.   But it is not necessary for you
and I to join them !"—ED.

habits in the utmost magnificence, to the number
of one hundred and eight. No house could hold
such large decorations; but the ladies all sitting
in the open air exposes them to great inconveniences; for there is but one canopy for the imperial family; and the first night it was represented,
a shower of rain happening, the opera was broken
off, and the company crowded away in such confu-
sion, that I was almost squeezed to death. ([17])

But if their operas are thus delightful their
comedies are in as high a degree ridiculous. They
have but one playhouse, where I had the curiosity
to go to a German comedy, and was very glad it
happened to be the story of Amphitryon. As that
subject has been already handled by a Latin,
French, and English poet, I was curious to see
what an Austrian author would make of it. I
understood enough of that language to comprehend the greatest part of it; and, besides, I took
with me a lady, who had the goodness to explain
to me every word. The way is, to take a box,
which holds four, for yourself and company. The
fixed price is a gold ducat. I thought the house
very low and dark; but, I confess, the comedy admirably recompensed that defect. I never laughed

---

([17]) In a climate like that of Vienna nothing could be more
maladroit than this imitation of the ancients, whose hypæthral
theatres suited very well with their sunny and unhumid atmosphere. Nevertheless, even in Greece and southern Italy, a *vela-
rium* was at length found necessary, since flying showers sometimes scattered the audiences, and spotted their saffron-coloured
chitons, though the theatres were open only in the spring and
summer months.—ED.

so much in my life. It began with Jupiter's falling in love out of a peep-hole in the clouds, and
ended with the birth of Hercules. But what was
most pleasant was the use Jupiter made of his
metamorphosis ; for you no sooner saw him under
the figure of Amphitryon, but, instead of flying to
Alcmena, with the raptures Mr. Dryden puts into
his mouth, he sends for Amphitryon's tailor, and
cheats him of a laced coat, and his banker of a
bag of money, a Jew of a diamond-ring, and bespeaks a great supper in his name : and the greatest
part of the comedy turns upon poor Amphitryon's being tormented by these people for their
debts. Mercury uses Sosia in the same manner. But I could not easily pardon the liberty
the poet has taken of larding his play with, not
only indecent expressions, but such gross words,
as I don't think our mob would suffer from a
mountebank. Besides, the two Sosias very fairly
let down their breeches in the direct view of the
boxes, which were full of people of the first rank,
that seemed very well pleased with their entertainment, and assured me this was a celebrated
piece. ([18])

I shall conclude my letter with this remarkable
relation, very well worthy the serious consideration

([18]) Her ladyship has here given a practical proof that no
degree of coarseness is sufficient to deter women from frequenting
the theatre. We may therefore recommend this passage to the
consideration of those German *savans* who infer from the character of the Aristophanic plays, that the ladies of Athens could not
have been present at the performance of them.—ED.

of Mr. Collier. ([19])   I will not trouble you with
farewell compliments, which I think generally
as impertinent as courtesies at leaving the room,
when the visit had been too long already.

X.

TO THE COUNTESS OF MAR.

Vienna, Sept. 14, 1716.

THOUGH I have so lately troubled you, my dear sister, with a long letter, yet I will keep my promise
in giving you an account of my first going to court.

In order to that ceremony, I was squeezed up in
a gown, and adorned with a gorget and the other
implements thereunto belonging ; a dress very in-
convenient, but which certainly shows the neck
and shape to great advantage. I cannot forbear
giving you some description of the fashions here,
which are more monstrous, and contrary to all
common sense and reason, than it is possible for
you to imagine. They build certain fabrics of
gauze on their heads, about a yard high, consisting
of three or four stories, fortified with numberless
yards of heavy ribbon. The foundation of this
structure is a thing they call a *bourle,* which is

([19]) Jeremy Collier, an English divine, eminent for his piety
and wit. In 1698 he wrote " A short View of the Immorality
and Profaneness of the English Stage, together with the sense of
Antiquity on this subject," 8vo. This tract excited the resentment of the wits, and engaged him in a controversy with Congreve and Vanbrugh.—ED.

exactly of the same shape and kind, but about four times as big as those rolls our prudent milk-maids make use of to fix their pails upon. This machine they cover with their own hair, which they mix with a great deal of false, it being a particular beauty to have their heads too large to go into a moderate tub. Their hair is prodigiously powdered, to conceal the mixture, and set out with three or four rows of bodkins (wonderfully large, that stick out two or three inches from their hair,) made of diamonds, pearls, red, green, and yellow stones, that it certainly requires as much art and experience to carry the load upright as to dance upon May-day with the garland.[20] Their whale-bone petticoats outdo ours by several yards' circumference, and cover some acres of ground.

You may easily suppose how this extraordinary dress sets off and improves the natural ugliness with which God Almighty has been pleased to endow them, generally speaking. Even the lovely empress herself is obliged to comply, in some de-

---

[20] A history of the absurdities and extravagance of female dress would be an amusing and instructive work, which might remove many prejudices, and among others the too common one, that our fair contemporaries are more irrational in this respect than their predecessors. Upon comparison, too, it might be found that the reasoning sex have made as little use of their reason, in the matter of dress, as the ladies themselves ; and with far less excuse. Two or three years ago the *bourle* appeared to be revived in England, when one saw young women perambulating the streets with an acre of silk and pasteboard on their heads ; which furnished the caricaturists with excellent materials to work upon.—ED.

gree, with these absurd fashions, which they would
not quit for all the world. I had a private audience
(according to ceremony) of half-an-hour, and then
all the other ladies were permitted to come and make
their court. I was perfectly charmed with the empress : ([21]) I cannot, however, tell you that her features are regular ; her eyes are not large, but have
a lively look, full of sweetness ; her complexion
the finest I ever saw ; her nose and forehead well
made, but her mouth has ten thousand charms
that touch the soul. When she smiles, it is with a
beauty and sweetness that forces adoration. She
has a vast quantity of fine fair hair; but then her
person !—one must speak of it poetically to do it
rigid justice ; all that the poets have said of the
mien of Juno, the air of Venus, come not up to the
truth. The Graces move with her ; the famous
statue of Medicis was not formed with more delicate proportions ; nothing can be added to the
beauty of her neck and hands. Till I saw them I
did not believe there were any in nature so perfect,
and I was almost sorry that my rank here did not
permit me to kiss them. But they are kissed suffi-

([21]) One of the principal charms of Lady Mary's letters is,
doubtless, the ingenuous enthusiasm for beauty with which they
everywhere abound. She speaks without a spark of envy of
women evidently far her superiors in personal accomplishments ;
and that not from reflecting how amiable it would appear, but
because to gaze on a lovely form was delightful to her. This,
therefore, whatever faults and imperfections she might have,
must be regarded as a proof that her character was originally
good, and will infallibly secure for her the admiration of
posterity.—ED.

ciently; for every body that waits on her pays that homage at their entrance, and when they take leave.

When the ladies were come in, she sat down to quinze. I could not play at a game I had never seen before, and she ordered me a seat at her right hand, and had the goodness to talk to me very much, with that grace so natural to her. I expected every moment, when the men were to come in to pay their court; but this drawing-room is very different from that of England; no man enters it but the grand-master, who comes in to advertise the empress of the approach of the emperor. His imperial majesty did me the honour of speaking to me in a very obliging manner; but he never speaks to any of the other ladies; and the whole passes with a gravity and air of ceremony that has something very formal in it.

The Empress Amelia, dowager of the late Emperor Joseph, came this evening to wait on the reigning empress, followed by the two archduchesses, her daughters, who are very agreeable young princesses. Their imperial majesties rose, and went to meet her at the door of the room, after which she was seated in an armed chair, next the empress, and in the same manner at supper, and there the men had the permission of paying their court. The archduchesses sat on chairs with backs without arms. The table was entirely served, and all the dishes set on by the empress's maids of honour, which are twelve young ladies of the first quality.([22])

([22]) A genuine trait of despotism.—Ed.

They have no salary but their chamber at court,
where they live in a sort of confinement, not being
suffered to go to the assembles or public places in
town, except in compliment to the wedding of a
sister maid, whom the empress always presents
with her picture set in diamonds. The three first
of them are called *ladies of the key,* and wear gold
keys by their sides ; but what I find most pleasant
is the custom which obliges them, as long as they
live, after they have left the empress's service, to
make her some present every year on the day of her
feast. Her majesty is served by no married women,
but the *grande maitresse,* who is generally a widow
of the first quality, always very old, and is at the
same time groom of the stole, and mother of the
maids. The dressers are not at all in the figure
they pretend to in England, being looked upon no
otherwise than as downright chambermaids.

I had an audience next day of the empress-
mother, a princess of great virtue and goodness,
but who piques herself too much on a violent devotion. She is perpetually performing extraordinary acts of penance, without having ever done
any thing to deserve them. She has the same
number of maids of honour, whom she suffers to
go in colours ; but she herself never quits her
mourning : and sure nothing can be more dismal
than the mourning here, even for a brother. There
is not the least bit of linen to be seen; all black
crape instead of it. The neck, ears, and side of
the face, are covered with a plaited piece of the
same stuff, and the face, that peeps out in the

midst of it, looks as if it were pilloried. The
widows wear, over and above, a crape forehead-
cloth ; and in this solemn weed go to all the public places of diversion without scruple.

The next day I was to wait on the empress
Amelia, who is now at her palace of retirement,
half-a-mile from the town. I had there the pleasure of seeing a diversion wholly new to me, but
which is the common amusement of this court.
The empress herself was seated on a little throne
at the end of the fine alley in the garden, and
on each side of her were ranged two parties of
her ladies of quality, headed by two young archduchesses, all dressed in their hair, full of jewels,
with fine light guns in their hands; ([23]) and at
proper distances were placed three oval pictures,
which were the marks to be shot at. The first was
that of a CUPID, filling a bumper of Burgundy, and
the motto, " 'Tis easy to be valiant here." The
second, a FORTUNE, holding a garland in her hand,
the motto, " For her whom Fortune favours." The
third was a SWORD, with a laurel wreath on the
point, the motto, " Here is no shame to be van-
quished." Near the empress was a gilded trophy
wreathed with flowers, and made of little crooks,
on which were hung rich Turkish handkerchiefs,
tippets, ribbons, laces, &c. for the small prizes.
The empress gave the first with her own hand,
which was a fine ruby ring, set round with diamonds, in a gold snuff-box. There was for the

---

([23]) Extremely absurd and unfeminine.—ED.

second a little Cupid set with brilliants : and, besides these, a set of fine china for the tea-table,
enchased in gold, japan trunks, fans, and many
gallantries of the same nature. All the men of
quality at Vienna were spectators ; but the ladies
only had permission to shoot, and the Archduchess
Amelia carried off the first prize. I was very well
pleased with having seen this entertainment, and I
do not know but it might make as good a figure as
the prize-shooting in the Æneid, if I could write as
well as Virgil. This is the favourite pleasure of
the emperor, and there is rarely a week without
some feast of this kind, which makes the young
ladies skilful enough to defend a fort. They
laughed very much to see me afraid to handle a
gun.

My dear sister, you will easily pardon an abrupt
conclusion. I believe, by this time, you are ready
to fear I shall never conclude at all.

XI.

TO THE LADY RICH.

Vienna, Sept. 20, 1716.

I AM extremely pleased, but not at all surprised,
at the long delightful letter you have had the goodness to send me. I know that you can think of an
absent friend even in the midst of a court, and you
love to oblige, where you can have no view of a
return ; and I expect from you that you should

love me, and think of me, when you do not see
me.

I have compassion for the mortifications that you
tell me befel our little friend; and I pity her much
more, since I know that they are only owing to
the barbarous customs of our country. Upon my
word, if she were here, she would have no other
fault but that of being something too young for
the fashion, and she has nothing to do but to trans-
plant herself hither about seven years hence, to be
again a young and blooming beauty. I can assure
you that wrinkles, or a small stoop in the shoulders,
nay, even gray hairs are no objection to the making
new conquests. I know you cannot easily figure
to yourself a young fellow of five-and-twenty ogling
my Lady Suffolk with passion, or pressing to hand
the Countess of Oxford from an opera. But such
are the sights I see every day, and I do not perceive any body surprised at them but myself. A
woman, till five-and-thirty, is only looked upon as
a raw girl; and can possibly make no noise in the
world till about forty. I do not know what your
ladyship may think of this matter; but it is a considerable comfort to me to know that there is upon
earth such a paradise for old women; and I am
content to be insignificant at present, in the design
of returning when I am fit to appear nowhere else.
I cannot help lamenting, on this occasion, the
pitiful case of too many good English ladies, long
since retired to prudery and ratafia, (²⁴) whom, if

(²⁴) That ratafia was no weak beverage may be inferred from

their stars had luckily conducted hither, would shine in the first rank of beauties. Besides, that perplexing word *reputation* has quite another meaning here than what you give it at London; and getting a lover is so far from losing, that it is properly getting reputation; ladies being much more respected in regard to the rank of their lovers, than that of their husbands.

But, what you will think very odd, the two sects that divide our whole nation of petticoats are utterly unknown in this place. Here are neither coquettes nor prudes. No woman dares appear coquette enough to encourage two lovers at a time. And I have not seen any such prudes as to pretend fidelity to their husbands, who are certainly the best natured set of people in the world, and look upon their wives' gallants as favourably as men do upon their deputies, that take the troublesome part of their business off their hands. They have not, however, the less to do on that account; for they are generally deputies in another place themselves; in one word, it is the established custom for every lady to have two husbands, one that bears the name, and another that performs the duties. (²⁵) And these engagements are so well

---

the old song, where the valiant captain, who has been too successful in his campaigns among the ladies, has recourse to it to drown the qualms of conscience : —

" His cruel thoughts tormented him, his stomach left him daily,
He took to drinking ratafie, and thought upon Miss Baillie."—ED.

(²⁵) Since we have grown more familiar with continental manners, particularly as they are modified in Italy, the system of *Cecisbeism*, of which Lady Montagu here speaks, no longer

known that it would be a downright affront, and
publicly resented, if you invited a woman of quality
to dinner, without, at the same time, inviting her
two attendants of lover and husband, between
whom she sits in state with great gravity. The
sub-marriages generally last twenty years together,
and the lady often commands the poor lover's
estate, even to the utter ruin of his family.

These connexions, indeed, are seldom begun by
any real passion, as other matches; for a man makes
but an ill figure that is not in some commerce of
this nature; and a woman looks out for a lover as
soon as she is married, as part of her equipage,
without which she could not be genteel; and the
first article of the treaty is establishing the pension
which remains to the lady in case the gallant
should prove inconstant. This chargeable point
of honour I look upon as the real foundation of so
many wonderful instances of constancy. I really
know some women of the first quality, whose pen-
sions are as well known as their annual rents, and
yet nobody esteems them the less; on the contrary,
their discretion would be called in question, if they
should be suspected to be mistresses for nothing.
A great part of their emulation consists in trying
who shall get most; and having no intrigue at all
is so far a disgrace, that I will assure you a lady who
is very much my friend here, told me but yester-

---

appears extraordinary to us. Even our countrywomen, in those
haunts of sin, have not been slow to discover the advantages of
a certain practice, which no person with the slightest pretension
to principle can fail to view in the proper light.—ED.

day how much I was obliged to her for justifying
my conduct in a conversation relating to me, where
it was publicly asserted that I could not possibly
have common sense, since I had been in town
above a fortnight, and had made no steps towards
commencing an amour. My friend pleaded for me
that my stay was uncertain, and she believed that
was the cause of my seeming stupidity; and this
was all she could find to say in my justification.

But one of the pleasantest adventures I ever met
with in my life was last night, and it will give you
a just idea in what a delicate manner the *belles
passions* are managed in this country. I was at
the assembly of the Countess of ——, and the
young Count of ——, leading me down stairs,
asked me how long I was to stay at Vienna? I
made answer, that my stay depended on the emperor, and it was not in my power to determine it.
" Well, madam," said he, " whether your time here
is to be long or short, I think you ought to pass it
agreeably ; and to that end you must engage in a
little affair of the heart." " My heart," answered I,
gravely enough, " does not engage very easily;
and I have no design of parting with it." " I see,
madam," said he, sighing, " by the ill nature of
that answer, I am not to hope for it, which is a
great mortification to me that am charmed with
you. But, however, I am still devoted to your
service ; and, since I am not worthy of entertaining
you myself, do me the honour of letting me know
whom you like best among us, and I will engage to
manage the affair entirely to your satisfaction."

You may judge in what manner I should have received this compliment in my own country; but I was well enough acquainted with the way of this to know that he really intended me an obligation, and I thanked him with a very grave courtesy for his zeal to serve me, and only assured him I had no occasion to make use of it.

Thus you see, my dear, that gallantry and good breeding are as different, in different climates, as morality and religion. Who have the rightest notions of both, we shall never know till the day of judgment; for which great day of *eclaircissement* I own there is very little impatience in your, &c., &c.

XII.

TO MRS. THISTLETHWAYTE.

Vienna, Sept. 26th, 1716.

I WAS never more agreeably surprised than by your obliging letter. It is a peculiar mark of my esteem that I tell you so; and I can assure you that if I loved you one grain less than I do, I should be very sorry to see it so diverting as it is. The mortal aversion I have to writing, makes me tremble at the thoughts of a new correspondent; and I believe I have disobliged no less than a dozen of my London acquaintance by refusing to hear from them, though I did verily think they intended to send me very entertaining letters. But I had rather lose the pleasure of reading several witty things, than be forced to write many stupid ones.

Yet, in spite of these considerations, I am charmed with this proof of your friendship, and beg a continuation of the same goodness, though I fear the dulness of this will make you immediately repent of it. It is not from Austria that one can write with vivacity; and I am already infected with the phlegm of the country. Even their amours and their quarrels are carried on with a surprising temper; and they are never lively but upon points of ceremony. There, I own, they show all their passions; and it it not long since two coaches, meeting in a narrow street at night, the ladies in them not being able to adjust the ceremonial of which should go back, sat there, with equal gallantry, till two in the morning, and were both so fully determined to die upon the spot, rather than yield in a point of that importance, that the street would never have been clear till their deaths, if the emperor had not sent his guards to part them; and even then they refused to stir, till the expedient could be found of taking them both out in chairs, exactly in the same moment. ([26]) After the ladies were agreed, it was with some difficulty that the *pas* was decided between the two coach-men, no less tenacious of their rank than the ladies.

This passion is so omnipotent in the breasts of the women that even their husbands never die but

---

([26]) An excellent stroke of satire. — ED.

they are ready to break their hearts, because that
fatal hour puts an end to their rank, no widows
having any place at Vienna. The men are not
much less touched with this point of honour, and
they do not only scorn to marry, but even to make
love to any woman of a family not as illustrious as
their own; and the pedigree is much more considered by them than either the complexion or
features of their mistresses. Happy are the shes
that can number amongst their ancestors counts of
the empire; they have neither occasion for beauty,
money, nor good conduct to get them husbands.
It is true, as to money, it is seldom any advantage
to the man they marry; the laws of Austria confine the woman's portion to two thousand florins
(about two hundred pounds English,) and whatever they have beside remains in their own possession and disposal. Thus, here are many ladies
much richer than their husbands, who are, however, obliged to allow them pin-money agreeably
to their quality; and I attribute to this considerable branch of prerogative the liberty that they
take upon other occasions.

I am sure you, that know my laziness, and extreme indifference on this subject, will pity me,
entangled amongst all these ceremonies, which are
a wonderful burden to me, though I am the envy
of the whole town, having, by their own customs,
the *pas* before them all. They indeed so revenge
upon the poor envoys this great respect shown
to ambassadors, that (with all my indifference) I
should be very uneasy to suffer it. Upon days of

ceremony they have no entrance at court, and on other days must content themselves with walking after every soul, and being the very last taken notice of. But I must write a volume to let you know all the ceremonies; and I have already said too much on so dull a subject, which, however, employs the whole care of the people here. I need not, after this, tell you how agreeably time slides away with me; you know as well as I do the taste of

Yours, &c., &c.

XIII.

TO THE LADY X——.

Vienna, Oct. 1, 1716.

You desire me, madam, to send you some account of the customs here, and at the same time a description of Vienna. I am always willing to obey your commands; but you must, upon this occasion, take the will for the deed. If I should undertake to tell you all the particulars in which the manners here differ from ours, I must write a whole quire of the dullest stuff that ever was read, or printed without being read. Their dress agrees with the French or English in no one article but wearing petticoats. They have many fashions peculiar to themselves; they think it indecent for a widow ever to wear green or rose colour, but all the other gayest colours at her own discretion.

The assemblies here are the only regular diversion, the operas being always at court, and commonly on some particular occasion. Madame Rabutin has the assembly constantly every night at her house; and the other ladies, whenever they have a mind to display the magnificence of their apartments, or oblige a friend by complimenting them on the day of their saint they declare that on such a day the assembly shall be at their house in honour of the feast of the count or countess such a one. These days are called days of gala, and all the friends or relations of the lady whose saint it is are obliged to appear in their best clothes, and all their jewels. The mistress of the house takes no particular notice of any body, nor returns any body's visit; and whoever pleases may go, without the formality of being presented. The company are entertained with ice in several forms, winter and summer; afterwards they divide into several parties of ombre, piquet, or conversation, all games of hazard being forbidden.

I saw the other day the gala for Count Altheim, the emperor's favourite, and never in my life saw so many fine clothes ill fancied: they embroider the richest gold stuffs; and provided they can make their clothes expensive enough, that is all the taste they show in them. On other days, the general dress is a scarf, and what you please under it

But, now I am speaking of Vienna, I am sure you expect I should say something of the convents; they are of all sorts and sizes, but I am

best pleased with that of St. Lawrence, where the
ease and neatness they seem to live with appears
to be much more edifying than those stricter
orders, where perpetual penance and nastiness
must breed discontent and wretchedness. The
nuns are all of quality. I think there are to the
number of fifty. They have each of them a little
cell perfectly clean, the walls of which are covered
with pictures more or less fine, according to their
quality. A long white stone gallery runs by all
of them, furnished with the pictures of exemplary
sisters; the chapel is extremely neat and richly
adorned. But I could not forbear laughing at
their showing me a wooden head of our Saviour,
which they assured me spoke during the siege of
Vienna; and, as a proof of it, bid me mark his
mouth, which had been open ever since. Nothing
can be more becoming than the dress of these
nuns : it is a white robe, the sleeves of which are
turned up with fine white calico, and their head-
dress the same, excepting a small veil of black
crape that falls behind. They have a lower sort
of serving nuns, that wait on them as their cham-
ber-maids : they receive all visits of women, and
play at ombre in their chambers, with permission
of their abbess, which is very easy to be obtained.
I never saw an old woman so good natured ; she
is near fourscore, and yet shows very little sign of
decay, being still lively and cheerful. She caressed
me as if I had been her daughter, giving me some
pretty things of her own work, and sweetmeats in
abundance. The grate is not of the most rigid ;

E 2

it is not very hard to put a head through, and I do
not doubt but a man, a little more slender than
ordinary, might squeeze in his whole person. The
young Count of Salmes came to the grate while I
was there, and the abbess gave him her hand to
kiss. But I was surprised to find here the only
beautiful young woman I have seen at Vienna,
and not only beautiful but genteel, witty, and
agreeable, of a great family, and who had been the
admiration of the town. I could not forbear showing my surprise at seeing a nun like her: she
made me a thousand obliging compliments, and
desired me to come often : " It will be an infinite
pleasure to me," said she, sighing; " but I avoid,
with the greatest care, seeing any of my former
acquaintance, and whenever they come to our con-
vent, I lock myself in my cell." I observed tears
come into eyes, which touched me extremely, and
I began to talk to her in that strain of tender pity
she inspired me with; but she would not own to
me that she was not perfectly happy. I have since
endeavoured to learn the real cause of her retirement, without being able to get any other account
but that every body was surprised at it, and nobody guessed the reason.

I have been several times to see her ; but it gives
me too much melancholy to see so agreeable a
young creature buried alive. I am not surprised
that nuns have so often inspired violent passions :
the pity one naturally feels for them, when they
seem worthy of another destiny, making an easy
way for yet more tender sentiments. I never in

my life had so little charity for the Roman Catholic religion, as since I see the misery it occasions so many poor unhappy women [1] and then the gross superstition of the common people, who are some or other of them, day and night, offering bits of candle to the wooden figures that are set up almost in every street.

The processions I see very often are a pageantry as offensive, and apparently contradictory to common sense, as the pagods of China: God knows whether it be the *womanly* spirit of contradiction that works in me; but there never before was such zeal against popery in the heart of,

Dear madam, &c., &c.

XIV.

TO MR. POPE. ([27])

Vienna, Oct. 10, 1716.

I DESERVE not all the reproaches you make me. If I have been some time without answering your letter, it is not that I do not know how many thanks are due to you for it; or that I am stupid enough to prefer any amusements to the pleasure of hearing from you; but after the professions of esteem you have so obligingly made me, I cannot help delaying, as long as I can, showing you that you

---

([27]) Pope's letter, to which this is in reply, is printed in Warton's edition, vol. viii. p. 388.

are mistaken. If you are sincere when you say you
expect to be extremely entertained by my letters,
I ought to be mortified at the disappointment that
I am sure you will receive when you hear from
me ; though I have done my best endeavours to
find out something worth writing to you.

I have seen every thing that was to be seen with
a very diligent curiosity. Here are some fine villas,
particularly the late prince of Lichtenstein's ; but
the statues are all modern, and the pictures not
of the first hands ; it is true, the emperor has
some of great value. I was yesterday to see the
repository, which they call his treasure, where
they seem to have been more diligent in amassing
a great quantity of things, than in the choice of
them. I spent about five hours there, and yet
there were very few things that stopped me long
to consider them : but the number is prodigious,
being a very long gallery filled on both sides, and
five large rooms. There is a vast quantity of
paintings, among which are many fine miniatures :
but the most valuable pictures are a few of Corregio, those of Titian being at the Favorita.

The cabinet of jewels did not appear to me so
rich as I expected to see it. They showed me here
a cup, about the size of a tea-dish, of one entire
emerald, which they had so particular a respect
for that only the emperor has the liberty of touching it. (²⁸) There is a large cabinet full of curiosi-

---

(²⁸) Perhaps, had persons been allowed to touch it, they might
have discovered that, like the jewels of several saints which her
ladyship speaks of, it was but a piece of coloured glass. At all

ties of clockwork, only one of which I thought
worth observing, that was a craw-fish, with all
the motions so natural that it was hard to distinguish it from the life. ([29])

The next cabinet was a large collection of
agates, some of them extremely beautiful, and of
an uncommon size, and several vases of lapis lazuli.
I was surprised to see the cabinet of medals so
poorly furnished ; I did not remark one of any
value, and they are kept in a most ridiculous dis-
order. As to the antiques, very few of them
deserve that name. Upon my saying they were
modern, I could not forbear laughing at the answer
of the profound antiquary that showed them, that
" they were ancient enough ; for, to his knowledge,
they had been there these forty years." But the
next cabinet diverted me yet better, being nothing
else but a parcel of wax babies, and toys in ivory,
very well worthy to be presented to children of
five years old. Two of the rooms were wholly
filled with these trifles of all kinds, set in jewels,
amongst which I was desired to observe a crucifix
that they assured me had spoken very wisely to
the Emperor Leopold. I will not trouble you
with a catalogue of the rest of the lumber ; but I

---

events, I remember no mention of this emerald cup in any sub-
sequent traveller.—ED.

([29]) The imperial cabinet at Vienna has been greatly improved
since 1716, by the Emperors Joseph and Ferdinand. In the
classes of mineralogy, and a collection of medals, it now yields
to few others in Europe. See Eckel. Catal. Musæi Cæsarei
Vindobon. Numm. Vet., fol. 1779, and Baron Bornu's Shells of
the Imperial Museum at Vienna, fol. 1780.—ED.

must not forget to mention a small piece of load-
stone that held up an anchor of steel too heavy for
me to lift : this is what I thought most curious in
the whole treasure.   There are some few heads of
ancient statues ; but several of them are defaced
by modern additions.

I foresee that you will be very little satisfied with
this letter, and I dare hardly ask you to be good-
natured enough to charge the dulness of it on
the barrenness of the subject, and to overlook the
stupidity of,

Yours, &c., &c.

XV.

TO THE COUNTESS OF MAR.

Prague, Nov. 17, 1716.

I HOPE my dear sister wants no new proofs of my
sincere affection for her : but I am sure, if you do,
I could not give you a stronger than writing at this
time, after three days, or, more properly speaking,
three nights and days, hard post-travelling.

The kingdom of Bohemia is the most desert of
any I have seen in Germany.   The villages are so
poor, and the post-houses so miserable, that clean
straw and fair water are blessings not always to be
met with, and better accommodation not to be
hoped for.   Though I carried my own bed with
me, I could not sometimes find a place to set it up
in ; and I rather chose to travel all night, as cold

as it is, wrapped up in my furs, than go into the common stoves, which are filled with a mixture of all sorts of ill scents.

This town was once the royal seat of the Bohemian kings, and is still the capital of the kingdom. There are yet some remains of its former splendour, being one of the largest towns in Germany, but, for the most part, old built, and thinly inhabited, which makes the houses very cheap. Those people of quality who cannot easily bear the expense of Vienna, choose to reside here, where they have assemblies, music, and all other diversions, (those of a court excepted,) at very moderate rates, all things being here in great abundance, especially the best wild fowl I ever tasted. I have already been visited by some of the most considerable ladies, whose relations I know at Vienna: they are dressed after the fashions there, after the manner that the people at Exeter imitate those of London; that is, their imitation is more excessive than the original: it is not easy to describe what extraordinary figures they make. The person is so much lost between head-dress and petticoat that they have as much occasion to write upon their backs, " This is a woman," for the information of travellers as ever sign-post painter had to write, " This is a bear."

I will not forget to write to you again from Dresden and Leipzig, being much more solicitous to content your curiosity than to indulge my own repose.

I am, &c.

XVI.

TO THE COUNTESS OF MAR.

Leipzig, Nov. 21, 1716.

I BELIEVE, dear sister, you will easily forgive my not writing to you from Dresden, as I promised, when I tell you that I never went out of my chaise from Prague to this place.

You may imagine how heartily I was tired with twenty-four hours' post-travelling, without sleep or refreshment, (for I can never sleep in a coach, however fatigued.) We passed, by moonshine, the frightful precipices that divide Bohemia from Saxony, at the bottom of which runs the river Elbe; but I cannot say that I had reason to fear drowning in it, being perfectly convinced that, in case of a tumble, it was utterly impossible to come alive to the bottom. In many places the road is so narrow that I could not discern an inch of space between the wheels and the precipice: yet I was so good a wife as not to wake Mr. Wortley, who was fast asleep by my side, to make him share in my fears, since the danger was unavoidable, till I perceived, by the bright light of the moon, our postillions nodding on horseback, while the horses were on a full gallop: then, indeed, I thought it very convenient to call out to desire them to look where they were going. My calling waked Mr. Wortley, and he was much more surprised than myself at the situation we were in, and assured me

that he passed the Alps five times in different
places, without ever having gone a road so dangerous.   I have been told since that it is common to
find the bodies of travellers in the Elbe; but,
thank God, that was not our destiny : and we
came safe to Dresden, so much tired with fear and
fatigue it was not possible for me to compose myself to write.

After passing these dreadful rocks, Dresden appeared to me a wonderfully agreeable situation, in
a fine large plain on the banks of the Elbe : I was
very glad to stay there a day to rest myself.   The
town is the neatest I have seen in Germany; most
of the houses are new built ; the elector's palace is
very handsome, and his repository full of curiosities
of different kinds, with a collection of medals very
much esteemed.   Sir Robert Sutton, our king's envoy, came to see me here, and Madame de L——,
whom I knew in London, when her husband was
minister to the king of Poland there : she offered
me all things in her power to entertain me, and
brought some ladies with her, whom she presented
to me.   The Saxon ladies resemble the Austrian
no more than the Chinese do those of London ;
they are very genteely dressed after the English
and French modes, and have generally pretty
faces, but they are the most determined *minaudieres*
in the whole world : they would think it a mortal
sin against good breeding, if they either spoke or
moved in a natural manner : they all affect a little
soft lisp, and a pretty pitty-pat step ; which female
frailties ought, however, to be forgiven them, in

favour of their civility and good nature to strangers, which I have a great deal of reason to praise.

The Countess of Cozelle is kept prisoner in a melancholy castle, some leagues from hence; and I cannot forbear telling you what I have heard of her, because it seems to me very extraordinary, though I forsee I shall swell my letter to the size of a packet.—She was mistress to the king of Poland (elector of Saxony,) with so absolute a dominion over him, that never any lady had so much·power in that court. They tell a pleasant story of his majesty's first declaration of love, which he made in a visit to her, bringing in one hand a bag of a hundred thousand crowns, and in the other a horse-shoe, which he snapped asunder before her face, leaving her to draw the consequences of such remarkable proofs of strength and liberality. I know not which charmed her most; but she consented to leave her husband, and to give herself up to him entirely, being divorced publicly, in such a manner as, by their laws, permits either party to marry again. God knows whether it was at this time, or in some other fond fit, but it is certain the king had the weakness to make her a formal contract of marriage; which, though it could signify nothing during the life of the queen, pleased her so well, that she could not be contented without telling it to all the people she saw, and giving herself the airs of a queen. Men endure every thing while they are in love; but when the excess of passion was cooled by long possession, his majesty began to reflect on the ill consequences of leaving such a

paper in her hands, and desired to have it restored
to him. But she rather chose to endure all the
most violent effects of his anger, than give it up;
and though she is one of the richest and most
avaricious ladies of her country, she has refused
the offer of the continuation of a large pension, and
the security of a vast sum of money she has
amassed; and has, at last, provoked the king to
confine her person to a castle, where she endures all
the terrors of a strait imprisonment, and remains
still inflexible, either to threats or promises. Her
violent passions have brought her indeed into fits
which, it is supposed, will soon put an end to her
life. I cannot forbear having some compassion for
a woman that suffers for a point of honour, however mistaken, especially in a country where points
of honour are not overscrupulously observed among
ladies.

I could have wished Mr. Wortley's business had
permitted him a longer stay at Dresden.

Perhaps I am partial to a town where they profess the Protestant religion ; but every thing seemed
to me with quite another air of politeness than I
have found in other places. Leipzig, where I am
at present, is a town very considerable for its trade ;
and I take this opportunity of buying pages' live-
ries, gold stuffs for myself, &c. all things of that
kind being at least double the price at Vienna;
partly because of the excessive customs, and partly
through want of genius and industry in the people,
who make no one sort of thing there ; so that the
ladies are obliged to send even for their shoes out

of Saxony. The fair here is one of the most considerable in Germany, and the resort of all the people of quality, as well as of the merchants. This is also a fortified town, but I avoid ever mentioning fortifications, being sensible that I know not how to speak of them. I am the more easy under my ignorance, when I reflect that I am sure you will willingly forgive the omission; for if I made you the most exact description of all the ravelins and bastions I see in my travels, I dare swear you would ask me, What is a ravelin? and what is a bastion?

Adieu, my dear sister!

XVII.

TO THE COUNTESS OF MAR.

Brunswick, Nov. 23, 1716.

I AM just come to Brunswick, a very old town, but which has the advantage of being the capital of the Duke of Wolfenbuttle's dominions, a family (not to speak of its ancient honours) illustrious, by having its younger branch on the throne of England, and having given two empresses to Germany. I have not forgotten to drink your health here in mum, which, I think, very well deserves its reputation of being the best in the world. This letter is the third I have written to you during my journey; and I declare to you, that if you do not send me immediately a full and true account of all the changes and chances among our London acquaintance, I will not write you any description of Hanover, (where I hope to be to-night,) though I know you have more curiosity to hear of that place than any other.

XVIII.

TO THE COUNTESS OF BRISTOL.

Hanover, Nov. 25, 1716.

I RECEIVED your ladyship's letter but the day before I left Vienna, though, by the date, I ought to have had it much sooner; but nothing was ever worse regulated than the post in most parts of Germany. I can assure you the packet at Prague was behind my chaise, and in that manner conveyed to Dresden, so that the secrets of half the country were at my mercy, if I had any curiosity for them. I would not longer delay my thanks for yours, though the number of my acquaintances here, and my duty of attending at court, leave me hardly any time to dispose of. I am extremely pleased that I can tell you, without flattery or partiality, that our young prince ([30]) has all the accomplishments that it is possible to have at his age, with an air of sprightliness and understanding, and something so very engaging and easy in his behaviour, that he needs not the advantage of his rank to appear

---

([30]) The father of his late majesty.

charming. I had the honour of a long conversation with him last night, before the king came in.
His governor retired on purpose (as he told me afterwards) that I might make some judgment of
his genius, by hearing him speak without constraint; and I was surprised at the quickness and
politeness that appeared in every thing he said;
joined to a person perfectly agreeable, and the fine
fair hair of the princess.

This town is neither large nor handsome; but
the palace is capable of holding a much greater
court than that of St. James's. The king has had
the goodness to appoint us a lodging in one part
of it, without which we should have been very ill
accommodated; for the vast number of English
crowds the town so much, it is very good luck to
get one sorry room in a miserable tavern. I dined
to-day with the Portuguese ambassador, who thinks
himself very happy to have two wretched parlours
in an inn. I have now made the tour of Germany,
and cannot help observing a considerable difference between travelling here and in England. One
sees none of those fine seats of noblemen, so common amongst us, nor any thing like a country
gentleman's house, though they have many situations perfectly fine. But the whole people are divided into absolute sovereignties, were all the riches
and magnificence are at court, or into communities of merchants, such as Nuremberg and Frankfort, where they live always in town for the convenience of trade. The king's company of French
comedians play here every night: they are very

well dressed, and some of them not ill actors. His majesty dines and sups constantly in public. The court is very numerous, and his affability and goodness make it one of the most agreeable places in the world.

Dear madam, your, &c. &c.

XIX.

TO THE LADY RICH.

Hanover, Oct. 1, 1716.

I AM very glad, my dear Lady Rich, that you have been so well pleased, as you tell me, at the report of my returning to England; though, like other pleasures, I can assure you it has no real foundation. I hope you know me enough to take my word against any report concerning me. It is true, as to distance of place, I am much nearer to London than I was some weeks ago; but as to the thoughts of a return, I never was farther off in my life. I own, I could with great joy indulge the pleasing hope of seeing you, and the very few others that share my esteem; but while Mr. Wortley is determined to proceed in his design, I am determined to follow him.

I am running on upon my own affairs, that is to say, I am going to write very dully, as most people do when they write of themselves. I will make haste to change the disagreeable subject, by telling you that I am now got into the region

of beauty.   All the women have literally rosy
cheeks, snowy foreheads and bosoms, jet eyebrows,
and scarlet lips, to which they generally add coal-
black hair. Those perfections never leave them till
the hour of their deaths, and have a very fine effect
by candlelight; but I could wish they were handsome with a little more variety : they resemble one
another as much as Mrs. Salmon's court of Great
Britain, and are in as much danger of melting
away by too nearly approaching the fire, which
they for that reason carefully avoid, though it
is now such excessively cold weather that I believe they suffer extremely by that piece of self-denial.

The snow is already very deep, and the people
begin to slide about in their traineaus. This is a
favourite diversion all over Germany. They are
little machines fixed upon a sledge, that hold a lady
and gentleman, and are drawn by one horse. The
gentleman has the honour of driving, and they
move with a prodigious swiftness. The lady, the
horse, and the traineau are all as fine as they can
be made ; and when there are many of them together,
it is a very agreeable show. At Vienna, where all
pieces of magnificence are carried to excess, there
are sometimes machines of this kind that cost five
or six hundred pounds English.

The Duke of Wolfenbuttle is now at this court;
you know he is nearly related to our king, and
uncle to the reigning empress, who is, I believe,
the most beautiful princess upon earth. She is
now with child, which is all the consolation of the

imperial court, for the loss of the archduke.
I took my leave of her the day before I left Vienna,
and she began to speak to me with so much grief
and tenderness, of the death of that young prince,
I had much ado to withhold my tears. You know
that I am not at all partial to people for their titles;
but I own that I love that charming princess; (if I
may use so familiar an expression;) and if I had
not, I should have been very much moved at the
tragical end of an only son, born after being so long
desired, and at length killed by want of good management, weaning him in the beginning of the
winter.

Adieu, dear Lady Rich; continue to write to
me, and believe none of your goodness is lost
upon

Your, &c.

XX.

TO THE COUNTESS OF MAR.

Blankenburg, Oct. 17, 1716.

I RECEIVED yours, dear sister, the very day I left
Hanover. You may easily imagine I was then
in too great a hurry to answer it; but you see I
take the first opportunity of doing myself that pleasure.

I came here the 15th, very late at night, after a
terrible journey, in the worst roads and weather
that ever poor traveller suffered. I have taken this

F 2

little fatigue merely to oblige the reigning empress, and carry a message from her imperial majesty to the Duchess of Blankenburg, her mother, who is a princess of great address and good breeding, and may be still called a fine woman. It was so late when I came to this town, I did not think it proper to disturb the duke and duchess with the news of my arrival; so I took up my quarters in a miserable inn : but as soon as I had sent my compliments to their highnesses, they immediately sent me their own coach and six horses, which had, however, enough to do to draw us up the very high hill on which the castle is situated. The duchess is extremely obliging to me, and this little court is not without its diversions. The duke taillys at basset every night; and the duchess tells me she is so well pleased with my company, that it makes her play less than she used to do. I should find it very diffiicult to steal time to write, if she were not now at church, where I cannot wait on her, not understanding the language enough to pay my devotions in it.

You will not forgive me, if I do not say something of Hanover; I cannot tell you that the town is either large or magnificent. The opera-house, which was built by the late elector, is much finer than that of Vienna. I was very sorry that the ill weather did not permit me to see Hernhausen in all its beauty ; but in spite of the snow, I thought the gardens very fine. I was particularly surprised at the vast number of orange-trees, much larger than any I have ever seen in England, though this climate is certainly colder. But I had more reason to wonder that night at the king's table, to see a present from a gentleman of this country, of two large baskets full of ripe oranges and lemons of different sorts, many of which were quite new to me; and, what I thought worth all the rest, two ripe ananas, which, to my taste, are a fruit perfectly delicious. You know they are naturally the growth of Brazil, and I could not imagine how they came here, but by enchantment. Upon inquiry, I learned that they have brought their stoves to such perfection, they lengthen their summer as long as they please, giving to every plant the degree of heat it would receive from the sun in its native soil. The effect is very nearly the same; I am surprised we do not practise in England so useful an invention.

This reflection leads me to consider our obstinacy in shaking with cold five months in the year, rather than make use of stoves, ([31]) which are cer-

---

([31]) Upon this hint, perhaps, our stove-makers set to work. But Lady Mary, who felt the warmth and comfort of stoves, remained too short a time in the countries where they are used, to discover how injurious they are to health. It is to the use of them, however, that we are in a great measure to attribute the sallow faces one every day sees in Paris, and many other continental cities, where no one can have entered the smaller houses that are warmed by stoves without experiencing that feeling of lassitude, and prostration of energy, always caused by considerable heat, in a moist atmosphere. I should be sorry to see the fashion prevail to any great extent in England; though, as mere articles of furniture, or ornaments, stoves are often very handsome things.

tainly one of the greatest conveniences of life. Besides, they are so far from spoiling the form of a room,
that they add very much to the magnificence of it,
when they are painted and gilt, as they are at
Vienna, or at Dresden, where they are often in
the shapes of china jars, statues, or fine cabinets,
so naturally represented, that they are not to be
distinguished. If ever I return, in defiance to the
fashion, you shall certainly see one in the chamber
of,

Dear sister, your, &c.

I will write often, since you desire it : but I must
beg you to be a little more particular in yours ;
you fancy me at forty miles distance, and forget
that, after so long an absence, I cannot understand
hints.

XXI.

TO THE LADY RICH.

Vienna, Jan. 1, 1717.

I HAVE just received here at Vienna, your ladyship's
compliments on my return to England, sent me
from Hanover.

You see, madam, all things that are asserted
with confidence are not absolutely true ; and that
you have no sort of reason to complain of me for
making my designed return a mystery to you, when
you say, all the world are informed of it. You

may tell all the world in my name, that they are never so well informed of my affairs as I am myself: that I am very positive I am at this time at Vienna, where the carnival is begun, and all sorts of diversions are carried to the greatest height, except that of masquing, which is never permitted during a war with the Turks.([32])   The balls are in public places, where the men pay a gold ducat([33]) at entrance, but the ladies nothing.   I am told that these houses get sometimes a thousand ducats in a night.   They are very magnificently furnished, and the music good, if they had not that detestable custom of mixing hunting horns with it, that almost deafen the company.([34])   But that noise is so agreeable here, they never make a concert without them. The ball always concludes with English country dances, to the number of thirty or forty couple, and so ill danced, that there is very little pleasure in them.   They know but half a dozen, and they have danced them over and over these fifty years : I would fain have taught them some new ones, but I found it would be some months' labour to make them comprehend them.

([32]) Lest the adventurous Musulmans should make their way in masquerade into the imperial palace, and terrify the court libertines to death with their scimitars !—ED.

([33]) About nine shillings.

([34]) German music, horns and all, we have since learned to admire ; but their dancers have not hitherto begun to make their fortunes in England.   This, however, time, which teaches all things, will no doubt bring to pass yet ; and we shall one day be edified at the opera, with the uncouth antics of a Croatian boor. We have long made the first step towards this desirable consummation.—ED.

Last night there was an Italian comedy acted
at court. The scenes were pretty, but the comedy
itself such intolerably low farce, without either wit
or humour, that I was surprised how all the court
could sit there attentively for four hours together.
No women are suffered to act on the stage, ([35]) and
the men dressed like them were such awkward figures,
they very much added to the ridicule of the spectacle. What completed the diversion was the excessive cold, which was so great, I thought I should
have died there.

It is now the very extremity of the winter here ;
the Danube is entirely frozen, and the weather not
to be supported without stoves and furs; but, however, the air is so clear, almost every body is well,
and colds not half so common as in England. I
am persuaded there cannot be a purer air, nor
more wholesome, than that of Vienna. The plenty
and excellence of all sorts of provisions are greater
here than in any place I ever was before, and it is
not very expensive to keep a splendid table. It
is really a pleasure to pass through the markets,
and see the abundance of what we should think
rarities, of fowls and venison, that are daily brought
in from Hungary and Bohemia. They want
nothing but shell-fish, and are so fond of oysters,

([35]) Another absurd imitation of classical practices, far more
honoured in the breach than in the observance. They admitted
no women on the stage at Athens, *therefore* they could not be
allowed at Vienna! As if this nest of vicious barbarians had
anything in common with the Athenians.—ED.

that they have them sent from Venice, and eat them very greedily, stink or not stink. ([36])

Thus I obey your commands, madam, in giving you an account of Vienna, though I know you will not be satisfied with it. You chide me for my laziness, in not telling you a thousand agreeable and surprising things, that you say you are sure I have seen and heard. Upon my word, madam, it is my regard to truth, and not laziness, that I do not entertain you with as many prodigies as other travellers use to divert their readers with. I might easily pick up wonders in every town I pass through, or tell you a long series of popish miracles; but I cannot fancy that there is anything new in letting you know that priests will lie, and the mob believe, all the world over. Then, as for news, that you are so inquisitive about, how can it be entertaining to you (that do not know the people) that the Prince of —— has forsaken the Countess of ——? or that the prince such a one has an intrigue with the countess such a one? Would you have me write novels like the countess of D——? and is it not better to tell you a plain truth,

That I am, &c.

([36]) The passion of the continental people for stinking fish continues unimpaired. You may smell a cart laden with these dainties a mile off upon the highway. Yet, when brought to table, the most delicate gourmands of both sexes, will regale on them in defiance of their own noses, and every body else's.—ED.

XXII.

TO THE COUNTESS OF MAR.

Vienna, Jan. 16, 1717.

I AM now, dear sister, to take leave of you for a long time, and of Vienna for ever; designing to-morrow to begin my journey through Hungary, in spite of the excessive cold, and deep snows, which are enough to damp a greater courage than I am mistress of. But my principles of *passive obedience* carry me through every thing.

I have had my audience of leave of the empress. His imperial majesty was pleased to be present, when I waited on the reigning empress; and after a very obliging conversation, both their imperial majesties invited me to take Vienna in my road back; but I have no thoughts of enduring, over again, so great a fatigue. I delivered a letter from the Duchess of Blankenburg. I staid but a few days at that court, though her highness pressed me very much to stay: and when I left her, engaged me to write to her.

I wrote you a long letter from thence, which I hope you have received, though you do not mention it; but I believe I forgot to tell you one curiosity in all the German courts, which I cannot forbear taking notice of: all the princes keep favourite dwarfs. The emperor and empress have two of these little monsters, as ugly as devils, especially the female: but they are all bedaubed with diamonds, and stand at her majesty's elbow, in all public places. The Duke of Wolfenbuttle has one, and the Duchess of Blankenburg is not without hers, but indeed the most proportionable I ever saw. I am told the King of Denmark has so far improved upon this fashion, that his dwarf is his chief minister. I can assign no reason for their fondness for these pieces of deformity, but the opinion all the absolute ([37]) princes have, that it is below them to converse with the rest of mankind; and, not to be quite alone, they are forced to seek their companions among the refuse of human nature, these creatures being the only part of their court privileged to talk freely to them.

I am at present confined to my chamber by a sore throat; and am really glad of the excuse, to avoid seeing people that I love well enough to be very much mortified when I think I am going to part with them for ever. It is true, the Austrians are not commonly the most polite people in the world, nor the most agreeable. But Vienna is inhabited by all nations, and I had formed to myself a little society of such as were perfectly to my own taste. And though the number was not very great, I could never pick up, in any other place, such a number of reasonable, agreeable people. We were almost always together, and you know I have ever

---

([37]) Whether the word *absolute* be in the original or not, Lord Wharncliffe perhaps can tell. At all events, the remark is just, and bespeaks no little boldness and sagacity in Lady Mary, who was much used to courts, and, had nature endued her with less good sense, would very probably have been dazzled by them.—Ed.

been of opinion, that a chosen conversation, composed of a few that one esteems, is the greatest
happiness of life.

Here are some Spaniards of both sexes, that have
all the vivacity and generosity of sentiments anciently ascribed to their nation; and could I believe the whole kingdom were like them, I would
wish nothing more than to end my days there. ([38])
The ladies of my acquaintance have so much goodness for me, they cry whenever they see me, since
I have determined to undertake this journey.
And, indeed, I am not very easy when I reflect on
what I am going to suffer. Almost every body I
see, frights me with some new difficulty. Prince
Eugene has been so good as to say all the things
he could to persuade me to stay till the Danube is
thawed, that I may have the conveniency of going
by water; assuring me, that the houses in Hungary
are such, as are no defence against the weather;
and that I shall be obliged to travel three or four
days between Buda and Essek, without finding any
house at all, through desert plains covered with snow,
where the cold is so violent, many have been killed
by it. I own these terrors have made a very deep
impression on my mind, because I believe he tells
me things truly as they are, and nobody can be
better informed of them.

Now I have named that great man, I am sure

([35]) Had Lady Montagu travelled in Spain, or freely asso-
ciated elsewhere with many Spaniards, her admiration would
have been short-lived.—ED.

you expect I should say something particular of
him, having the advantage of seeing him very often; but I am as unwilling to speak of him at
Vienna, as I should be to talk of Hercules in the
court of Omphale, if I had seen him there. ([39]) I do
not know what comfort other people find in considering the weakness of great men, (because, perhaps, it brings them nearer to their level,) but it is
always a mortification to me, to observe that there
is no perfection in humanity. The young Prince
of Portugal is the admiration of the whole court;
he is handsome and polite, with a great vivacity.
All the officers tell wonders of his gallantry at the
last campaign. He is lodged at court with all the
honours due to his rank.—Adieu, dear sister: this
is the last account you will have from me of Vienna.
If I survive my journey, you shall hear from me
again. I can say, with great truth, in the words
of Moneses, " I have long learned to hold myself as
nothing;" but when I think of the fatigue my poor
infant must suffer, I have all a mother's fondness in
my eyes, and all her tender passions in my heart. ([40])
 P. S. I have written a letter to my Lady——,

([39]) What impression she intended to make upon her readers
with regard to this prince, of course I cannot undertake to say ;
I suspect it was precisely the impression which she *does* make ;
that is, the most unfavourable possible. From her account we
can think nothing of this celebrated soldier, but that he was as
vicious as he was brave, idling and sauntering about Vienna
among courtiers of bad character, and imitating or surpassing
them in all their vices ; just as we have known equally celebrated soldiers of our own day do in other effeminate courts.—ED.

([40]) The *mother*, not a prominent feature in Lady Mary's
character, peeps forth here.—ED.

that I believe she will not like; and, upon cooler
reflection, I think I had done better to have let it
alone; but I was downright peevish at all her
questions, and her ridiculous imagination that I have
certainly seen abundance of wonders which I keep
to myself out of mere malice. She is very angry
that I will not lie like other travellers. I verily
believe she expects I should tell her of the *Anthro-
pophagi*, men whose heads grow below their shoulders; however, pray say something to pacify her.

XXIII.

MR. POPE TO LADY MONTAGU.

If you must go from us, I wish at least you might
pass to your banishment by the most pleasant way;
might all your road be roses and myrtles, and a
thousand objects rise round you, agreeable enough
to make England less desirable to you. I am glad,
madam, your native country uses you so well as to
justify your regret for it; it is not for me to talk of
it with tears in my eyes; I can never think that
place my country, where I cannot call a foot of pa-
ternal earth my own. Indeed, it may seem some
alleviation, that when the wisest thing I can do is
to leave my country, that which was most agreeable
in it should be taken from thence beforehand. I
could overtake you with pleasure in Italy (if you
took that way,) and make that tour in your company. Every reasonable entertainment and beau-

tiful view would be doubly instructive when you talked of it. I should at least attend you to the sea-coast, and cast a last look after the sails that transported you, if I liked Italy enough to reside in it. But I believe I should be as uneasy in a country where I saw others persecuted by the rogues of my own religion, as where I was so myself by those of yours. And it is not impossible but I might run into Turkey in search of liberty;([41]) for who would not rather live a free man among a nation of slaves, than a slave among a nation of free men ?

In good earnest, if I knew your motions towards Italy, (on the supposition you go that course,) and your exact time, I verily think I shall be once more happy in a sight of you, next spring. I will conclude with a wish, God send you with us, or me with you.

By what I have seen of Monsieur Rousseau's works, I should envy you his conversation. But I am sure I envy him yours.

Mr. Addison has not had one epithalamium that

([41]) And he might have found it—at least one may *now*. But liberty in the East exists only for strangers; the natives know nothing of it, not even sufficient to give rise to a natural wish for more. Were this not the case, we should observe them more on the alert to profit by the changes of governors constantly taking place, to introduce some beneficial changes into their government. Like many persons in Europe, they appear to imagine there is some satisfaction in having a master. They laugh, and eat, and sleep, and die—like the beast. Freedom to them is a dream. Worse even than those who sprang up in Rome after the battle of Actium—they have never *seen*, never *heard* of a republic.—ED.

I can hear of, and must even be reduced, like a
poorer and a better poet, Spenser, to make his own.

Mr. Congreve is entirely yours, and has writ
twice to you; he is not in town, but well. I am
in great health, and sit up all night; a just reward
for a fever I just come out of, that kept me in bed
seven days.

How may I send a large bundle to you?

I beg you will put dates to your letters: they are
not long enough.

A. POPE.

XXIV.

TO MR. POPE.

Vienna, Jan. 16, 1717.

I HAVE not time to answer your letter, being in the
hurry of preparing for my journey; but I think I
ought to bid adieu to my friends with the same so-
lemnity as if I was going to mount a breach, at
least, if I am to believe the information of the people here, who denounce all sorts of terrors to me;
and, indeed, the weather is at present such, as very
few ever set out in. I am threatened, at the same
time, with being frozen to death, buried in the
snow, and taken by the Tartars, who ravage that
part of Hungary I am to pass.([42])   It is true, we

([42]) It is quite clear that she had good sense enough to despise all the imaginary perils with which a host of silly and ef-

shall have a considerable *escorte,* so that possibly
I may be diverted with a new scene, by finding myself in the midst of a battle.

How my adventures will conclude, I leave entirely to Providence; if comically, you shall hear of
them. Pray be so good as to tell Mr. Congreve I
have received his letter. Make him my adieus; if
I live I will answer it. The same compliment to
my Lady Rich.

XXV.

TO THE COUNTESS OF MAR.

Peterwaradin, Jan. 30, 1717.

At length, dear sister, I am safely arrived, with all
my family, in good health, at Peterwaradin ; having suffered so little from the rigour of the season,
(against which we were well provided by furs,)
and found such tolerable accommodation everywhere, by the care of sending before, that I can
hardly forbear laughing when I recollect all the
frightful ideas that were given me of this journey.([43])

---

feminate courtiers menaced her ; though it was very well to make
the most of them in letters to England. We shall presently,
however, have room to fear that her own invention aided, somewhat, in peopling the road with terrors at which she alternately
laughs and pretends to quake, according as it is her cue to appear
courageous or otherwise.—Ed.

([43]) Travelling as she travelled, there was nothing frightful in
the journey, either to man or woman.—Ed.

G

These, I see, were wholly owing to the tenderness of my Vienna friends, and their desire of keeping me with them for this winter.

Perhaps it will not be disagreeable to you to give a short journal of my journey, being through a country entirely unknown to you, and very little passed even by the Hungarians themselves, who generally choose to take the conveniency of going down the Danube. We have had the blessing of being favoured with finer weather than is common at this time of the year; though the snow was so deep, we were obliged to have our own coaches fixed upon traineaus, which move so swift and so easily, it is by far the most agreeable manner of travelling post. We came to Raab (the second day from Vienna) on the seventeenth instant, where Mr. Wortley sending word of our arrival to the governor, the best house in the town was provided for us, the garrison put under arms, a guard ordered at our door, and all other honours paid to us. The governor and all other officers immediately waited on Mr. Wortley, to know if there was anything to be done for his service. The Bishop of Temeswar came to visit us with great civility, earnestly pressing us to dine with him next day; which we refusing, as being resolved to pursue our journey, he sent us several baskets of winter fruit, and a great variety of Hungarian wines, with a young hind just killed. This is a prelate of great power in this country, of the ancient family of Nadasti, so considerable for many ages in this kingdom. He is a very polite, agreeable, cheerful old man, wearing the Hungarian habit, with a venerable white beard down to his girdle.

Raab is a strong town, well garrisoned and fortified, and was a long time the frontier town between the Turkish and German empires. It has its name from the river Rab, on which it is situated, just on its meeting with the Danube, in an open campaign country. It was first taken by the Turks, under the command of Pasha Sinan, in the reign of Sultan Amurath III. in the year fifteen hundred and ninety-four. The governor, being supposed to have betrayed it, was afterwards beheaded by the emperor's command. The counts of Schwartzenburg and Palfi retook it by surprise, 1598; since which time it has remained in the hands of the Germans, though the Turks once more attempted to gain it by stratagem in 1642. The cathedral is large and well built, which is all I saw remarkable in the town.

Leaving Comora on the other side the river, we went, the eighteenth, to Nosmuhl, a small village, where, however, we made shift to find tolerable accommodation. We continued two days travelling between this place and Buda, through the finest plains in the world, as even as if they were paved, and extremely fruitful ; but for the most part desert and uncultivated, laid waste by the long wars between the Turk and the emperor, and the more cruel civil war occasioned by the barbarous persecution of the Protestant religion by the Emperor Leopold. That prince has left behind him the character of an extraordinary piety, and was naturally of a mild, merciful temper; but, putting his conscience into the hands of a Jesuit, he was more cruel and treacherous to his poor Hungarian subjects than ever the Turk has been to the Christians; breaking, without scruple, his coronation oath, and his faith, solemnly given in many public treaties. Indeed, nothing can be more melancholy than, in travelling through Hungary, to reflect on the former flourishing state of that kingdom, and to see such a noble spot of earth almost uninhabited. Such are also the present circumstances of Buda, (where we arrived very early the twenty-second,) once the royal seat of the Hungarian kings whose palace was reckoned one of the most beautiful buildings of the age, now wholly destroyed, no part of the town having been repaired since the last siege, but the fortifications and the castle, which is the present residence of the Governor General Ragule, an officer of great merit. He came immediately to see us, and carried us in his coach to his house, where I was received by his lady with all possible civility, and magnificently entertained.

This city is situated upon a little hill on the south side of the Danube. The castle is much higher than the town, and from it the prospect is very noble. Without the walls lie a vast number of little houses, or rather huts, that they call the Rascian town, being altogether inhabited by that people. The governor assured me, it would furnish twelve thousand fighting men. These towns look very odd; their houses stand in rows, many thousands of them so close together, that they appear, at a little distance, like old-fashioned thatched tents. They consist, every one of them, of one hovel above, and another under ground ; these are their summer and winter apartments.([44]) Buda was first taken by Solyman the Magnificent, in 1526, and lost the following year to Ferdinand I. King of Bohemia. Solyman regained it by the treachery of the garrison, and voluntarily gave it into the hands of King John of Hungary ; after whose death, his son being an infant, Ferdinand laid siege to it, and the queen-mother was forced to call Solyman to her aid. He indeed raised the siege, but left a Turkish garrison in the town, and commanded her to remove her court from thence, which she was forced to submit to in 1541. It resisted afterwards the sieges laid to it by the Marquis of Brandenburg, in the year 1542; Count Schwartzenburg, in 1598; General Rosworm, in 1602 ; and the Duke of Lorrain, commander of the emperor's forces, in 1684 ; to whom it yielded in 1686, after an obstinate defence, Apti Bassa, the governor, being killed, fighting in the breach with a Roman bravery.

([44]) The description of these curious habitations recalls to the mind of the classical reader Xenophon's account of the Armenian villages, where the Ten Thousand found the people, in winter living under ground, in houses spacious below, but with an entrance resembling the mouth of a well. There was a sloping passage-way for the cattle, but the inhabitants descended by ladders ; and there they passed the cold months, together with their sheep, goats, cattle, and poultry, possessing abundance of wheat, barley, and vegetables, with beer in jars, which they sucked through a reed when thirsty.—*Anab.* IV.—ED.

The loss of this town was so important, and so much resented by the Turks, that it occasioned the deposing of their Emperor Mahomet IV. the year following.

We did not proceed on our journey till the twenty-third, when we passed through Adam and Todowar, both considerable towns when in the hands of the Turks, but now quite ruined. The remains, however, of some Turkish towns show something of what they have been. This part of the country is very much overgrown with wood, and little frequented. It is incredible what vast numbers of wild-fowl we saw, which often live here to a good old age,—and, *undisturbed by guns, in quiet sleep*. We came the five-and-twentieth to Mohatch, and were showed the field near it where Lewis, the young king of Hungary, lost his army and his life, being drowned in a ditch, trying to fly from Balybeus, general of Solyman the Magnificent. This battle opened the first passage for the Turks into the heart of Hungary. I do not name to you the little villages, of which I can say nothing remarkable; but, I will assure you, I have always found a warm stove, and great plenty, particularly of wild-boar, venison, and all kinds of *gibier*. The few people that inhabit Hungary live easily enough; they have no money, but the woods and plains afford them provision in great abundance : they were ordered to give us all things necessary, even what horses we pleased to demand, *gratis;* but Mr. Wortley would not oppress the poor country people by making use of this order, and always paid them to the full worth of what he

had. They were so surprised at this unexpected
generosity, which they are very little used to, that
they always pressed upon us, at parting, a dozen
of fat pheasants, or something of that sort, for a
present. Their dress is very primitive, being only
a plain sheep's skin, and a cap and boots of the
same stuff. You may easily imagine this lasts
them many winters; and thus they have very little
occasion for money.

The twenty-sixth, we passed over the frozen
Danube, with all our equipage and carriages. We
met on the other side General Veterani, who invited us, with great civility, to pass the night at a
little castle of his a few miles off, assuring us we
should have a very hard day's journey to reach
Essek. This we found but too true, the woods
being very dangerous, and scarcely passable, from
the vast quantity of wolves that herd in them. We
came, however, safe, though late, to Essek, where
we staid a day, to despatch a courier with letters to
the pasha of Belgrade; and I took that opportunity
of seeing the town, which is not very large, but
fair built, and well fortified. This was a town of
great trade, very rich and populous, when in the
hands of the Turks. It is situated on the Drave,
which runs into the Danube. The bridge was
esteemed one of the most extraordinary in the
world, being eight thousand paces long, and all
built of oak. It was burnt, and the city laid
in ashes, by Count Lesly, 1685, but was again
repaired and fortified by the Turks, who, however,
abandoned it in 1687. General Dunnewalt then

took possession of it for the emperor, in whose hands it has remained ever since, and is esteemed one of the bulwarks of Hungary.

The twenty-eighth, we went to Bocorwar, a very large Rascian town, all built after the manner I have described to you. We were met there by Colonel ——, who would not suffer us to go anywhere but to his quarters, where I found his wife, a very agreeable Hungarian lady, and his niece and daughter, two pretty young women, crowded into three or four Rascian houses cast into one, and made as neat and convenient as those places are capable of being made. The Hungarian ladies are much handsomer than those of Austria. All the Vienna beauties are of that country; they are generally very fair and well shaped, and their dress, I think, is extremely becoming. This lady was in a gown of scarlet velvet, lined and faced with sables, made exact to her shape, and the skirt falling to her feet. The sleeves are strait to their arms, and the stays buttoned before, with two rows of little buttons of gold, pearl, or diamonds. On their heads they wear a tassel of gold that hangs low on one side, lined with sable, or some other fine fur.([45]) They gave us a handsome dinner, and I thought the conversation very polite and

---

([45]) No one can fail to remark her ladyship's extraordinary felicity in describing dress. By the magical graces of her style she brings the wearer so vividly before the eye, and infuses so much interest into what in itself may be trifling, that there is, perhaps, no part of her works more truly interesting or elegant than these descriptions.—ED.

agreeable. They would accompany us part of
our way.

The twenty-ninth, we arrived here, where we were
met by the commanding-officer, at the head of all
the officers of the garrison. We are lodged in the
best apartment of the governor's house, and entertained in a very splendid manner by the emperor's
order. We wait here till all points are adjusted,
concerning our reception on the Turkish frontiers.
Mr. Wortley's courier, which he sent from Essek,
returned this morning, with the pasha's answer in
a purse of scarlet satin, which the interpreter here
has translated. It is to promise him to be honourably received. I desired him to appoint where he
would be met by the Turkish convoy. He has
despatched the courier back, naming Betsko, a
village in the midway between Peterwaradin and
Belgrade. We shall stay here till we receive his
answer.

Thus, dear sister, I have given you a very particular, and (I am afraid you will think) a tedious
account of this part of my travels. It was not an
affectation of showing my reading that has made
me tell you some little scraps of the history of
the towns I have passed through; I have always
avoided any thing of that kind, when I spoke of
places that I believe you knew the story of as well
as myself. But Hungary being a part of the
world which, I believe, is quite new to you, I
thought you might read with some pleasure an
account of it, which I have been very solicitous to
get from the best hands. However, if you do not

like it, it is in your power to forbear reading it. I
am, dear sister, &c.

P.S. I am promised to have this letter carefully
sent to Vienna.

XXVI.

MR. POPE TO LADY MONTAGU.

MADAM,

I NO more think I can have too many of your
letters than that I could have too many writings
to entitle me to the greatest estate in the world;
which I think so valuable a friendship as yours is
equal to. I am angry at every scrap of paper
lost, as at something that interrupts the history of
my title; and, though it is an odd compliment to
compare a fine lady to a Sybil, your leaves,
methinks, like hers, are too good to be committed
to the winds; though I have no other way of receiving them but by those unfaithful messengers.
I have had but three, and 1 reckon in that a short
one from Dort, which was rather a dying ejacula-
tion than a letter. But I have so great an opinion
of your goodness that, had I received none, I
should not have accused you of neglect or insensibility. I am not so wrong-headed as to quarrel
with my friends the minute they do not write; I
would as soon quarrel at the sun the minute he
did not shine, which he is hindered from by acci-

dental causes, and is in reality all that time performing the same course, and doing the same good offices as ever.

You have contrived to say in your last the two most pleasing things to me in nature; the first is, that, whatever be the fate of your letters, you will continue to write in the discharge of your conscience. This is generous to the last degree, and a virtue you ought to enjoy. Be assured, in return, my heart shall be as ready to think you have done every good thing, as yours can be to do it; so that you shall never be able to favour your absent friend, before he has thought himself obliged to you for the very favour you are then conferring.

The other is, the justice you do me in taking what I write to you in the serious manner it was meant: it is the point upon which I can bear no suspicion, and in which, above all, I desire to be thought serious: it would be the most vexatious of all tyranny, if you should pretend to take for raillery, what is the mere disguise of a discontented heart, that is unwilling to make you as melancholy as itself; and for wit, what is really only the natural overflowing and warmth of the same heart, as it is improved and awakened by an esteem for you: but, since you tell me you believe me, I fancy my expressions have not at least been entirely unfaithful to those thoughts, to which I am sure they can never be equal. May God increase your faith in all truths that are as great as this! and, depend upon it, to whatever degree your belief may extend, you can never be a bigot.

If you could see the heart I talk of, you would
really think it a foolish good kind of thing, with
some qualities as well deserving to be half laughed
at, and half esteemed, as any in the world : its
grand foible, in regard to you, is the most like
reason of any foible in nature. Upon my faith,
this heart is not, like a great warehouse, stored
only with my own goods, with vast empty spaces
to be supplied as fast as interest or ambition can
fill them up ; but it is every inch of it let out into
lodgings for its friends, and shall never want a
corner at your service ; where, I dare affirm, madam,
your idea lies as warm and as close as any idea in
Christendom.

If I do not take care, I shall write myself all out
to you ; and, if this correspondence continues on
both sides at the free rate I would have it, we shall
have very little curiosity to encourage our meeting
at the day of judgment.   I foresee that the further
you go from me the more freely I shall write : and
if (as I earnestly wish) you would do the same, I
cannot guess where it will end : let us be like
modest people, who, when they are close together,
keep all decorums ; but if they step a little aside,
or get to the other end of a room, can untie garters
or take off shifts without scruple.

If this distance (as you are so kind as to say)
enlarges your belief of my friendship, I assure you
it has extended my notion of your value, that I
begin to be impious on your account, and to wish
that even slaughter, ruin, and desolation might
interpose between you and Turkey ; I wish you

restored to us at the expense of a whole people :([46])
I barely hope you will forgive me for saying this,
but I fear God will scarce forgive me for desiring
it.

Make me less wicked, then. Is there no other
expedient to return you and your infant in peace
to the bosom of your country ? I hear you are
going to Hanover; can there be no favourable
planet at this conjuncture, or do you only come
back so far to die twice ? Is Eruydice once more
snatched to the shades ? If ever mortal had reason
to hate the king, it is I ; for it is my particular
misfortune to be almost the only innocent man
whom he has made to suffer, both by his government at home, and his negociations abroad.

A. Pope.

XXVII.

TO MR. POPE.

Belgrade, Feb. 12, 1717.

I DID verily intend to write you a long letter from
Peterawardin, where I expected to stay three or

([46]) But that we know all this to be merely an absurd attempt
at saying something out of the common, it would be exceedingly
wicked. I blush for genius when I read these letters of Pope.
To *any* woman they would have been in bad taste—to a married
woman they are detestable : but setting aside the morality of
the matter, and supposing a certain point to have been aimed
at, nothing could have been worse calculated to succeed.—
ED.

four days; but the pasha here was in such haste
to see us that he despatched the courier back,
(which Mr. Wortley had sent to know the time he
would send the convoy to meet us,) without suffering him to pull off his boots.

My letters were not thought important enough
to stop our journey ; and we left Peterwaradin the
next day, being waited on by the chief officers of
the garrison, and a considerable convoy of Germans
and Rascians. The emperor has several regiments
of these people; but, to say the truth, they are
rather plunderers than soldiers ; having no pay,
and being obliged to furnish their own arms and
horses, they rather look like vagabond gipsies, or
stout beggars than regular troops.

I cannot forbear speaking a word of this race of
creatures, who are very numerous all over Hungary.
They have a patriarch of their own at Grand Cairo,
and are really of the Greek church : but their
extreme ignorance gives their priests occasion to
impose several new notions upon them. These
fellows, letting their hair and beard grow inviolate,
make exactly the figure of the Indian bramins.
They are heirs-general to all the money of the
laity; for which, in return, they give them formal
passports, signed and sealed, for heaven ;([47]) and
the wives and children only inherit the house and
cattle. In most other points they follow the Greek
church.

([47]) They borrowed the original hint from the pope, and no
doubt profited considerably by following the example of his
Holiness.—ED.

This little digression has interrupted my telling you we passed over the fields of Carlowitz,
where the last great victory was obtained by Prince
Eugene over the Turks. The marks of that glorious bloody day are yet recent, the field being yet
strewed with the skulls and carcasses of unburied
men, horses, and camels. I could not look, without horror, on such numbers of mangled human
bodies, nor without reflecting on the injustice of
war, that makes murder not only necessary, but
meritorious. Nothing seems to be a plainer proof
of the *irrationality* of mankind (whatever fine
claims we pretend to reason) than the rage with
which they contest for a small spot of ground,
when such vast parts of fruitful earth lie quite uninhabited. It is true, custom has now made it unavoidable ; but can there be a greater demonstra-
tion of want of reason, than a custom being firmly
established so plainly contrary to the interest of
man in general ? I am a good deal inclined to believe Mr. Hobbes, that the *state of nature* is a *state of
war* ; ([18]) but thence I conclude human nature not
rational, if the word reason means common sense,

([18]) Hobbes's theory will always be the theory of wits—of
persons who would rather seem wise than be so. Perhaps,
however, the whole fallacy lurks in the words, "state of nature"—for what is that state ? Aristotle, a better politician and
philosopher than Hobbes, thought the "state of nature" to be
the highest state of civilization, the perfect manhood of society,
in which war is rather an accident than a habit. Even understanding by the "state of nature" the savage's condition, there
is no foundation for Hobbes's theory—for savages never fight, or

as I suppose it does. I have a great many admirable arguments to support this reflection : I will not, however, trouble you with them, but return, in a plain style, to the history of my travels.

We were met at Betsko (a village in the midway between Belgrade and Peterwaradin) by an aga of the janisaries, with a body of the Turks, exceeding the Germans by one hundred men, though the pasha had engaged to send exactly the same number. You may judge by this of their fears. I am really persuaded, that they hardly thought the odds of one hundred men set them even with the Germans; however, I was very uneasy till they were parted, fearing that some quarrel might arise, notwithstanding the parole given.

We came late to Belgrade, the deep snows making the ascent to it very difficult. It seems a strong city, fortified on the east side by the Danube, and on the south by the river Save, and was formerly the barrier of Hungary. It was first taken by Solyman the Magnificent, and since by the emperor's forces, led by the elector of Bavaria. The emperor held it only two years, it being retaken by the grand vizier. It is now fortified with the utmost care and skill the Turks are capable of, and strengthened by a very numerous garrison of their bravest janisaries, commanded by a pasha seraskiér, (i. e. general,) though this last expression is not

seek to fight, but when the rights of their tribe are supposed to be invaded. But this is, perhaps, laying on her ladyship's remark with more stress than it deserves.—ED.

very just; for, to say truth, the seraskiér is commanded by the janisaries. These troops have an
absolute authority here, and their conduct carries
much more the aspect of rebellion than the appearance of subordination. You may judge of this
by the following story, which, at the same time,
will give you an idea of the *admirable* intelligence
of the governor of Peterwaradin, though so few
hours distant. We were told by him at Peterwaradin, that the garrison and inhabitants of Belgrade were so weary of the war, they had killed
their pasha about two months ago, in a mutiny, because he had suffered himself to be prevailed upon,
by a bribe of five purses (five hundred pounds sterling) to give permission to the Tartars to ravage
the German frontiers. We were very well pleased
to hear of such favourable dispositions in the people; but when we came hither, we found that the
governor had been ill informed, and the real truth
of the story to be this: The late pasha fell under
the displeasure of his soldiers, for no other reason
but restraining their incursions on the Germans.
They took it into their heads, from that mildness,
that he had intelligence with the enemy, and sent
such information to the grand signior at Adrianople; but, redress not coming quick enough from
thence, they assembled themselves in a tumultuous
manner, and, by force, dragged their pasha before
the cadi and mufti, and there demanded justice in
a mutinous way; one crying out, Why he pro-
tected the infidels? another, Why he squeezed
them of their money? The pasha, easily guessing

H

their purpose, calmly replied to them, that they asked him too many questions, and that he had but one life, which must answer for all. They then immediately fell upon him with their scimitars (without waiting the sentence of their heads of the law,) and in a few moments cut him in pieces. ([49]) The present pasha has not dared to punish the murder; on the contrary, he affected to applaud the actors of it, as brave fellows, that knew how to do themselves justice. He takes all pretences of throwing money among the garrison, and suffers them to make little excursions into Hungary, where they burn some poor Rascian houses.

You may imagine, I cannot be very easy in a town which is really under the government of an insolent soldiery. We expected to be immediately dismissed, after a night's lodging here: but the pasha detains us till he receives orders from Adrianople, which may possibly be a month a-coming. In the mean time, we are lodged in one of the best houses, belonging to a very considerable man amongst them, and have a whole chamber of janisaries to guard us. My only diversion is the conversation of our host, Achmet Bey, a title something like that of count in Germany. His father was a

---

([49]) These glances at an order of things formerly prevalent in Turkey will become more and more curious every day, in proportion as we recede from the period when they ceased to exist. The present sultan found the janisaries precisely what Lady Mary describes, except in strength and good fortune; and, as a preliminary to his reforms, was compelled to cut them off at a blow.—ED.

great pasha, and he has been educated in the most
polite eastern learning, being perfectly skilled in
the Arabic and Persian languages, and an extraordinary scribe, which they call *effendi*. This accomplishment makes way to the greatest preferments : but he has had the good sense to prefer an
easy, quiet, secure life, to all the dangerous honours
of the Porte. He sups with us every night, and
drinks wine very freely. ([50]) You cannot imagine
how much he is delighted with the liberty of conversing with me. He has explained to me many
pieces of Arabian poetry, which, I observe, are in
numbers not unlike ours, generally of an alternate
verse, and of a very musical sound. Their expressions of love are very passionate and lively. I
am so much pleased with them, I really believe I
should learn to read Arabic if I was to stay here a
few months. He has a very good library of their
books of all kinds ; and, as he tells me, spends the
greatest part of his life there. I pass for a great
scholar with him, by relating to him some of
the Persian tales, which I find are genuine.([51])

([50]) A wine-bibbing Turk is now no rarity. The difficulty,
perhaps, is, to find one who does not drink ; for, in this respect
at least, they have shown themselves apt pupils of the Europeans
whom they propose for their models. Fashion still requires, however, that the indulgence of intemperate habits should be concealed from the public eye; and accordingly, though they do
not, in many cases, even pretend to abstinence, it is still uncommon to meet with a Musulman out of doors in a state of drunk-
enness.—Ed.

([51]) The Persian Tales appeared first in Europe as a translation by Monsieur Petit de la Croix ; and what are called "The
Arabian Nights," in a similar manner, by Monsieur Galland.

At first he believed I understood Persian. I have frequent disputes with him concerning the difference of our customs, particularly the confinement of women. He assures me there is nothing at all in it; only, says he, we have the advantage, that when our wives cheat us nobody knows it. He has wit, and is more polite than many Christian men of quality. I am very much entertained with him. He has had the curiosity to make one of our servants set him an alphabet of our letters, and can already write a good Roman hand.

But these amusements do not hinder my wishing heartily to be out of this place; though the weather is colder than I believe it ever was anywhere but in Greenland. We have a very large stove constantly kept hot, yet the windows of the room are frozen on the inside. God knows when I may have an opportunity of sending this letter: but I have written it for the discharge of my own conscience: and you cannot now reproach me, that one of yours makes ten of mine. Adieu.

XXVIII.

TO THE PRINCESS OF WALES.([52])

Adrianople, April 1, 1717.

I HAVE now, madam, finished a journey that has not been undertaken by any Christian since the

---

([52]) The late Queen Caroline.

time of the Greek emperors; and I shall not regret all the fatigues I have suffered in it, if it gives
me an opportunity of amusing your royal highness
by an account of places utterly unknown amongst
us; the emperor's ambassadors, and those few
English that have come hither always going on the
Danube to Nicopolis. ([53]) But the river was now frozen, and Mr. Wortley was so zealous for the service
of his majesty, that he would not defer his journey
to wait for the conveniency of that passage.

We crossed the deserts of Servia, almost quite
overgrown with wood, through a country naturally
fertile. The inhabitants are industrious; but the
oppression of the peasants is so great, they are
forced to abandon their houses, and neglect their
tillage, all they have being a prey to the janisaries,
whenever they please to seize upon it. We had a
guard of five hundred of them, and I was almost in
tears every day, to see their insolencies in the poor
villages through which we passed.

After seven days' travelling through thick woods,
we came to Nissa, once the capital of Servia, situ-

([53]) She would appear for the moment to have forgotten the
embassy of the emperor Ferdinand, which produced a collection of letters scarcely less interesting, and once much more
celebrated than her own; I mean those of Busbequius, which
every reader of Lady Montagu should compare with her
lively sketches. The ambassador, quitting Vienna in December, performed but a small portion of the journey—from
Buda to Belgrade—by water, and moved almost with the rapidity
of a Tartar courier. Busbequius looked upon society from a
higher intellectual level, and had by no means the same temptation to extravagance, since he had not taught his correspondents
to expect wit in his letters.—ED.

ated in a fine plain on the river Nissava, in a very
good air, and so fruitful a soil, that the great plenty
is hardly credible. I was certainly assured, that
the quantity of wine last vintage was so prodigious,
that they were forced to dig holes ([54]) in the earth
to put it in, not having vessels enough in the town
to hold it. The happiness of this plenty is scarcely
perceived by the oppressed people. I saw here a
new occasion for my compassion; the wretches
that had provided twenty waggons for our baggage
from Belgrade hither for a certain hire, being all
sent back without payment, some of their horses
lamed, and others killed, without any satisfaction
made for them. The poor fellows came round the
house weeping and tearing their hair and beards
in a most pitiful manner, without getting anything
but drubs from the insolent soldiers. I cannot express to your royal highness how much I was
moved at this scene. I would have paid them the
money out of my own pocket with all my heart;
but it would only have been giving so much to the
aga, who would have taken it from them without
any remorse.

After four days' journey from this place over the
mountains, we came to Sophia, situated in a large
beautiful plain on the river Isca, and surrounded
with distant mountains. It is hardly possible to
see a more agreeable landscape. The city itself is
very large, and extremely populous. Here are hot
baths, very famous for their medicinal virtues.—Four

([54]) For " holes" read " cisterns," *meo periculo.*—ED.

days' journey from hence, we arrived at Philippopolis, after having passed the ridges between the
mountains of Hæmus and Rhodope, which are
always covered with snow. This town is situated
on a rising ground near the river Hebrus, and is
almost wholly inhabited by Greeks: here are
still some ancient Christian churches. They have
a bishop; and several of the richest Greeks live
here: but they are forced to conceal their wealth
with great care, the appearance of poverty (which
includes part of its inconveniences) being all their
security against feeling it in earnest. The country
from hence to Adrianople is the finest in the world.
Vines grow wild on all the hills; (⁵⁵) and the perpetual spring they enjoy makes every thing gay
and flourishing. But this climate, happy as it
seems, can never be preferred to England with all
its frosts and snows, while we are blessed with an
easy government, under a king who makes his own
happiness consist in the liberty of his people, and
chooses rather to be looked upon as their father
than their master.

This theme would carry me very far, and I am
sensible I have already tired out your royal high-

(⁵⁵) These vines were no doubt the relics of ancient vineyards,
planted when the country was in the hands of a more intelligent
and industrious people. A tree bearing fruit something like
grapes is found, however, in many parts of the world. Lieutenant Wellsted, in his account of Socotra, speaks of one called the
ukshare, whose berries, round and clustering, bear much resemblance to bunches of grapes. (*Journ. Geogr. Soc.* v. ii. 149, 153,
199.)—Ed.

ness's patience. But my letter is in your hands,
and you may make it as short as you please, by
throwing it into the fire, when weary of reading it.

I am, madam,

With the greatest respect, &c.

XXIX.

TO THE LADY RICH.

Adrianople, April 1, 1717.

I AM now got into a new world, where every thing
I see appears to me a change of scene ; and I write
to your ladyship with some content of mind,
hoping, at least, that you will find the charms of
novelty in my letters, and no longer reproach me
that I tell you nothing extraordinary.

I will not trouble you with a relation of our
tedious journey ; but must not omit what I saw remarkable at Sophia, one of the most beautiful
towns in the Turkish empire, and famous for its
hot baths, that are resorted to both for diversion
and health. I stopped here one day on purpose to
see them ; and designing to go *incognito*, I hired a
Turkish coach. These voitures are not at all like
ours,([56]) but much more convenient for the country,
the heat being so great that glasses would be very

([56]) These carriages, of which there are two kinds, have since
been both described and engraved by Castellan. (*Mœurs des
Othomans.* IV. 230. v. 202.) In most cases they are drawn by

troublesome. They are made a good deal in the manner of the Dutch stage-coaches, having wooden lattices painted and gilded; the inside being also painted with baskets and nosegays of flowers, inter-mixed commonly with little poetical mottoes. They are covered all over with scarlet cloth, lined with silk, and very often richly embroidered and fringed: this covering entirely hides the persons in them, but may be thrown back at pleasure, and thus permits the ladies to peep through the lattices. They hold four people very conveniently, seated on cushions, but not raised.

In one of these covered waggons, I went to the bagnio about ten o'clock; it was already full of women. It is built of stone, in the shape of a dome, with no windows but in the roof, which gives light enough. There were five of these domes joined together, the outmost being less than the rest, and serving only as a hall, where the portress stood at the door. Ladies of quality generally give this woman a crown or ten shillings; and I did not forget that ceremony. The next room is a very large one, paved with marble, and all around it are two raised sofas of marble, one above another. There were four fountains of cold water in this room, falling first into marble basons, and then running on the floor in little channels made for that purpose, which carried the streams into the

---

oxen, whose labours the drivers soften by suspending a number of small bells from a sort of network supported by a bent rod over their necks. The harness of these animals is generally of bright coloured leather embroidered.—ED.

next room, something less than this, with the same
sort of marble sofas, but so hot with streams of
sulphur proceeding from the baths joining to it, it
was impossible to stay there with one's clothes on :
the two other domes were the hot baths, one of
which had two cocks of cold water turning into it,
to temper it to what degree of warmth the bathers
please to have.

I was in my travelling habit, which is a riding
dress, and certainly appeared very extraordinary to
them : yet there was not one of them that showed
the least surprise or impertinent curiosity, but received me with all the obliging civility possible.   I
know no European court where the ladies would
have behaved themselves in so polite a manner to
such a stranger.   I believe, upon the whole, there
were two hundred women, and yet none of those
disdainful smiles and satirical whispers, that never
fail in our assemblies when any body appears that
is not dressed exactly in the fashion.   They re-
peated over and over to me, " Guzél, péc guzél,"
which is nothing but " Charming, very charming."
The first sofas were covered with cushions and rich
carpets, on which sat the ladies ; and on the second
their slaves behind them, but without any distinction of rank by their dress, all being in the state
of nature, that is, in plain English, stark naked,
without any beauty or defect concealed.   Yet
there was not the least wanton smile or immodest
gesture among them : they walked and moved with
the same majestic grace which Milton describes
our general mother with.   There were many

amongst them as exactly proportioned as ever any goddess was drawn by the pencil of a Guido or Titian,—and most of their skins shiningly white, only adorned by their beautiful hair divided into many tresses, hanging on their shoulders, braided either with pearl or ribbon, perfectly representing the figures of the Graces.

I was here convinced of the truth of a reflection I have often made, " That if it were the fashion to go naked, the face would be hardly observed." ([57]) I perceived that the ladies of the most delicate skins and finest shapes had the greatest share of my admiration, though their faces were sometimes less beautiful than those of their companions. To tell you the truth, I had wickedness enough to wish secretly that Mr. Jervas ([58]) could have been there invisible : I fancy it would have very much im- proved his art, to see so many fine women naked, in different postures, some in conversation, some working, others drinking coffee or sherbet, and many negligently lying on their cushions, while their slaves (generally pretty girls of seventeen or eighteen) were employed in braiding their hair in

---

([57]) This remark is only partly just. Where the face is moderately handsome, more admiration is bestowed on the form ; but, wherever there is consummate beauty of countenance, the figure is regarded as little more than its pedestal.—ED.

([58]) Charles Jervas was a pupil of Sir Godfrey Kneller. He was the friend of Pope, and much celebrated for his portraits of females. The beauties of his day were proud to be painted by his hand, after Pope had published his celebrated epistle to him, in which he is complimented as " selling a thousand years of bloom."

several pretty fancies. In short, it is the woman's
coffeehouse, where all the news of the town is told,
scandal invented, &c.——They generally take this
diversion once a week, and stay there at least four
or five hours, without getting cold by immediately
coming out of the hot bath into the cold room,
which was very surprising to me. The lady that
seemed the most considerable among them, en-
treated me to sit by her, and would fain have un-
dressed me for the bath : I excused myself with
some difficulty. They being, however, all so
earnest in persuading me, I was at last forced to
open my shirt, and show them my stays, which
satisfied them very well ; for I saw they believed I
was locked up in that machine, and that it was not
in my own power to open it, which contrivance
they attributed to my husband. I was charmed
with their civility and beauty, and should have
been very glad to pass more time with them ; but
Mr. Wortley resolving to pursue his journey next
morning early, I was in haste to see the ruins of
Justinian's church, which did not afford me so agreeable a prospect as I had left, being little more than
a heap of stones.

Adieu, madam : I am sure I have now entertained you with an account of such a sight as you
never saw in your life, and what no book of
travels could inform you of, as it is no less than
death for a man to be found in one of these
places. ([59])

([59]) The *Hammams*, or Turkish baths, are now much bet-

XXX.

TO THE ABBOT ——

Adrianople, April 1, 1717.

You see that I am very exact in keeping the promise you engaged me to make. I know not, however, whether your curiosity will be satisfied with the accounts I shall give you, though I can assure you the desire I have to oblige you to the utmost of my power has made me very diligent in my inquiries and observations. It is certain we have but very imperfect accounts of the manners and religion of these people; this part of the world being seldom visited but by merchants, who mind little but their own affairs ; or travellers, who make too short a stay to be able to report anything exactly of their own knowledge. ([60]) The Turks are too proud to converse familiarly with mer-

---

ter known than when Lady Montagu wrote. From her account it would appear that she supposed men to be excluded altogether from these buildings ; but in this she was mistaken ; for throughout the Turkish empire the public baths are frequented by both sexes, though not, of course, at the same time. In some cities men bathe in the morning, and women in the afternoon; in others, the sexes divide the days of the week between them, and enjoy this luxury alternately. I have elsewhere (*Egypt and Mohammed Ali*, ii. 370. *ff.*) described the splendid salt-water baths of the pasha, in a passage too long to be introduced here.—ED.

([60]) This remark is peculiarly amusing from a person who had been scarcely one month in the country, and that, too, merely on its borders.—ED.

chants, who can only pick up some confused in-
formations, which are generally false; and can
give no better account of the ways here than a
French refugee, lodging in a garret in Greek-street,
could write of the court of England.

The journey we have made from Belgrade hither
cannot possibly be passed by any out of a public
character. The desert woods of Servia are the
common refuge of thieves, who rob fifty in a company, so that we had need of all our guards to
secure us; and the villages are so poor that only
force could extort from them the necessary provisions. Indeed, the janisaries had no mercy on
their poverty, killing all the poultry and sheep
they could find, without asking to whom they
belonged; while the wretched owners durst not
put in their claim, for fear of being beaten.
Lambs just fallen, geese and turkeys big with egg,
all massacred without distinction! I fancied I
heard the complaints of Meliboeus for the hope of
his flock. When the pashas travel it is yet worse.
These oppressors are not content with eating all
that is to be eaten belonging to the peasants; after
they have crammed themselves and their numerous retinue, they have the impudence to exact
what they call *teeth-money*, a contribution for the
use of their teeth, worn with doing them the
honour of devouring their meat. This is literally
and exactly true, however extravagant it may seem;
and such is the natural corruption of a military
government, their religion not allowing of this
barbarity, any more than ours does.

I had the advantage of lodging three weeks at Belgrade, with a principal effendi, that is to say, a scholar. This set of men are equally capable of preferments in the law or the church, these two sciences being cast into one, and a lawyer and a priest being the same word in the Turkish language. They are the only men really considerable in the empire; all the profitable employments and church revenues are in their hands. The grand-signior, though general heir to his people, never presumes to touch their lands or money, which go, in an uninterrupted succession to their children. It is true they lose this privilege by accepting a place at court, or the title of pasha; but there are few examples of such fools among them. You may easily judge of the power of these men, who have engrossed all the learning, and almost all the wealth of the empire : they are the real authors, though the soldiers are the actors of revolutions. They deposed the late Sultan Mustapha; and their power is so well known, that it is the emperor's interest to flatter them.

This is a long digression. I was going to tell you that an intimate daily conversation with the effendi, Achmet Bey, gave me an opportunity of knowing their religion and morals in a more particular manner than, perhaps, any Christian ever did. ([61]) I explained to him the difference between

([61]) Quick as Lady Montagu was, she failed to perceive the ridicule of passages like this, in which she assumes that no other traveller ever before formed an acquaintance with a sensible Turk.   After all, too, it is quite clear that her friend Achmet

the religion of England and Rome: and he was
pleased to hear there were Christians that did not
worship images, or adore the Virgin Mary. The
ridicule of transubstantiation appeared very strong
to him.—Upon comparing our creeds together, I am
convinced that if our friend Dr. —— had free
liberty of preaching here, it would be very easy
to persuade the generality to Christianity, whose
notions are very little different from his. Mr.
Whiston would make a very good apostle here. I
do not doubt but his zeal will be much fired, if
you communicate this account to him; but tell
him, he must first have the gift of tongues, before
he can possibly be of any use. ([62])

Mahometism is divided into as many sects as
Christianity; and the first institution as much
neglected and obscured by interpretations. I cannot here forbear reflecting on the natural inclination of mankind to make mysteries and novelties.
—The Zeidi, Kudi, Jabari, &c., put me in mind of
the Catholics, Lutherans, and Calvinists, and are
equally zealous against one another. But the
most prevailing opinion, if you search into the
secret of the effendis, is plain deism. This is, indeed, kept from the people, who are amused with a
thousand different notions, according to the differ-

Bey, who probably already experienced some symptoms of the
Frankomania, was playing off a hoax upon her. With regard
to religion, he had clearly none at all; and on comparing *creeds*
with our fair traveller, he probably discovered that they were
both in the same predicament.—ED.

([62]) A proof of what is advanced in the preceding note.—ED.

ent interest of their preachers.—There are very few amongst them (Achmet Bey denied there were any) so absurd as to set up for wit by declaring they believe no God at all : and Sir Paul Rycaut is mistaken (as he commonly is) in calling the sect *muterin* ([63]) (i. e. *the secret with us.*) Atheists, they being Deists, whose impiety consists in making a jest of their prophet. ([64]) Achmet Bey did not own to me that he was of this opinion ; but made no scruple of deviating from some part of Mahomet's law, by drinking wine with the same freedom we did. When I asked him how he came to allow himself that liberty ? he made answer that all the creatures of God are good, and designed for the use of man ; however, that the prohibition of wine was a very wise maxim, and meant for the common people, being the source of all disorders among them ; but that the prophet never designed to confine those that knew how to use it with moderation : nevertheless, he said, that scandal ought to be avoided, and that he never drank it in public. This is the general way of thinking among them, and very few forbear drinking wine that are able

---

([63]) See D'Ohsson, Tableau Général de l'Empire Othoman, 5 vols. 8vo., 1791, in which the religious code of the Mohammedans, and of each sect, is very satisfactorily detailed.

([64]) Atheists, however, are not rare in the East. The tendency of all voluptuous and mystical people is always very equivocal, on this point ; and among the sects of dreamers in Persia, India, and other Asiatic countries, they who by courtesy are termed *philosophers*, entertain opinions little different from those of Spinoza, which was very much the case with the ancient Egyptians, as Jablonski has already observed.—ED.

I

to afford it. He assured me that, if I understood
Arabic, I should be very well pleased with reading
the Alcoran, which is so far from the nonsense we
charge it with, that it is the purest morality, delivered in the very best language. (⁶⁵) I have
since heard impartial Christians speak of it in the
same manner; and I do not doubt but that all
our translations are from copies got from the Greek
priests, who would not fail to falsify it with the
extremity of malice. No body of men ever were
more ignorant, or more corrupt : yet they differ so
little from the Romish church that, I confess, nothing gives me a greater abhorrence of the cruelty
of your clergy than the barbarous persecution of
them, whenever they have been their masters, for
no other reason than their not acknowledging the
pope. The dissenting in that one article has got
them the titles of heretics and schismatics; and,
what is worse, the same treatment. I found at
Philippopolis a sect of Christians that call themselves Paulines. (⁶⁶) They show an old church,
where, they say, St. Paul preached; and he is their
favourite saint, after the same manner that St. Peter
is at Rome; neither do they forget to give him the
same preference over the rest of the apostles.

But of all the religions I have seen, that of the
Arnaöuts seems to me the most particular. They

(⁶⁵) Of the value of this assertion the English reader may
now form a just estimate from the able translation and very
learned commentary of *Sale*, who, as Gibbon observes, was half
a Musulman.—ED.

(⁶⁶) See Bayle, Dict. Hist. et Crit. art. *Pauliciens.*—ED.

are natives of Arnaöutlich, the ancient Macedonia, and still retain the courage and hardiness, though they have lost the name of Macedonians, being the best militia in the Turkish empire, and the only check upon the janisaries. They are foot-soldiers; we had a guard of them, relieved in every considerable town we passed : they are all clothed and armed at their own expense, dressed in clean white coarse cloth, carrying guns of a prodigious length, which they run with upon their shoulders as if they did not feel the weight of them, the leader singing a sort of rude tune, not unpleasant, and the rest making up the chorus. These people, living between Christians and Mahometans, and not being skilled in controversy, declare, that they are utterly unable to judge which religion is best ; but, to be certain of not entirely rejecting the truth, they very prudently follow both. They go to the mosques on Fridays, and to the church on Sundays, saying for their excuse that at the day of judgment they are sure of protection from the true prophet ; but which that is they are not able to determine in this world. I believe there is no other race of mankind who have so modest an opinion of their own capacity.

These are the remarks I have made on the diversity of religions I have seen. I do not ask your pardon for the liberty I have taken in speaking of the Roman. I know you equally condemn the quackery of all churches, as much as you revere the sacred truths, in which we both agree.

You will expect I should say something to you

of the antiquities of this country; but there are
few remains of ancient Greece. We passed near
the piece of an arch which is commonly called
Trajan's Gate, from a supposition that he made it
to shut up the passage over the mountains between
Sophia and Philippopolis. But I rather believe it
the remains of some triumphal arch; (though I
could not see any inscription;) for, if that passage
had been shut up, there are many others that
would serve for the march of an army; and, notwithstanding the story of Baldwin, Earl of Flan-
ders, being overthrown in these straits, after he
won Constantinople, I do not fancy the Germans
would find themselves stopped by them at this
day. It is true the road is now made (with great
industry) as commodious as possible, for the march
of the Turkish army; there is not one ditch or
puddle between this place and Belgrade that has
not a large strong bridge of planks built over it:
but the precipices are not so terrible as I had
heard them represented. At these mountains we
lay at the little village Kiskoi, wholly inhabited
by Christians, as all the peasants of Bulgaria are.
Their houses are nothing but little huts, raised of
dirt baked in the sun: and they leave them and
fly into the mountains, some months before the
march of the Turkish army, who would else entirely
ruin them, by driving away their whole flocks.
This precaution secures them in a sort of plenty;
for, such vast tracts of land lying in common, they
have the liberty of sowing what they please, and
are generally very industrious husbandmen. I

drank here several sorts of delicious wine. The women dress themselves in a great variety of coloured glass beads, and are not ugly, but of a tawny complexion.

I have now told you all that is worth telling you, and perhaps more, relating to my journey. When I am at Constantinople, I will try to pick up some curiosities, and then you shall hear again from

Yours, &c.

XXXI,

TO THE COUNTESS OF BRISTOL.

Adrianople, April 1, 1717.

As I never can forget the smallest of your lady-ship's commands, my first business here has been to inquire after the stuffs you ordered me to look for, without being able to find what you would like. The difference of the dress here and at London is so great, the same sort of things are not proper for *caftáns* and *manteaus*. However, I will not give over my search, but renew it again at Constantinople, though I have reason to believe there is nothing finer than what is to be found here, as this place is at present the residence of the court. The grand signior's eldest daughter was married some few days before I came hither; and upon that occasion, the Turkish ladies display all their magnificence. The bride was conducted to

her husband's house in very great splendour. She
is widow of the late vizier, who was killed at Peterwaradin, though that ought rather to be called a
contract than a marriage, ([67]) since she never has
lived with him; however, the greatest part of his
wealth is hers. He had the permission of visiting
her in the seraglio; and, being one of the hand-
somest men in the empire, had very much engaged
her affections. When she saw this second husband, who is at least fifty, she could not forbear
bursting into tears. He is indeed a man of merit,
and the declared favourite of the sultan; (which
they call *mosáyp;*) but that is not enough to make
him pleasing in the eyes of a girl of thirteen.

The government here is entirely in the hands of
the army; the grand signior, with all his absolute
power, is as much a slave as any of his subjects,
and trembles at a janisary's frown. Here is, indeed, a much greater appearance of subjection
than among us: a minister of state is not spoken
to but upon the knee; should a reflection on his
conduct be dropped in a coffee-house, (for they

([67]) In Mohammedan countries marriage is nothing more than
a contract. Betrothment often takes place when the female is
only three or four years old, and the marriage is solemnized
before she has reached the age of fourteen. All the prelimina-
ries are settled by other persons, as custom, in this instance
more powerful than law, forbids the future bridegroom and
bride to meet before their nuptials. Their prophet, however,
formally set aside the practice, which had prevailed before the
preaching of Islamism, and advised one of his followers, about
to be married, to see the lady first, and ascertain from her appearance and manner whether he could hope to be happy with
her.—Ed.

have spies everywhere,) the house would be razed
to the ground, and perhaps the whole company
put to the torture. No " huzzaing mobs, senseless
pamphlets, and tavern disputes about politics ;"

> " A consequential ill that freedom draws ;
> A bad effect,—but from a noble cause."

None of our harmless calling names! but when a
minister here displeases the people, in three hours'
time he is dragged even from his master's arms.
They cut off hands, head, and feet, and throw
them before the palace-gate with all the respect in
the world ; while the sultan (to whom they all
profess an unlimited adoration) sits trembling in
his apartment, and dares neither defend nor revenge his favourite. This is the blessed condition
of the most absolute monarch upon earth, who
owns no *law* but his *will*.

I cannot help wishing, in the loyalty of my
heart, that the parliament would send hither a
ship-load of your passive-obedient men, that they
might see arbitrary government in its clearest
and strongest light, ([68]) where it is hard to judge
whether the prince, people, or ministers are most
miserable. I could make many reflections on this
subject ; but I know, madam, your own good
sense has already furnished you with better than I
am capable of.

([68]) The voyage does not effect a cure, in cases of this kind,
because the patient looks upon all he sees as on a drama, in
which he is no way concerned. To effect any good he should
be made to feel what the natives feel.—ED.

I went yesterday along with the French ambassadress to see the grand signior ([69]) in his passage to
the mosque. He was preceded by a numerous
guard of janisaries, with vast white feathers on
their heads, as also by the *spahis* and *bostangees*,
(these are foot and horse guards,) and the royal
gardeners, which are a very considerable body of
men, dressed in different habits of fine lively
colours, so that at a distance they appeared like a
parterre of tulips. After them, the aga of the
janisaries, in a robe of purple velvet, lined with
silver tissue, his horse led by two slaves richly
dressed. Next him the *kyzlár-aga* (your ladyship
knows this is the chief guardian of the seraglio
ladies,) in a deep yellow cloth, (which suited very
well to his black face,) lined with sables. Last came
his sublimity himself, arrayed in green, lined with
the fur of a Muscovite fox, which is supposed
worth a thousand pounds sterling, and mounted
on a fine horse, with furniture embroidered with
jewels. Six more horses richly caparisoned were
led after him ; and two of his principal courtiers
bore, one his gold, and the other his silver coffee-
pot, on a staff; another carried a silver stool on
his head for him to sit on. ([70])

([69]) Achmèt III., who reigned from 1703 to 1730, recovered
the Morea from the Venetians, but lost Belgrade, Peterwaradin,
and Temesvar, to the Imperialists. He preferred his palace at
Adrianople to the Ottoman Porte, which lost him the favour of
the janisaries.

([70]) Choiseul-Gouffier (Voyage Pittoresque de la Grèce) has
a very good view of this procession, the original drawing of
which, in the possession of M. Blaise of Paris, publisher of the

It would be too tedious to tell your ladyship the various dresses and turbans by which their rank is distinguished : but they were all extremely rich and gay, to the number of some thousands ; so that, perhaps, there cannot be seen a more beautiful procession. The sultan appeared to us a handsome man of about forty, with something, however, severe in his countenance, and his eyes very full and black. He happened to stop under the window where we stood, and (I suppose being told who we were) looked upon us very attentively, so that we had full leisure to consider him. The French ambassadress agreed with me as to his good mien: I see that lady very often; she is young, and her conversation would be a great relief to me, if I could persuade her to live without those forms and ceremonies that make life so formal and tiresome.([71]) But she is so delighted with her guards, her four-and-twenty footmen, gentlemen ushers, &c., that she would rather die than make me a visit without them ; not to reckon a coachful of attending damsels, ycleped maids of honour. What vexes me is, that, as long as she will visit me with a troublesome equipage, I am obliged to do the same ; however, our mutual interest makes us much together.

---

work, is not merely valuable as an illustration of costume, but as a picture. I should be glad to see the whole original illustrations of this splendid work, which might easily be purchased, transferred to the British Museum.—ED.

([71]) How could her ladyship be so unreasonable ! What, deprive the poor woman of all her consequence ? The idea is perfectly shocking.—ED.

I went with her the other day all round the
town in an open gilt chariot, with our joint train
of attendants, preceded by our guards, who might
have summoned the people to see what they had
never seen, nor ever perhaps would see again, two
young Christian ambassadresses at the same time.
Your ladyship may easily imagine we drew a vast
crowd of spectators, but all silent as death. If
any of them had taken the liberties of our mobs
upon any strange sight, our janisaries had made
no scruple of falling on them with their scimitars,
without danger for so doing, being above law.

These people, however, (I mean the janisaries,)
have some good qualities; they are very zealous
and faithful where they serve, and look upon it as
their business to fight for you on all occasions. Of
this I had a very pleasant instance in a village on
this side Philippopolis, where we were met by our
domestic guards. I happened to bespeak pigeons
for supper, upon which one of my janisaries went
immediately to the cadi, (the chief civil officer of
the town,) and ordered him to send in some
dozens. The poor man answered, that he had
already sent about, but could get none. My janisary, in the height of his zeal for my service, immediately locked him up prisoner in his room, telling
him he deserved death for his impudence, in offering to excuse his not obeying my command; but,
out of respect to me, he would not punish him but
by my order. Accordingly, he came very gravely
to me, to ask what should be done to him; adding,
by way of compliment, that if I pleased he would

bring me his head. ([72]) This may give you some
idea of the unlimited power of these fellows, who
are all sworn brothers, and bound to revenge the
injuries done to one another, whether at Cairo,
Aleppo, or any part of the world. This inviolable
league makes them so powerful that the greatest man
at court never speaks to them but in a flattering
tone; and in Asia, any man that is rich is forced
to enrol himself a janisary, to secure his estate.

But I have already said enough; and I dare
swear, dear madam, that, by this time, it is a very
comfortable reflection to you, that there is no possibility of your receiving such a tedious letter but
once in six months; it is that consideration has
given me the assurance of entertaining you so long,
and will, I hope, plead the excuse of, dear madam,
Yours, &c.

XXXII.

TO THE COUNTESS OF MAR.

Adrianople, April 1, 1717.

I WISH to God, dear sister, that you were as regular in letting me know what passes on your side
of the globe, as I am careful in endeavouring to
amuse you by the account of all I see here that
I think worth your notice. You content yourself

([72]) He would have been very much embarrassed, though, if
her ladyship had taken him at his word.—ED.

with telling me over and over, that the town is very
dull: it may possibly be dull to you, when every
day does not present you with something new;
but for me, that am in arrears at least two months'
news, all that seems very stale with you would be
very fresh and sweet here. Pray let me into more
particulars, and I will try to awaken your gratitude, by giving you a full and true relation of the
novelties of this place, none of which would surprise you more than a sight of my person, as I am
now in my Turkish habit, though I believe you
would be of my opinion, that it is admirably becoming. I intend to send you my picture; in the
mean time accept of it here.

The first part of my dress is a pair of drawers,
very full, that reach to my shoes, and conceal the
legs more modestly than your petticoats. They are
of a thin rose-coloured damask, brocaded with silver flowers. My shoes are of white kid leather, embroidered with gold. Over this hangs my smock,
of a fine white silk gauze, edged with embroidery.
This smock has wide sleeves, hanging half-way
down the arm, and is closed at the neck with a diamond button; but the shape and colour of the bosom are very well to be distinguished through it.
The *antery* is a waistcoat, made close to the shape,
of white and gold damask, with very long sleeves
falling back, and fringed with deep gold fringe, and
should have diamond or pearl buttons. My *caftan*,
of the same stuff with my drawers, is a robe exactly
fitted to my shape, and reaching to my feet, with
very long strait falling sleeves. Over this is my

girdle, of about four fingers broad, which all that
can afford it have entirely of diamonds or other
precious stones; those who will not be at that
expense have it of exquisite embroidery on satin; but it must be fastened before with a clasp
of diamonds. The *curdee* is a loose robe they
throw off or put on according to the weather,
being of a rich brocade (mine is green and gold,)
either lined with ermine or sables; the sleeves
reach very little below the shoulders. The head-
dress is composed of a cap, called *talpock*, which is
in winter of fine velvet, embroidered with pearls
or diamonds, and in summer of a light shining
silver stuff. This is fixed on one side of the head,
hanging a little way down with a gold tassel, and
bound on, either with a circle of diamonds (as I
have seen several) or a rich embroidered handkerchief. On the other side of the head, the hair is
laid flat; and here the ladies are at liberty to show
their fancies; some putting flowers, others a plume
of heron's feathers, and, in short, what they please;
but the most general fashion is a large *bouquet* of
jewels, made like natural flowers; that is, the buds,
of pearl; the roses, of different coloured rubies;
the jessamines, of diamonds; the jonquils, of to-
pazes, &c. so well set and enamelled, it is hard to
imagine anything of that kind so beautiful. The
hair hangs at its full length behind, divided into
tresses braided with pearl or ribbon, which is always in great quantity. ([73])

([73]) Castellan, despairing in the article of dress to rival our

I never saw in my life so many fine heads of hair. In one lady's I have counted an hundred and ten of the tresses all natural; ([74]) but it must be owned, that every kind of beauty is more common here than with us. It is surprising to see a young woman that is not very handsome. They have naturally the most beautiful complexion in the world, and generally large black eyes. I can assure you, with great truth, that the court of England (though I believe it the fairest in Christendom) does not contain so many beauties as are under our protection here. They generally shape their eyebrows; and both Greeks and Turks have the custom of putting round their eyes a black tincture, that at a distance, or by candlelight, adds very much to the blackness of them.([75]) I fancy many of our ladies would be overjoyed to know this secret; but it is too visible by day. They dye their nails a rose colour; but, I own, I cannot enough accustom myself to the fashion to find any beauty in it.

---

lively and elegant traveller, has translated and adopted this description, which, for easy grace, and minute delicacy of detail has never been surpassed. (*Mœurs des Othomans*, VI. 29. ff.)—ED.

([74]) On this point she must, I think, have been misinformed. At least it is now customary among oriental ladies, both Christian and Mohammedan, to introduce a great quantity of false hair in the plaiting of their tresses, as I learned from some who appeared to be as richly endowed, in this respect, as she of the hundred and ten tails.—ED.

([75]) Skilfully and sparingly used, this curious cosmetic does not look amiss, even by day; and at night, as her ladyship observes, it adds much to the beauty of the countenance by conferring the appearance of increased lustre to the eyes.—ED.

As to their morality or good conduct, I can say, like Harlequin, that it is just as it is with you; and the Turkish ladies do not commit one sin the less for not being Christians. Now that I am a little acquainted with their ways, I cannot forbear admiring, either the exemplary discretion or extreme stupidity of all the writers that have given accounts of them. It is very easy to see they have in reality more liberty than we have. No woman, of what rank soever is permitted to go into the streets without two *murlins;* one that covers her face all but her eyes, and another that hides the whole dress of her head, and hangs half way down her back. Their shapes are also wholly concealed by a thing they call a *ferigee,* which no woman of any sort appears without; this has strait sleeves, that reach to their finger-ends, and it laps all round them, not unlike a riding-hood. In winter it is of cloth, and in summer of plain stuff or silk. You may guess then how effectually this disguises them, so that there is no distinguishing the great lady from her slave. It is impossible for the most jealous husband to know his wife when he meets her; and no man dare touch or follow a woman in the street.

This perpetual masquerade gives them entire liberty of following their inclinations without danger of discovery. The most usual method of intrigue is, to send an appointment to the lover to meet the lady at a Jew's shop, which are as notoriously convenient as our Indian-houses; and yet even those who do not make use of them, do not scruple to go

to buy pennyworths, and tumble over rich goods
which are chiefly to be found amongst that sort of
people. The great ladies seldom let their gallants
know who they are; and it is so difficult to find
it out, that they can very seldom guess at her
name, whom they have corresponded with for above
half a year together. You may easily imagine the
number of faithful wives very small in a country
where they have nothing to fear from a lover's indiscretion, since we see so many have the courage
to expose themselves to that in this world, and all
the threatened punishment of the next, which is
never preached to the Turkish damsels. Neither
have they much to apprehend from the resentment
of their husbands; those ladies that are rich having
all their money in their own hands.

Upon the whole, I look upon the Turkish women as the only free people in the empire; the
very divan pays respect to them, and the grand
signior himself, when a pasha is executed, never
violates the privileges of the *harém*, (or women's
apartment,) which remains untouched and entire to the widow. ([76]) They are queens of their
slaves, whom the husband has no permission so
much as to look upon, except it be an old woman
or two that his lady chooses. It is true their law

([76]) In India, too, the harem is considered inviolable. For
this reason, when princes are reduced to the last extremity,
they often throw their treasures and jewels into the female apartments, where they remain safe, the fear of retaliation restraining
the victors from trampling on this privilege of the sex. Alexander was actuated by some such motive when he respected the
harem of Darius that fell into his hands.—ED.

permits them four wives; but there is no instance
of a man of quality that makes use of this liberty,
or of a woman of rank that would suffer it. When
a husband happens to be inconstant, (as those
things will happen,) he keeps his mistress in a
house apart, and visits her as privately as he can,
just as it is with you. Amongst all the great men
here, I only know the *tefterdar*, (i. e. treasurer) that
keeps a number of she slaves for his own use (that
is, on his own side of the house; for a slave once
given to serve a lady is entirely at her disposal,)
and he is spoken of as a libertine, or what we
should call a rake, and his wife will not see him,
though she continues to live in his house.

Thus you see, dear sister, the manners of mankind do not differ so widely as our voyage writers
would make us believe. Perhaps it would be
more entertaining to add a few surprising customs
of my own invention; but nothing seems to me so
agreeable as truth, and I believe nothing so acceptable to you. I conclude therefore with repeating
the great truth of my being,

Dear sister, &c.

XXXIII.

MR. POPE TO LADY MONTAGU.

MADAM,

If to live in the memory of others have any thing
desirable in it, it is what you possess with regard

K

to me in the highest sense of the words. There is
not a day in which your figure does not appear before me; your conversations return to my thoughts,
and every scene, place, or occasion, where I have
enjoyed them, are as lively painted, as an imagination equally warm and tender can be capable to
represent them. Yet how little accrues to you from
all this, when not only my wishes, but the very expressions of them can hardly ever arrive to be
known to you! I cannot tell whether you have
seen half the letters I have written; but if you had,
I have not said in them half of what I designed to
say; and you can have seen but a faint, slight, tim-
orous *eschantillon* of what my spirit suggests, and
my hand follows slowly and imperfectly, indeed unjustly, because discreetly and reservedly.
When you told me there was no way left for our
correspondence but by merchant ships, I watched
ever since for any that set out, and this is the first
I could learn of. I owe the knowledge of it to Mr.
Congreve (whose letters, with my lady Rich's, accompany this). However, I was impatient enough
to venture two from Mr. Methuen's office: they
have miscarried: you have lost nothing but such
words and wishes as I repeat every day in your memory, and for your welfare. I have had thoughts
of causing what I write for the future to be tran-
scribed, and to send copies by more ways than one,
that one at least might have a chance to reach you.
The letters themselves would be artless and natural enough to prove there could be no vanity in
this practice, and to show it proceeded from the be-

lief of their being welcome to you, not as they came from me, but from England. My eyesight is grown so bad, that I have left off all correspondence except with yourself; in which, methinks, I am like those people who abandon and abstract themselves from all that are about them, (with whom they might have business and intercourse,) to employ their addresses only to invisible and distant beings, whose good offices and favours cannot reach them in a long time, if at all. If I hear from you, I look upon it as little less than a miracle or extraordinary visitation from another world; it is a sort of dream of an agreeable thing, which subsists no more to me: but, however, it is such a dream as exceeds most of the dull realities of my life. Indeed, what with ill-health and ill-fortune, I am grown so stupidly philosophical as to have no thought about me that deserves the name of warm or lively, but that which sometimes awakens me into an imagination that I may yet see you again. Compassionate a poet, who has lost all manner of romantic ideas; except a few that hover about the Bosphorus and Hellespont, not so much for the fine sound of their names, as to raise up images of Leander, who was drowned in crossing the sea to kiss the hand of fair Hero. This were a destiny less to be lamented, than what we are told of the poor Jew, one of your interpreters, who was beheaded at Belgrade as a spy. I confess such a death would have been a great disappointment to me; and I believe Jacob Tonson will hardly venture to visit you after this news.

You tell me, the pleasure of being nearer the sun has a great effect upon your health and spirits. You have turned my affections so far eastward, that I could almost be one of his worshippers: for I think the sun has more reason to be proud of raising your spirits, than of raising all the plants and ripening all the minerals in the earth. It is my opinion, a reasonable man might gladly travel three or four thousand leagues to see your nature and your wit in their full perfection. What may not we expect from a creature that went out the most perfect of this part of the world, and is every day improving by the sun in the other! If you do not now write and speak the finest things imaginable, you must be content to be involved in the same imputation with the rest of the East, and be concluded to have abandoned yourself to extreme effeminacy, laziness, and lewdness of life.

I make not the least question but you could give me great eclaircissements upon many passages in Homer, since you have been enlightened by the same sun that inspired the father of poetry. You are now glowing under the climate that animated him; you may see his images rising more boldly about you in the very scenes of his story and action; you may lay the immortal work on some broken column([76]) of a hero's sepulchre, and read the fall of Troy in the shade of a Trojan ruin, but if, to visit

---

([76]) This sounds odd in Pope, who might surely have remembered that *barrows* and not *columns* constituted the monuments of heroes.—ED.

the tomb of so many heroes, you have not the heart
to pass over that sea where once a lover perished,
you may at least, at ease in your own window, contemplate the fields of Asia in such a dim and remote
prospect as you have of Homer in my translation.

I send you, therefore, with this, the third volume
of the Iliad, and as many other things as fill a
wooden box, directed to Mr. Wortley. Among the
rest, you have all I am worth, that is, my works :
there are few things in them but what you have already seen, except the Epistle of Eloisa to Abelard,
in which you will find one passage, that I cannot
tell whether to wish you should understand or
not. ([77])

For the news in London, I will sum it up in
short : we have masquerades at the theatre in the
Haymarket, of Mr. Heideker's institution ; they
are very frequent, yet the adventures are not so
numerous but that of my Lady Mohun still makes
the chief figure. Her marriage to young Mordant,
and all its circumstances, I suppose you will have
from Lady Rich, or Miss Griffin, The political
state is under great divisions, the parties of Walpole and Stanhope as violent as whig and tory.
The king and prince continue two names ; there is
nothing like a coalition but at the masquerade :
however, the princess is a dissenter from it, and
has a very small party in so unmodish a separation.

([77]) Nevertheless she would have understood it without his
being at the pains to point it out.—ED.

The last I received from your hands was from
Peterwaradin; it gave me the joy of thinking you
in good health and humour: one or two expressions in it are too generous ever to be forgotten by
me. I wrote a very melancholy one just before,
which was sent to Mr. Stanyan, to be forwarded
through Hungary. It would have informed you
how meanly I thought of the pleasures of Italy,
without the qualification of your company, and that
mere statues and pictures are not more cold to me,
than I to them. I have had but four of your letters; I have sent several, and wish I knew how
many you have received. For God's sake, madam,
send to me as often as you can, in the dependence
that there is no man breathing more constantly or
more anxiously mindful of you. Tell me that you
are well, tell me that your little son is well, tell me
that your very dog (if you have one) is well. De-
fraud me of no one thing that pleases you; for,
whatever that is, it will please me better than anything else can do.

I am always yours,

A. POPE.

XXXIV.

TO MR. POPE.

Adrianople, April 1, 1717.

I DARE say you expect at least something very new
in this letter, after I have gone a journey not

undertaken by any Christian for some hundred years. ([78]) The most remarkable accident that happened to me was my being very near over-turned into the Hebrus; and, if I had much regard for the glories that one's name enjoys after death, I should certainly be sorry for having missed the romantic conclusion of swimming down the same river in which the musical head of Orpheus re-peated verses so many ages since:

> " Caput a cervice revulsum,
> Gurgite cum medio, portans Œagrius Hebrus
> Volveret, Eurydicen vox ipsa, et frigida lingua,
> Ah! miseram Eurydicen! animâ fugiente vocabat,
> Eurydicen toto referebant flumine ripæ."

Who knows but some of your bright wits might have found it a subject affording many poetical turns, and have told the world, in an heroic elegy, that,

> As equal were our souls, so equal were our fates?

I despair of ever hearing so many fine things said of me, as so extraordinary a death would have given occasion for.

I am at this present moment writing in a house situated on the banks of the Hebrus, which runs under my chamber window. My garden is full of tall cypress-trees, upon the branches of which seve-ral couple of true turtles are saying soft things to one another from morning till night. How natu-

---

([78]) Vide note 38.—ED.

rally do *boughs* and *vows* come into my mind at
this minute ! and must not you çonfess, to my
praise, that it is more than an ordinary discretion
that can resist the wicked suggestions of poetry, in
a place where truth, for once, furnishes all the ideas
of pastoral ? The summer is already far advanced
in this part of the world ; and for some miles round
Adrianople, the whole ground is laid out in gardens, and the banks of the rivers are set with rows
of fruit-trees, under which all the most considerable
Turks divert themselves every evening; not with
walking, that is not one of their pleasures, but a
set party of them choose out a green spot, where
the shade is very thick, and there they spread a
carpet, on which they sit drinking their coffee, and
are generally attended by some slave with a fine
voice, or that plays on some instrument. ([79]) Every
twenty paces you may see one of these little companies listening to the dashing of the river; and
this taste is so universal, that the very gardeners
are not without it. I have often seen them and
their children sitting on the banks of the river, and
playing on a rural instrument, perfectly answering
the description of the ancient *fistula,* being composed of unequal reeds, with a simple but agreeable
softness in the sound.

Mr. Addison might here make the experiment he

([79]) No doubt there are such things as fine voices in Turkey,
though it was never my luck to hear them. In fact, they appear to me, who am but a novice in the matter, to have no notion at all of any kind of music.—ED.

speaks of in his travels; there not being one instrument of music among the Greek or Roman sta-
tues([80]) that is not to be found in the hands of the
people of this country. The young lads generally
divert themselves with making garlands for their
favourite lambs, which I have often seen painted
and adorned with flowers lying at their feet while
they sung or played. It is not that they ever read
romances, but these are the ancient amusements
here, and as natural to them as cudgel-playing and
football to our British swains; the softness and
warmth of the climate forbidding all rough exer-
cises, which were never so much as heard of amongst
them, and naturally inspiring a laziness and aversion to labour, which the great plenty indulges.
These gardeners are the only happy race of country
people in Turkey. They furnish all the city with
fruits and herbs, and seem to live very easily.
They are most of them Greeks, and have little
houses in the midst of their gardens, where their
wives and daughters take a liberty not permitted in the town, I mean, to go unveiled. These
wenches are very neat and handsome, and pass
their time at their looms under the shade of the
trees.

I no longer look upon Theocritus as a romantic
writer; he has only given a plain image of the way
of life amongst the peasants of his country; who,

([80]) I much fear that her ladyship had but a slight acquaintance with the musical instruments of the ancients, though, to be
sure, the list of such as are represented in sculpture is not very
voluminous.—ED.

before oppression had reduced them to want, were, I suppose, all employed as the better sort of them are now. I do not doubt, had he been born a Briton, but his *Idylliums* had been filled with descriptions of thrashing and churning, both which are unknown here, the corn being all trodden out by oxen ; and butter (I speak it with sorrow) unheard of.

I read over your Homer here with an infinite pleasure, and find several little passages explained, that I did not before entirely comprehend the beauty of; many of the customs, and much of the dress, then in fashion being yet retained.([81]) I do not wonder to find more remains here of an age so distant, than is to be found in any other country, the Turks not taking that pains to introduce their own manners as has been generally practised by other nations, that imagine themselves more polite. It would be too tedious to you to point out all the passages that relate to present customs. But I can assure you that the princesses and great ladies pass their time at their looms, embroidering veils and robes, surrounded by their maids, which are always very numerous, in the same manner as we find Andromache and Helen described. The description of the belt of Menelaus exactly resembles those that are now worn by the great men, fastened before with broad golden clasps, and embroidered round with rich work. The snowy veil that Helen

---

([81]) I need not say how much she was mistaken on this point. —Ed.

throws over her face is still fashionable; and I
never see half a dozen of old bashaws (as I do very
often) with their reverend beards, sitting basking
in the sun, but I recollect good King Priam and
his counsellors. Their manner of dancing is certainly the same that Diana is *sung* to have danced
on the banks of Eurotas. The great lady still
leads the dance, and is followed by a troop of
young girls, who imitate her steps, and, if she sings,
make up the chorus. The tunes are extremely gay
and lively, yet with something in them wonderfully
soft. The steps are varied according to the pleasure of her that leads the dance, but always in exact time, and infinitely more agreeable than any of
our dances, at least in my opinion. I sometimes
make one in the train, but am not skilful enough
to lead : these are the Grecian dances, the Turkish
being very different.

I should have told you, in the first place, that the
Eastern manners give a great light into many
Scripture passages that appear odd to us, their
phrases being commonly what we should call
Scripture language.([82]) The vulgar Turk is very
different from what is spoken at court, or amongst
the people of figure, who always mix so much
Arabic and Persian in their discourse, that it may
very well be called another language. And it is

([82]) These are not the points on which Lady Montagu shines.
The Orientals, no doubt, still make use of Scripture language,
but not such Orientals as she found at Adrianople. To find
real traces of this it is necessary to pass the boundaries of Europe.—ED.

as ridiculous to make use of the expressions commonly used, in speaking to a great man or lady, as it would be to speak broad Yorkshire, or Somersetshire in the drawing-room. Besides this distinction, they have what they call the *sublime*, that is, the style proper for poetry, and which is the exact Scripture style. I believe you will be pleased to see a genuine example of this ; and I am very glad I have it in my power to satisfy your curiosity, by sending you a faithful copy of the verses that Ibrahim Pasha, the reigning favourite, has made for the young princess, his contracted wife, whom he is not yet permitted to visit without witnesses, though she is gone home to his house. He is a man of wit and learning ; and whether or no he is capable of writing good verse, you may be sure, that on such an occasion, he would not want the assistance of the best poets in the empire. Thus the verses may be looked upon as a sample of their finest poetry ; and I do not doubt you will be of my mind, that it is most wonderfully resembling " The Song of Solomon," which was also addressed to a royal bride.

TURKISH VERSES ADDRESSED TO THE SULTANA, ELDEST
DAUGHTER OF SULTAN ACHMET III.

STANZA. I.

1. The nightingale now wanders in the vines :
   Her passion is to seek roses.

2. I went down to admire the beauty of the vines :
   The sweetness of your charms has ravish'd my soul.

3. Your eyes are black and lovely,
But wild and disdainful as those of a stag.([83])

STANZA. II.

1. The wished possession is delayed from day to day ;
The cruel sultan Achmet will not permit me
To see those cheeks, more vermilion than roses.

2. I dare not snatch one of your kisses ;
The sweetness of your charms has ravished my soul.

3. Your eyes are black and lovely,
But wild and disdainful as those of a stag.

STANZA. III.

1. The wretched Ibrahim sighs in these verses :
One dart from your eyes has pierc'd through my heart.

2. Ah ! when will the hour of possession arrive ?
Must I yet wait a long time ?
The sweetness of your charms has ravish'd my soul.

3. Ah ! Sultana !—stag-eyed—an angel amongst angels !
I desire,—and my desire remains unsatisfied.—
Can you take delight to prey upon my heart ?—

STANZA. IV.

1. My cries pierce the heavens !
My eyes are without sleep !
Turn to me, Sultana !—let me gaze on thy beauty.

([83]) Sir W. Jones, in the preface to his Persian Grammar,
objects to this translation. The expression is merely analogous
to the " Βονωπις " of Homer.

The word here translated " stag " signifies rather " gazelle."
It is a very common epithet for the eyes in Eastern poetry ; and
it will be understood by those who have seen the animal, or the
female eyes painted by Corregio, large, dark, and liquid as
those of the Cairoen women.—ED.

2. Adieu !—I go down to the grave.
   If you call me—I return.
   My heart is—hot as sulphur;—sigh, and it will flame.

3. Crown of my life ! fair light of my eyes !
   My Sultana ! my princess !
   I rub my face against the earth;—I am drown'd in
      scalding tears—I rave !
   Have you no compassion ?   Will you not turn to look
      upon me ?

I have taken abundance of pains to get these
verses in a literal translation ; and if you were acquainted with my interpreters, I might spare myself the trouble of assuring you, that they have
received no poetical touches from their hands.   In
my opinion (allowing for the inevitable faults of a
prose translation into a language so very different)
there is a good deal of beauty in them.   The epithet of *stag-eyed* (though the sound is not very
agreeable in English) pleases me extremely ; and
I think it a very lively image of the fire and indifference in his mistress's eyes.   Monsieur Boileau
has very justly observed, that we are never to judge
of the elevation of an expression in an ancient author by the sound it carries with us, since it may
be extremely fine with them, when, at the same time,
it appears low or uncouth to us.   You are so well
acquainted with Homer, you cannot but have observed the same thing, and you must have the
same indulgence for all Oriental poetry.

The repetitions at the end of the two first stanzas
are meant for a sort of chorus, and are agreeable to
the ancient manner of writing.   The music of the

verses apparently changes in the third stanza,
where the burthen is altered; and I think he very
artfully seems more passionate at the conclusion,
as it is natural for people to warm themselves by
their own discourse, especially on a subject in
which one is deeply concerned : it is certainly far
more touching than our modern custom of concluding a song of passion with a turn which is in-
consistent with it. The first verse is a description
of the season of the year ; all the country now being
full of nightingales, whose amours with roses is an
Arabian fable, as well known here as any part
of Ovid amongst us, and is much the same as if an
English poem should begin by saying,—" Now Phi-
lomela sings." Or what if I turned the whole into
the style of English poetry, to see how it would look ?

STANZA. I.

" Now Philomel renews her tender strain,
Indulging all the night her pleasing pain :

I sought the groves to hear the wanton sing,
There saw a face more beauteous than the spring.

Your large stag-eyes, where thousand glories play,
As bright, as lively, but as wild as they.

STANZA. II.

In vain I'm promis'd such a heav'nly prize ;
Ah ! cruel Sultan ! who delay'st my joys !

While piercing charms transfix my amorous heart,
I dare not snatch one kiss to ease the smart.

Those eyes ! like, &c.

STANZA. III.

Your wretched lover in these lines complains ;
From those dear beauties rise his killing pains.

When will the hour of wish'd-for bliss arrive ?
Must I wait longer ?—Can I wait and live ?

Ah ! bright Sultana ! maid divinely fair !
Can you, unpitying, see the pains I bear ?

STANZA. IV.

The heavens, relenting, hear my piercing cries,
I loathe the light, and sleep forsakes my eyes ;
Turn thee, Sultana, ere thy lover dies :

Sinking to earth, I sigh the last adieu ;
Call me, my goddess, and my life renew.

My queen ! my angel ! my fond heart's desire !
I rave—my bosom burns with heav'nly fire !
Pity that passion which thy charms inspire."

I have taken the liberty, in the second verse, of
following what I suppose the true sense of the
author, though not literally expressed. By his saying, " He went down to admire the beauty of the
vines, and her charms ravished his soul," I understand a poetical fiction, of having first seen her in
a garden, where he was admiring the beauty of the
spring. But I could not forbear retaining the
comparison of her eyes with those of a stag, though,
perhaps, the novelty of it may give it a burlesque
sound in our language. I cannot determine upon
the whole how well I have succeeded in the translation, neither do I think our English proper to ex-

press such violence of passion, which is very seldom felt amongst us. ([84])   We want also those compound words which are very frequent and strong in the Turkish language.

You see I am pretty far gone in Oriental learning; and, to say truth, I study very hard.   I wish my studies may give me an occasion of entertaining your curiosity, which will be the utmost advantage hoped for from them by,

Yours, &c.

XXXV.

TO MRS. S. C——.

Adrianople, April 1.

In my opinion, dear S., I ought rather to quarrel with you for not answering my Nimeguen letter of August till December, than to excuse my not writing again till now.   I am sure there is on my side a very good excuse for silence, having gone such tiresome land journeys, though I do not find the conclusion of them so bad as you seem to imagine. I am very easy here, and not in the solitude you fancy me.   The great number of Greeks, French, English, and Italians, that are under our protection, make their court to me from morning till night; and, I will assure you, are many of them very fine

---

([84]) And still more seldom, perhaps, in the East, where marriage is a mere contract of bargain and sale.—ED.

L

ladies; for there is no possibility for a Christian to live easily under this government but by the protection of an ambassador——and the richer they are, the greater is their danger.

Those dreadful stories you have heard of the *plague* have very little foundation in truth. I own I have much ado to reconcile myself to the sound of a word which has always given me such terrible ideas, though I am convinced there is little more in it than in a fever. As a proof of this, let me tell you that we passed through two or three towns most violently infected. In the very next house where we lay (in one of those places) two persons died of it. Luckily for me, I was so well deceived that I knew nothing of the matter; and I was made believe that our second cook had only a great cold. However, we left our doctor to take care of him, and yesterday they both arrived here in good health; and I am now let into the secret that he has had the *plague*. There are many that escape it; neither is the air ever infected. I am persuaded that it would be as easy a matter to root it out here as out of Italy and France; but it does so little mischief, they are not very solicitous about it, and are content to suffer this distemper instead of our variety, which they are utterly unacquainted with.

A-propos of distempers: I am going to tell you a thing that will make you wish yourself here. The small-pox, so fatal and so general amongst us, is here entirely harmless by the invention of *ingrafting*, which is the term they give it. There is a set of old women who make it their business to perform the operation every autumn, in the month of September, when the great heat is abated. People send to one another to know if any of their family has a mind to have the small-pox : they make parties for this purpose, and when they are met (commonly fifteen or sixteen together,) the old woman comes with a nutshell full of the matter of the best sort of small-pox, and asks what vein you please to have opened. She immediately rips open that you offer to her with a large needle (which gives you no more pain than a common scratch,) and puts into the vein as much matter as can lie upon the head of her needle, and after that binds up the little wound with a hollow bit of shell; and in this manner opens four or five veins. The Grecians have commonly the superstition of opening one in the middle of the forehead, one in each arm, and one on the breast, to mark the sign of the cross; but this has a very ill effect, all these wounds leaving little scars, and is not done by those that are not superstitious, who choose to have them in the legs, or that part of the arm that is concealed. The children or young patients play together all the rest of the day, and are in perfect health to the eighth. Then the fever begins to seize them, and they keep their beds two days, very seldom three. They have very rarely above twenty or thirty in their faces, which never mark; and in eight days' time they are as well as before their illness. Where they are wounded, there remain running sores during the distemper, which I do not doubt is a great relief to it. Every year thousands undergo this operation; and the French ambassador says pleasantly, that they take the small-pox here by way of diversion, as they take the waters in other countries. There is no example of any one that has died in it; and you may believe I am well satisfied of the safety of this experiment, since I intend to try it on my dear little son. ([85])

I am patriot enough to take pains to bring this useful invention into fashion in England; and I should not fail to write to some of our doctors very particularly about it, if I knew any one of them that I thought had virtue enough to destroy such a considerable branch of their revenue for the good of mankind. But that distemper is too beneficial to them, not to expose to all their resentment the hardy wight that should undertake to put an end to it. Perhaps, if I live to return, I may, however, have courage to war with them. Upon this occasion admire the heroism in the heart of your friend, &c. &c.

XXXVI.

TO MRS. THISTLETHWAYTE.

Adrianople, April 1, 1718.

I can now tell dear Mrs. Thistlethwayte that I am safely arrived at the end of my very long journey.

([85]) It does her ladyship infinite honour that she was the first who introduced the knowledge of inoculation into the West of Europe, for this led to vaccination; and many a fair face owes its beauty to Lady Montagu.—Ed.

I will not tire you with the account of the many
fatigues I have suffered. You would rather be informed of the strange things that are to be seen
here; and a letter out of Turkey that has nothing
extraordinary in it would be as great a disappointment as my visitors will receive at London,
if I return thither without any rarities to show
them.

What shall I tell you of?—You never saw
camels in your life; ([86]) and perhaps the description
of them will appear new to you : I can assure you
the first sight of them was so to me; and though I
have seen hundreds of pictures of those animals, I
never saw any that was resembling enough to give
a true idea of them. I am going to make a bold
observation, and possibly a false one, because nobody has ever made it before me; but I do take
them to be of the stag kind; their legs, bodies, and
necks are exactly shaped like them, and their
colour very near the same. It is true, they are
much larger, being a great deal higher than a horse ;
and so swift, that, after the defeat of Peterwaradin,
they far outran the swiftest horses, and brought the
first news of the loss of the battle to Belgrade.
They are never thoroughly tamed ; ([87]) the drivers

([86]) So then, little more than a hundred years ago no person
had conceived the idea of instructing the public and garnishing
his own pockets by exhibiting this extraordinary animal about
the streets. Buffon's article on the camel, and a few pages of
Volney, have since conveyed an enlarged idea of its character
and usefulness to every corner of Europe, further, perhaps, than
the animal itself has yet travelled.—ED.

([87]) The remark, that they are never properly tamed is very

take care to tie them one to another with strong
ropes, fifty in a string, led by an ass, on which the
driver rides. I have seen three hundred in onè
caravan. They carry the third part more than any
horse; but it is a particular art to load them, because of the hunch on their backs. They seem to
me very ugly creatures; their heads being ill
formed, and disproportioned to their bodies. They
carry all the burdens; and the beasts destined to
the plough are buffaloes, an animal you are also
unacquainted with. They are larger and more
clur̄ ẙ than an ox; they have short thick black
horns, close to their heads, which grow turning
backwards. They say, this horn looks very beautiful when it is well polished. They are all black,
with very short hair on their hides, and have extremely little white eyes, that make them look like
devils. The country people dye their tails and
the hair of their forehead red, by way of ornament.

Horses are not put here to any laborious work,
nor are they at all fit for it. They are beautiful
and full of spirit, but generally little, and not
strong, as the breed of colder countries: ([88]) very
gentle, however, with all their vivacity, and also
swift and sure-footed. I have a little white fa-

---

correct, though at variance with common notions. I have seen
a string of perhaps fifteen hundred camels, all large and powerful, and as highly civilized as camels can be. But they are
nearly always vicious.—ED

([88]) The Turkish horse, though the breed appears to have
been since improved, is still smaller than our northern steeds.

vourite that I would not part with on any terms :
he prances under me with so much fire, you would
think that I had a great deal of courage to dare to
mount him; yet, I will assure you, I never rode a
horse so much at my command in my life. My
sidesaddle is the first that was ever seen in this
part of the world, and is gazed at with as much
wonder as the ship of Columbus in the first discovery of America. Here are some little birds held
in a sort of religious reverence, and for that reason
they multiply prodigiously : turtles, on the account
of their innocence; and storks, ([89]) because they
are supposed to make every winter the pilgrimage
to Mecca. To say truth, they are the happiest
subjects under the Turkish government, and are so
sensible of their privileges, that they walk the
streets without fear, and generally build in the low
parts of houses. Happy are those whose houses
are so distinguished, as the vulgar Turks are perfectly persuaded that they will not be that year at-
tacked either by fire or pestilence. I have the
happiness of one of their sacred nests under my
chamber window.

Now I am talking of my chamber, I remember
the description of the houses here will be as new
to you as any of the birds or beasts. I suppose you
have read, in most of our accounts of Turkey, that

This is also true of the Nejdis ; but though inferior in size,
they are scarcely less strong, and have far the advantage in
beauty.—ED.

([89]) These birds are equally favourites in Holland, in Spain,
and many other parts of the world.—ED.

the houses are the most miserable pieces of building in the world. I can speak very learnedly on
that subject, having been in so many of them ; and
I assure you it is no such thing. We are now
lodged in a palace belonging to the grand signior.
I really think the manner of building here very
agreeable, and proper for the country. It is true
they are not at all solicitous to beautify the outsides
of their houses, and they are generally built of
wood, which I own is the cause of many inconveniences ; but this is not to be charged on the ill
taste of the people, but on the oppression of the
government. Every house at the death of its
master is at the grand signior's disposal ; and,
therefore no man cares to make a great expense,
which he is not sure his family will be the better
for. (⁹⁰) All their design is to build a house
commodious, and that will last their lives; and
they are very indifferent if it falls down the year
after.

Every house, great and small, is divided into
two distinct parts, which only join together by a
narrow passage. The first house has a large court
before it, and open galleries all round it, which is
to me a thing very agreeable. This gallery leads
to all the chambers ; which are commonly large,
and with two rows of windows, the first being of
painted glass : they seldom build above two stories,
each of which has galleries. The stairs are broad,

(⁹⁰) If it be not put into " vacúf;" that is, annexed to some
mosque or fountain.

and not often above thirty steps. This is the house belonging to the lord, and the adjoining one is called the *haram*, that is, the ladies' apartment, (for the name of *seraglio* is peculiar to the grand signior;) it has also a gallery running round it towards the garden, to which all the windows are turned, and the same number of chambers as the other, but more gay and splendid, both in painting and furniture. The second row of windows is very low, with grates like those of convents: the rooms are all spread with Persian carpets, and raised at one end of them (my chambers are raised at both ends) about two feet. This is the sofa, which is laid with a richer sort of carpet, and all round it a sort of couch, raised half a foot, covered with rich silk, according to the fancy or magnificence of the owner. Mine is of scarlet cloth, with a gold fringe ; round about this are placed, standing against the wall, two rows of cushions, the first very large, and the next little ones; and here the Turks display their greatest magnificence. They are generally brocade, or embroidery of gold wire upon white satin : nothing can look more gay and splendid. These seats are also so convenient and easy, that I believe I shall never endure chairs as long as I live. The rooms are low, which I think no fault, and the ceiling is always of wood, generally inlaid or painted with flowers. They open in many places with folding-doors, and serve for cabinets, I think, more conveniently than ours. Between the windows are little arches to set pots of perfume, or baskets of flowers. But what pleases

me best is the fashion of having marble fountains
in the lower part of the room, which throw up
several spouts of water, giving at the same time an
agreeable coolness, and a pleasant dashing sound,
falling from one basin to another. Some of these
are very magnificent. Each house has a bagnio,
which consists generally in two or three little
rooms, leaded on the top, paved with marble, with
basins, cocks of water, and all conveniences for
either hot or cold baths.

You will, perhaps, be surprised at an account so
different from what you have been entertained
with by the common voyage writers, who are very
fond of speaking of what they do not know. It
must be under a very particular character, or on
some extraordinary occasion, that a Christian is
admitted into the house of a man of quality; and
their *harams* are always forbidden ground. ([91])
Thus they can only speak of the outside, which
makes no great appearance; and the women's
apartments are always built backward, removed
from sight, and have no other prospect than the

([91]) This was perfectly true in Lady Montagu's time; in
fact, I remember no male traveller who gives, upon his own
authority, any account of this part of a Turkish house. But the
present Pasha of Egypt, with a liberality unknown among persons of his class, granted me permission to visit all the apartments of his harem, the ladies retreating from one room to another, as we advanced, until we had made the round of the
whole. For a description, however, of what we saw, I must
refer to " Egypt and Mohammed Ali," vol. I., where the reader
will find more ample details on modern Oriental life than could
be introduced into these notes.—ED.

gardens, which are enclosed with very high walls.
There are none of our parterres in them ; but they
are planted with high trees, which give an agreeable shade, and, to my fancy, a pleasing view. In
the midst of the garden is the *chiosk*, that is, a
large room, commonly beautified with a fine fountain in the midst of it. It is raised nine or ten
steps, and enclosed with gilded lattices, round
which vines, jessamines, and honeysuckles make a
sort of green wall. Large trees are planted round
this place, which is the scene of their greatest pleasures, and where the ladies spend most of their
hours, employed by their music or embroidery. In
the public gardens there are public *chiosks*, where
people go that are not so well accommodated at
home, and drink their coffee, sherbet, &c. Neither
are they ignorant of a more durable manner of
building : their mosques are all of freestone, and
the public *hanns*, or inns, extremely magnificent,
many of them taking up a large square, built
round with shops, under stone arches, where poor
artificers are lodged *gratis*. They have always a
mosque joining to them, and the body of the *hann*
is a most noble hall, capable of holding three or
four hundred persons, the court extremely spacious,
and cloisters round it, that give it the air of
our colleges. I own I think it a more reasonable piece of charity than the founding of convents.

I think I have now told you a great deal for
once. If you do not like my choice of subjects,
tell me what you would have me write upon ; there

is nobody more desirous to entertain you than, dear Mrs. Thistlethwayte,

Yours, &c., &c.

XXXVII.

TO THE COUNTESS OF MAR.

Adrianople, April 18, 1717.

I WROTE to you, dear sister, and to all my other English correspondents, by the last ship, and only heaven can tell when I shall have another opportunity of sending to you; but I cannot forbear to write again, though perhaps my letter may lie upon my hands these two months. To confess the truth, my head is so full of my entertainment yesterday, that it is absolutely necesssary for my own repose to give it some vent. Without further preface I will begin my story.

I was invited to dine with the grand vizier's lady, ([92]) and it was with a great deal of pleasure I prepared myself for an entertainment which was never before given to any Christian. I thought I should very little satisfy her curiosity (which I did not doubt was a considerable motive to the invitation) by going in a dress she was used to see, and therefore dressed myself in the court habit of Vienna, which is much more magnificent than ours. However, I chose to go *incognita*, to avoid

---

([92]) This was the Sultana Hafitén, the favourite and widow of the Sultan Mustapha II., who died in 1703.

any disputes about ceremony, and went in a Turkish coach, only attended by my woman that held up my train, and the Greek lady who was my interpretress. I was met at the court-door by her black eunuch who helped me out of the coach with great respect, and conducted me through several rooms, where her she-slaves, finely dressed, were ranged on each side. In the innermost I found the lady sitting on her sofa, in a sable vest. She advanced to meet me, and presented me half-a-dozen of her friends with great civility. She seemed a very good-looking woman, near fifty years old. I was surprised to observe so little magnificence in her house, the furniture being all very moderate, and, except the habits and number of her slaves, nothing about her appeared expensive. She guessed at my thoughts, and told me she was no longer of an age to spend either her time or money in superfluities; that her whole expense was in charity, and her whole employment praying to God. There was no affectation in this speech; both she and her husband are entirely given up to devotion. He never looks upon any other woman; and, what is much more extraordinary, touches no bribes, notwithstanding the example of all his predecessors. He is so scrupulous on this point, he would not accept Mr. Wortley's present, till he had been assured over and over that it was a settled perquisite of his place at the entrance of every ambassador.

She entertained me with all kind of civility till dinner came in, which was served one dish at a

time, to a vast number, all finely dressed after
their manner, which I do not think so bad as you
have perhaps heard it represented. I am a very
good judge of their eating, having lived three
weeks in the house of an *effendi* at Belgrade, who
gave us very magnificent dinners, dressed by his
own cooks. The first week they pleased me extremely; but, I own, I then began to grow weary
of their table, and desired our own cook might add
a dish or two after our manner. But I attribute
this to custom, and am very much inclined to
believe that an Indian, who had never tasted of
either, would prefer their cookery to ours. Their
sauces are very high, all the roast very much done.
They use a great deal of very rich spice. The
soup is served for the last dish; and they have at
least as great a variety of ragouts as we have. I was
very sorry I could not eat of as many as the good
lady would have had me, who was very earnest in
serving me of every thing. The treat concluded
with coffee and perfumes, which is a high mark of
respect; two slaves kneeling *censed* my hair, clothes,
and handkerchief. (⁹³) After this ceremony, she
commanded her slaves to play and dance, which
they did with their guitars in their hands, and
she excused to me their want of skill, saying she
took no care to accomplish them in that art.

I returned her thanks, and soon after took my

(⁹³) This is a relic of a Greek custom. At the commence-
ment of an ancient entertainment the guests always had their
beards perfumed, in addition to which censers were kept burning with odoriferous gums during the whole repast.—ED.

leave. I was conducted back in the same manner
I entered, and would have gone straight to my
own house; but the Greek lady with me earnestly
solicited me to visit the *kiyáya's* lady, (⁹⁴) saying,
he was the second officer in the empire, and ought
indeed to be looked upon as the first, the grand
vizier having only the name, while he exercised
the authority. I had found so little diversion in
the vizier's *haram*, (⁹⁵) that I had no mind to go
into another. But her importunity prevailed with
me, and I am extremely glad I was so complaisant.

All things here were with quite another air than
the grand vizier's; and the very house confessed
the difference between an old devotee and a young
beauty. It was nicely clean and magnificent. I
was met at the door by two black eunuchs, who
led me through a long gallery between two ranks
of beautiful young girls, with their hair finely
plaited, almost hanging to their feet, all dressed in
fine light damasks, brocaded with silver. I was
sorry that decency did not permit me to stop to
consider them nearer. But that thought was lost
upon my entrance into a large room, or rather
pavilion, built round with gilded sashes, which
were most of them thrown up, and the trees
planted near them gave an agreeable shade, which

(⁹⁴) Kyhaïá, lieutenant. The deputy to the grand vizier.

(⁹⁵) Haram, literally, " The Forbidden," the apartment
sacredly appropriate to females, into which every man in
Turkey, but the master of the house, is interdicted from entering.

hindered the sun from being troublesome. ([96]) The jessamines and honeysuckles that twisted round their trunks shed a soft perfume, increased by a white marble fountain playing sweet water in the lower part of the room, which fell into three or four basins with a pleasing sound. The roof was painted with all sorts of flowers, falling out of gilded baskets, that seemed tumbling down. On a sofa, raised three steps, and covered with fine Persian carpets, sat the *kiyàya's* lady, leaning on cushions of white satin, embroidered; and at her feet sat two young girls about twelve years old, lovely as angels, dressed perfectly rich, and almost covered with jewels. But they were hardly seen near the fair *Fatima*, (for that is her name,) so much her beauty effaced every thing I have seen, nay, all that has been called lovely either in England or Germany. I must own that I never saw any thing so gloriously beautiful, nor can I recollect a face that would have been taken notice of near hers. She stood up to receive me, saluting me after their fashion, putting her hand to her heart with a sweetness full of majesty, that no court breeding could ever give. She ordered cushions to be given me, and took care to place me in the corner, which is the place of honour. I confess, though the Greek lady had before given me a great opinion of her beauty, I was so struck with admiration that I could not for some time speak to

---

([96]) This also is quite in the taste of antiquity, when, in Athens at least, the harem opened thus into shady gardens.— ED.

her, being wholly taken up in gazing. That surprising harmony of features! that charming result
of the whole! that exact proportion of body! that
lovely bloom of complexion, unsullied by art! the
unutterable enchantment of her smile!—But her
eyes!—large and black, with all the soft languish-
ment of the blue! every turn of her face discovering some new grace.

After my first surprise was over, I endeavoured,
by nicely examining her face, to find out some im-
perfection, without any fruit of my search, but my
being clearly convinced of the error of that vulgar
notion, that a face exactly proportioned, and perfectly beautiful, would not be agreeable; nature
having done for her, with more success, what
Apelles is said to have essayed, by a collection of
the most exact features, to form a perfect face.
Add to all this, a behaviour so full of grace and
sweetness, such easy motions, with an air so majestic, yet free from stiffness or affectation, that I
am persuaded, could she be suddenly transported
upon the most polite throne of Europe, nobody
would think her other than born and bred to be
a queen, though educated in a country we call
barbarous. To say all in a word, our most celebrated English beauties would vanish near her.

She was dressed in a *caftán* of gold brocade,
flowered with silver, very well fitted to her shape,
and showing to admiration the beauty of her
bosom, only shaded by the thin gauze of her shift.
Her drawers were pale pink, her waistcoat green
and silver, her slippers white satin, finely embroi-

M

dered : her lovely arms adorned with bracelets of
diamonds, and her broad girdle set round with
diamonds ; upon her head a rich Turkish handkerchief of pink and silver, her own fine black hair
hanging a great length in various tresses, and on
one side of her head some bodkins of jewels. ([97])
I am afraid you will accuse me of extravagance in
this description.   I think I have read somewhere
 that women always speak in rapture when they
speak of beauty, and I cannot imagine why they
should not be allowed to do so.   I rather think it
a virtue to be able to admire without any mixture
of desire or envy.   The gravest writers have spoken
with great warmth of some celebrated pictures and
statues.   The workmanship of Heaven certainly
excels all our weak imitations, and, I think, has a
much better claim to our praise.   For my part, I
am not ashamed to own I took more pleasure in
looking on the beauteous Fatima, than the finest
piece of sculpture could have given me.

She told me the two girls at her feet were her
daughters, though she appeared too young to be
their mother.   Her fair maids were ranged below
the sofa, to the number of twenty, and put me in
mind of the pictures of the ancient nymphs. I did
not think all nature could have furnished such a
scene of beauty.   She made them a sign to play
and dance.   Four of them immediately began to
play some soft airs on instruments between a lute

([97]) This description will remind the classical reader of the
dress in fashion among the Tarentine ladies, and even among
the young women of Athens, when within doors.—ED.

and a guitar, which they accompanied with their
voices, while the others danced by turns. This
dance was very different from what I had seen
before. ([98]) Nothing could be more artful, or more
proper to raise *certain ideas.* The tunes so soft!—
the motions so languishing!—accompanied with
pauses and dying eyes! half-falling back, and
then recovering themselves in so artful a manner,
that I am very positive the coldest and most rigid
prude upon earth could not have looked upon
them without thinking of *something not to be spoken
of.* I suppose you may have read that the Turks
have no music but what is shocking to the ears;
but this account is from those who never heard
any but what is played in the streets, and is just
as reasonable as if a foreigner should take his
ideas of English music from the *bladder and string,*
or the *marrowbones and cleavers.* I can assure you
that the music is extremely pathetic; it is true I
am inclined to prefer the Italian, but, perhaps, I
am partial. I am acquainted with a Greek lady
who sings better than Mrs. Robinson, and is very
well skilled in both, who gives the preference to
the Turkish. It is certain they have very fine
natural voices; these were very agreeable. When
the dance was over, four fair slaves came into the
room with silver censers in their hands, and perfumed the air with amber, aloes-wood, and other
scents. After this they served me coffee upon

([98]) This is the dance of the Almé, which I have described
at length in the first volume of " Egypt and Mohammed Ali."
—Ed.

their knees in the finest japan china, with *soucoups*
of silver, gilt. The lovely Fatima entertained me
all this while in the most polite agreeable manner,
calling me often *Guzél sultanum*, or the beautiful
sultana, and desiring my friendship with the best
grace in the world, lamenting that she could not
entertain me in my own language.

When I took my leave, two maids brought in a
fine silver basket of embroidered handkerchiefs;
she begged I would wear the richest for her sake,
and gave the others to my woman and interpretress. I retired through the same ceremonies as
before, and could not help thinking I had been
some time in Mahomet's paradise, so much was I
charmed with what I had seen. I know not how
the relation of it appears to you. I wish it may
give you part of my pleasure; for I would have
my dear sister share in all the diversions of,

Yours, &c.

XXXVIII.

TO THE ABBOT ——.

Adrianople, May 17, 1717.

I AM going to leave Adrianople, and I would not
do it without giving you some account of all that
is curious in it, which I have taken a great deal of
pains to see.

I will not trouble you with wise dissertations,
whether or no this is the same city that was

anciently called Orestesit or Oreste, which you
know better than I do. It is now called from the
Emperor Adrian, and was the first European seat
of the Turkish empire, and has been the favourite
residence of many sultans. Mahomet the Fourth,
and Mustapha, the brother of the reigning emperor, were so fond of it that they wholly abandoned
Constantinople; which humour so far exasperated
the janisaries, that it was a considerable motive to
the rebellions that deposed them: yet this man seems
to love to keep his court here. I can give you no
reason for this partiality. It is true the situation
is fine, and the country all round very beautiful;
but the air is extremely bad, and the seraglio itself
is not free from the ill effect of it. The town is
said to be eight miles in compass, I suppose they
reckon in the gardens. There are some good houses
in it, I mean large ones; for the architecture of
their palaces never makes any great show. It is
now very full of people; but they are most of
them such as follow the court, or camp; and when
they are removed, I am told it is no populous city.
The river Maritza, (anciently the Hebrus,) on
which it is situated, is dried up every summer,
which contributes very much to make it unwhole-
some. It is now a very pleasant stream: there
are two noble bridges built over it.

I had the curiosity to go to see the Exchange in
my Turkish dress, which is disguise sufficient: yet
I own I was not very easy when I saw it crowded
with janisaries; but they dare not be rude to a
woman, and made way for me with as much

respect as if I had been in my own figure. It is
half-a-mile in length, the roof arched, and kept
extremely neat. It holds three hundred and sixty-
five shops, furnished with all sorts of rich goods,
exposed to sale in the same manner as at the New
Exchange in London: ([99]) but the pavement is
kept much neater; and the shops are all so clean,
they seem just new painted. Idle people of all
sorts walk here for their diversion, or amuse themselves with drinking coffee, or sherbet, which is
cried about as oranges and sweetmeats are in
our playhouses.

I observed most of the rich tradesmen were Jews.
That people are in incredible power in this country : they have many privileges above all the
natural Turks themselves, and have formed a very
considerable commonwealth here, being judged by
their own laws. They have drawn the whole trade
of the empire into their hands, partly by the firm
union among themselves, and partly by the idle
temper and want of industry in the Turks. Every
pasha has his Jew, who is his *homme d'affaires;*
he is let into all his secrets, and does all his business. No bargain is made, no bribe received, no
merchandise disposed of, but what passes through
their hands : they are the physicians, the stewards,
and the interpreters, of all the great men.

You may judge how advantageous this is to a
people who never fail to make use of the smallest

([99]) The New Exchange, now taken down, formerly stood in
the Strand.

advantages. They have found the secret of making themselves so necessary, that they are certain of the protection of the court, whatever ministry is in power. Even the English, French, and Italian merchants, who are sensible of their artifices, are, however, forced to trust their affairs to their negociation, nothing of trade being managed without them, and the meanest among them being too important to be disobliged, since the whole body take care of his interests with as much vigour as they would those of the most considerable of their members. There are many of them vastly rich, but take care to make little public show of it; though they live in their houses in the utmost luxury and magnificence.—This copious subject has drawn me from my description of the exchange, founded by Ali Pasha, whose name it bears. Near it is the *tchartshi*, a street of a mile in length, full of shops of all kinds of fine merchandise, but excessively dear, nothing being made here. It is covered on the top with boards, to keep out the rain, that merchants may meet conveniently in all weathers. The *bessiten* near it is another exchange, built upon pillars, where all sorts of horse-furniture are sold; glittering everywhere with gold, rich embroidery, and jewels, it makes a very agreeable show.

From this place I went, in my Turkish coach, to the camp, which is to move in a few days to the frontiers. The sultan is already gone to his tents, and all his court; the appearance of them is, indeed, very magnificent. Those of the great men are rather like palaces than tents, taking up a great compass of ground, and being divided into a vast number of apartments. They are all of green, and the *pashas of three tails* have those ensigns of their power placed in a very conspicuous manner before their tents, which are adorned on the top with gilded balls, more or less, according to their different ranks. The ladies go in coaches to see the camp, as eagerly as ours did to that of Hyde Park ; but it is very easy to observe that the soldiers do not begin the campaign with any great cheerfulness. The war is a general grievance upon the people, but particularly hard upon the tradesmen, now that the grand signior is resolved to lead his army in person. Every company of them is obliged, upon this occasion, to make a present according to their ability.

I took the pains of rising at six in the morning to see the ceremony, which did not, however, begin till eight. The grand signior was at the seraglio window, to see the procession which passed through the principal streets. It was preceded by an *effendi,* mounted on a camel, richly furnished, reading aloud the Alcoran, finely bound, laid upon a cushion. He was surrounded by a parcel of boys, in white, singing some verses of it, followed by a man dressed in green boughs, representing a clean husbandman sowing seed. After him several reapers, with garlands of ears of corn, as Ceres is pictured with scythes in their hands seeming to mow. Then a little machine drawn by oxen, in which was a windmill, and boys employed in grinding corn, followed by another machine, drawn by buffaloes, carrying an oven, and two more boys, one employed in kneading bread, and another in drawing it out of the oven. These boys threw little cakes on both sides among the crowd, and were followed by the whole company of bakers, marching on foot, two by two, in their best clothes, with cakes, loaves, pasties, and pies of all sorts, on their heads, and after them two buffoons or jackpuddings, with their faces and clothes smeared with meal, who diverted the mob with their antic gestures. In the same manner followed all the companies of trade in the empire; the nobler sort, such as jewellers, mercers, &c., finely mounted, and many of the pageants that represent their trades, perfectly magnificent; among which, that of the furriers made one of the best figures, being a very large machine, set round with the skins of ermines, foxes, &c., so well stuffed that the animals seemed to be alive, and followed by music and dancers. I believe there were upon the whole twenty thousand men all ready to follow his highness, if he commanded them. The rear was closed by the volunteers, who came to beg the honour of dying in his service. This part of the show seemed to me so barbarous, that I removed from the window upon the first appearance of it. They were all naked to the middle. Some had their arms pierced through with arrows left sticking in them : others had them sticking in their heads, with the blood trickling down their faces. Some slashed their arms with sharp knives, making the blood spring out upon those that stood there; and this is looked upon as an expression of their zeal for glory. I am told that some make use of it to advance their love; and when they are near the window where their mistress stands, (all the women in town being veiled to see this spectacle,) they stick another arrow for her sake, who gives some sign of approbation and encouragement to this gallantry. The whole show lasted for near eight hours, to my great sorrow, who was heartily tired, though I was in the house of the widow of the captain pasha, (admiral,) who refreshed me with coffee, sweetmeats, sherbet, &c., with all possible civility.

I went two days after, to see the mosque of Sultan Selem I. ([100]) which is a building very well worth the curiosity of a traveller. I was dressed in my Turkish habit, and admitted without scruple; though I believe they guessed who I was, by the extreme officiousness of the doorkeeper to show me every part of it. It is situated very advantageously in the midst of the city, and in the highest part of it, making a very noble show. The first court has four gates, and the innermost three: they are both of them surrounded with cloisters, with marble pillars of the Ionic order, finely polished, and of very lively colours: the whole pavement is of white marble, and the roof of the cloisters divided into

---

([100]) The same sultan, between the years 1552 and 1566, constructed another mosque at Constantinople, which bears his name. The architecture exactly resembles this, and forms a perfect square of seventy-five feet, with a flat cupola rising from the side walls.

several cupolas or domes, headed with gilt balls on the top. In the midst of each court are fine fountains of white marble ; and before the great gate of the mosque, a portico, with green marble pillars, which has five gates, the body of the mosque being one prodigious dome.

I understand so little of architecture, I dare not pretend to speak of the proportions. It seemed to me very regular : this I am sure of, it is vastly high, and I thought it the noblest building I ever saw. It has two rows of marble galleries on pillars, with marble balusters : the pavement is also marble, covered with Persian carpets. In my opinion, it is a great addition to its beauty, that it is not divided into pews, and incumbered with forms and benches like our churches; nor the pillars (which are most of them red and white marble) disfigured by the little tawdry images and pictures, that give Roman Catholic churches the air of toyshops. The walls seemed to be inlaid with such very lively colours, in small flowers, that I could not imagine what stones had been made use of : but going nearer, I saw they were crusted with japan china, which has a very beautiful effect. In the midst hung a vast lamp of silver, gilt; besides which, I do verily believe, there were at least two thousand of a lesser size. This must look very glorious when they are all lighted ; but being at night, no women are suffered to enter. Under the large lamp is a great pulpit of carved wood, gilt; and just by, a fountain to wash, which, you know, is an essential part of their devotion. In one corner is a little

gallery, enclosed with gilded lattices, for the grand
signior. At the upper end, a large niche, very like
an altar, raised on two steps, covered with gold
brocade, and, standing before it, two silver gilt
candlesticks, the height of a man, and in them
white wax candles, as thick as a man's waist. The
outside of the mosque is adorned with towers, vastly high, gilt on the top, from whence the *imâms*
call the people to prayers. I had the curiosity to
go up one of them, which is contrived so artfully,
as to give surprise to all that see it. There is but
one door, which leads to three (¹⁰¹) different stair-
cases, going to the three different stories of the
tower, in such a manner, that the three priests may
ascend, rounding, without ever meeting each other;
a contrivance very much admired.

Behind the mosque is an exchange full of shops,
where poor artificers are lodged *gratis*. I saw several
dervises at their prayers here: they are dressed in
a plain piece of woollen, with their arms bare, and a
woollen cap on their heads, like a high-crowned hat
without brims. I went to see some other mosques,
built much after the same manner, but not comparable in point of magnificence to this I have described, which is infinitely beyond any church in
Germany or England; I will not talk of other
countries I have not seen. The seraglio does not

(¹⁰¹) There are always three little stone galleries one above
another round these *minarets*, though I never heard *three* muez-
zins proclaiming the hour of prayer at the same time, from the
same tower ; which, in fact, would be a great waste of lungs, as
one answers the purpose completely.—ED.

seem a very magnificent palace : but the gardens
are very large, plentifully supplied with water, and
full of trees; which is all I know of them, having
never been in them.

I tell you nothing of the order of Mr. Wortley's
entry, and his audience. These things are always
the same, and have been so often described, I will
not trouble you with the repetition. The young
prince, about eleven years old, sits near his father
when he gives audience: he is a handsome boy,
but probably will not immediately succeed the sultan, there being two sons of Sultan Mustapha (his
eldest brother) remaining; the eldest about twenty
years old, on whom the hopes of the people are
fixed. This reign has been bloody and avaricious.
I am apt to believe, they are very impatient to see
the end of it.

I am, sir, yours, &c. &c,

P. S. I will write to you again from Constantinople.

XXXIX.

TO THE ABBOT ——

Constantinople, May 29, 1717.

I HAVE had the advantage of very fine weather all
my journey ; and, as the summer is now in its
beauty, I enjoyed the pleasure of fine prospects; and
the meadows being full of all sorts of garden-flow-

ers, and sweet herbs, my berlin perfumed the air as
it pressed them. ([102])   The grand signior furnished
us with thirty covered waggons for our baggage,
and five coaches of the country for my women.
We found the road full of the great spahis and
their equipages coming out of Asia to the war.
They always travel with tents ; but I chose to lie
in houses all the way.

I will not trouble you with the names of the villages we passed, in which there was nothing remarkable but at Tchiorlú, where there was a *conac*,
or little seraglio, built for the use of the grand signior when he goes this road.   I had the curiosity to
view all the apartments destined for the ladies of
his court.   They were in the midst of a thick grove
of trees, made fresh by fountains; but I was most
surprised to see the walls almost covered with little
distichs of Turkish verse, written with pencils.   I
made my interpreter explain them to me, and I
found several of them very well turned; though I
easily believed him, that they had lost much of
their beauty in the translation.   One was literally
thus in English :

> " We come into this world ; we lodge, and we depart ;
>   He never goes, that's lodged within my heart."

The rest of our journey was through fine painted
meadows, by the side of the sea of Marmora, the
ancient Propontis.   We lay the next night at Seli-

([102]) Busbequius describes this part of Turkey in much the
same terms ; except that he is, perhaps, somewhat more elo-
quent. —ED.

vrea, anciently a noble town.   It is now a good
seaport, and neatly built enough, and has a bridge
of thirty-two arches.   Here is a famous Greek
church.   I had given one of my coaches to a Greek
lady, who desired the convenience of travelling
with me : she designed to pay her devotions, and
I was glad of the opportunity of going with her.
I found it an ill-built edifice, set out with the same
sort of ornaments, but less rich, as the Roman
Catholic churches, They showed me a saint's body,
where I threw a piece of money ; and a picture of
the Virgin Mary, drawn by the hand of St. Luke,
very little to the credit of his painting ; but, however, the finest Madonna of Italy is not more
famous for her miracles.   The Greeks have a monstrous taste in their pictures, which, for more finery,
are always drawn upon a gold ground.   You may
imagine what a good air this has; but they have
no notion either of shade or proportion.   They
have a bishop here, who officiated in his purple
robe, and sent me a candle almost as big as myself
for a present, when I was at my lodging.

We lay that night at a town called Bujuk Checkmedji, or Great Bridge ; and the night following, at
Kujuk Checkmedji, or Little Bridge; in a very
pleasant lodging, formerly a monastery of dervises,
having before it a large court, encompassed with
marble cloisters, with a good fountain in the middle.   The prospect from this place, and the gardens
round it, is the most agreeable I have seen ; and
shows, that monks of all religions know how to
choose their retirements.   It is now belonging to a

hogia, or schoolmaster, who teaches boys here. I asked him to show me his own apartment, and was surprised to see him point to a tall cypress tree in the garden, on the top of which was a place for a bed for himself, and a little lower, one for his wife and two children, who slept there every night. I was so much diverted with the fancy, I resolved to examine his nest nearer; but after going up fifty steps, I found I had still fifty to go up, and then I must climb from branch to branch, with some hazard of my neck. I thought it, therefore, the best way to come down again.

We arrived the next day at Constantinople; but I can tell you very little of it, all my time having been taken up with receiving visits, which are, at least, a very good entertainment to the eyes, the young women being all beauties, and their beauty highly improved by the high taste of their dress. Our palace is in Pera, which is no more a suburb of Constantinople, than Westminster is a suburb to London. All the ambassadors are lodged very near each other. One part of our house shows us the port, the city, the seraglio, and the distant hills of Asia; perhaps, all together, the most beautiful prospect in the world.

A certain French author says, Constantinople is twice as big as Paris. Mr. Wortley is unwilling to own it is bigger than London, though I confess it appears to me to be so; but I do not believe it is so populous. The burying-fields about it are certainly much larger than the whole city. It is surprising what a vast deal of land is lost this way in

Turkey. Sometimes I have seen burying-places of
several miles, belonging to very inconsiderable villages, which were formerly great towns, and retain
no other mark of their ancient grandeur than this
dismal one. On no occasion do they ever remove
a stone that serves for a monument. Some of them
are costly enough, being of very fine marble. They
set up a pillar, with a carved turban on the top of
it, to the memory of a man; and as the turbans,
by their different shapes, show the quality or profession, it is in a manner putting up the arms of
the deceased; besides, the pillar commonly bears
an inscription in gold letters. The ladies have a
simple pillar, without other ornament, except those
that die unmarried, who have a rose on the top of
their monument. The sepulchres of particular
families are railed in, and planted round with trees.
Those of the sultans, and some great men, have
lamps constantly burning in them.

When I spoke of their religion, I forgot to mention two particularities, one of which I have read of,
but it seemed so odd to me, I could not believe it;
yet it is certainly true : that when a man has divorced his wife in the most solemn manner, he can
take her again upon no other terms than permitting
another man to pass a night with her; and there
are some examples of those who have submitted to
this law, rather than not have back their beloved.
The other point of doctrine is very extraordinary ;
any woman that dies unmarried is looked upon to
die in a state of reprobation. To confirm this belief, they reason that the end of the creation of wo-

N

men is to increase and multiply; and that she is only properly employed in the works of her calling when she is bringing forth children, or taking care of them, which are all the virtues that God expects from her : and, indeed, their way of life, which shuts them out of all public commerce, does not permit them any other. Our vulgar notion, that they do not own women to have any souls, is a mistake ; it is true, they say they are not of so elevated a kind, and therefore must not hope to be admitted into the paradise appointed for the men, who are to be entertained by celestial beauties. But there is a place of happiness destined for souls of the inferior order, where all good women are to be in eternal bliss. Many of them are very superstitious, and will not remain widows ten days, for fear of dying in the reprobate state of a useless creature. But those that like their liberty, and are not slaves to their religion, content themselves with marrying when they are afraid of dying. This is a piece of theology very different from that which teaches nothing to be more acceptable to God than a vow of perpetual virginity : which divinity is most rational, I leave you to determine.

I have already made some progress in a collection of Greek medals. Here are several professed antiquaries who are ready to serve any body that desires them. But you cannot imagine how they stare in my face when I enquire about them, as if nobody was permitted to seek after medals till they were grown a piece of antiquity themselves. I have got some very valuable ones of the Macedonian kings, particularly one of Perseus, so lively, I fancy I can see all his ill qualities in his face. I have a porphyry head finely cut, of the true Greek sculpture ; but who it represents is to be guessed at by the learned when I return. For you are not to suppose these antiquaries (who are all Greeks) know anything. Their trade is only to sell ; they have correspondents at Aleppo, Grand Cairo, in Arabia, and Palestine, who send them all they can find, and very often great heaps that are only fit to melt into pans and kettles. They get the best price they can for them, without knowing those that are valuable from those that are not. Those that pretend to skill generally find out the image of some saint in the medals of the Greek cities. One of them showing me the figure of a Pallas, with a victory in her hand on a reverse, assured me it was the Virgin holding a crucifix. The same men offered me the head of a Socrates on a sardonyx ;([103]) and to enhance the value, gave him the title of St. Augustine.

I have bespoken a mummy, which I hope will come safe to my hands, notwithstanding the misfortune that befel a very fine one designed for the King of Sweden. He gave a great price for it, and the Turks took it into their heads that he must have some considerable project depending upon it. They fancied it the body of God knows who ; and that the state of their empire mystically depended

---

([103]) Did she purchase it ?—Ed.

on the conservation of it. Some old prophecies were remembered upon this occasion, and the mummy was committed prisoner to the Seven Towers, where it has remained under close confinement ever since; I dare not try my interest in so considerable a point as the release of it; but I hope mine will pass without examination.

I can tell you nothing more at present of this famous city. When I have looked a little about me, you shall hear from me again. I am, sir,

Yours, &c., &c.

XL.

TO MR. POPE.

Belgrade Village, June 17, 1717.

I HOPE before this time you have received two or three of my letters. I had yours but yesterday, though dated the 3d of February, in which you suppose me to be dead and buried. I have already let you know that I am still alive; but, to say truth, I look upon my present circumstances to be exactly the same with those of departed spirits.

The heats of Constantinople have driven me to this place, which perfectly answers the description of the Elysian fields. I am in the middle of a wood, consisting chiefly of fruit-trees, watered by a vast number of fountains, famous for the excellency of their water, and divided into many shady

walks, upon short grass, that seems to me artificial,
but, I am assured, is the pure work of nature ; and
within view of the Black Sea, from whence we
perpetually enjoy the refreshment of cool breezes,
that make us insensible of the heat of the summer.
The village is only inhabited by the richest amongst
the Christians, who meet every night at a fountain, forty paces from my house, to sing and dance.
The beauty and dress of the women exactly resemble the ideas of the ancient nymphs, as they are
given us by the representations of the poets and
painters. But what persuades me more fully of
my decease is the situation of my own mind, the
profound ignorance I am in of what passes among
the living, (which only comes to me by chance,)
and the great calmness with which I receive it.([104])
Yet I have still a hankering after my friends and
acquaintances left in the world, according to the authority of that admirable author,

> That spirits departed are wondrous kind
> To friends and relations left behind :
>   Which nobody can deny.

Of which solemn truth I am a *dead* instance. I
think Virgil is of the same opinion, that in human
souls there will still be some remains of human passions.

> —— Curæ non ipsæ in morte relinquunt.

And it is very necessary to make a perfect Elysium,

([104]) **The** original hint, perhaps, of an admirable scene in
" Vathek," where Nouronihar and her little cousin imagine
themselves dead.—Ed.

that there should be a river Lethe, which I am not so happy as to find.

To say truth, I am sometimes very weary of the singing and dancing, and sunshine, and wish for the smoke and impertinencies in which you toil, though I endeavour to persuade myself that I live in a more agreeable variety than you do; and that Monday, setting of partridges—Tuesday, reading English —Wednesday, studying in the Turkish language (in which, by the way, I am already very learned) — Thursday, classical authors — Friday, spent in writing—Saturday, at my needle—and Sunday admitting of visits, and hearing of music, is a better way of disposing of the week, than Monday at the drawing-room—Tuesday, Lady Mohun's — Wednesday, at the opera—Thursday, the play—Friday, Mrs. Chetwynd's &c.; a perpetual round of hearing the same scandal, and seeing the same follies acted over and over, which here affect me no more than they do other dead people. I can now hear of displeasing things with pity, and without indignation. The reflection on the great gulf between you and me cools all news that come hither. I can neither be sensibly touched with joy nor grief, when I consider that possibly the cause of either is removed before the letter comes to my hands. But (as I said before) this indolence does not extend to my few friendships; I am still warmly sensible of yours and Mr. Congreve's, and desire to live in your remembrance, though dead to all the world beside.

1 am, &c., &c.

XLI.

MR. POPE TO LADY MONTAGU.

MADAM,

I COULD quarrel with you quite through this paper, upon a period in yours, which bids me remember you if possibly I can. You would have shown more knowledge both of yourself and of me, had you bid me forget you if possibly I could. When I do, may this hand (as the Scripture says) forget its cunning, and this heart its—folly, I was going to say—but I mean, its reason, and the most rational sensation it ever had—that of your merit.

The poetical manner in which you paint some of the scenes about you, makes me despise my native country, and sets me on fire to fall into the dance about your fountain in Belgrade village. I fancy myself, in my romantic thoughts and distant admiration of you, not unlike the man in the Alchymist, that has a passion for the queen of the fairies: I lie dreaming of you in moonshiny nights, exactly in the posture of Endymion gaping for Cynthia in a picture; and with just such a surprise and rapture should I awake, if, after your long revolutions were accomplished, you should at last come rolling back again, smiling with all the gentleness and serenity peculiar to the moon and you, and gilding the same mountains from which you first set out on your solemn melancholy journey. I am told that fortune (more just to us than your virtue) will restore the most precious thing it ever robbed us of. Some think it will be the only equivalent the world affords for Pitt's diamond, so lately sent out of our country ; which, after you were gone, was accounted the most valuable thing here. Adieu to that toy ! let the costly bauble be hung about the neck of the baby king it belongs to, so England does but recover that jewel which was the wish of all her sensible hearts, and the joy of all her discerning eyes. I can keep no measures in speaking of this subject. I see you already coming ; I feel you as you draw nearer ; my heart leaps at your arrival. Let us have you from the East, and the sun is at her service.

I write as if I were drunk ; the pleasure I take in thinking of your return transports me beyond the bounds of common sense and decency. Yet believe me, madam, if there be any circumstance of chagrin in the occasion of that return, if there be any public or private ill fortune that may give you a displeasure, I must still be ready to feel a part of it, notwithstanding the joy I now express.

I have been mad enough to make all the inquiry I could at what time you set out, and what route you were to take. If Italy run yet in your thoughts, I hope you will see it in your return. If I but knew you intended it, I would meet you there, and travel back with you. I would fain behold the best and brightest thing I know in the scene of ancient virtue and glory : I would fain see how you look on the very spot where Curtius sacrificed himself for his country ; and observe what difference

there would be in your eyes when you ogled the
statue of Julius Cæsar, and Marcus Aurelius. Allow me but to sneak after you in your train, to fill
my pockets with coins, or to lug an old busto behind you, and I shall be proud beyond expression.
Let people think, if they will, that I did all this for
the pleasure of treading on classic ground; I would
whisper other reasons in your ear. The joy of following your footsteps would as soon carry me to
Mecca as to Rome; and let me tell you as a friend,
if you are really disposed to embrace the Mahometan religion, I will fly on pilgrimage with you
thither, with as good a heart and as sound devotion
as ever Jeffery Rudel, the Provençal poet, went
after the fine Countess of Tripoli to Jerusalem. If
you never heard of this Jeffrey, I will assure you he
deserves your acquaintance. He lived in our
Richard the First's time; put on a pilgrim's weed
took his voyage, and when he got ashore was just
upon the point of expiring. The Countess of Tripoli came to the ship, took him by the hand; he
lifted up his eyes, said he had been blessed with a
sight of her, he was satisfied, and so departed this
life. What did the Countess of Tripoli upon this?
She made him a splendid funeral; built him a
tomb of porphyry; put his epitaph upon it in Arabic verse; had his sonnets curiously copied out,
and illumined with letters of gold ; was taken with
melancholy, and turned nun. All this, madam,
you may depend upon for a truth, and I send it to
you in the very words of my author.

I do not expect all this should be punctually

copied on either side, but methinks something like
it is done already.   The letters of gold and the curious illumining of the sonnets, was not a greater
token of respect than what I have paid to your
eclogues : they lie enclosed in a monument of red
Turkey, written in my fairest hand ; the gilded
leaves are opened with no less veneration than the
pages of the Sibyls ; like them, locked up and concealed from all profane eyes ; none but my own
have beheld these sacred remains of yourself ; and
I should think it as great a wickedness to divulge
them, as to scatter abroad the ashes of my ancestors.   As for the rest, if I have not followed you to
the ends of the earth, it is not my fault : if I had,
I might possibly have died as gloriously as Jeffery
Rudel ; and if I had so died, you might probably have done every thing for me that the Countess of Tripoli did, except turning nun.

But since our romance is like to have a more fortunate conclusion, I desire you to take another
course to express your favour towards me ; I mean,
by bringing over the fair Circassian we used to
talk of.   I was serious in that request, and will
prove it by paying for her, if you will lay out my
money so well for me.   The thing shall be as secret as you please, and the lady made another half
of me, that is, both my mistress and my servant, as
I am both my own servant and my own master.
But I beg you to look oftener than you use to do
in your glass, in order to choose me one I may like.
If you have any regard to my happiness, let there
be something as near as possible to that face ; but,

if you please, the colours a little less vivid, the eyes a little less bright (such as reflection will show them ;) in short, let her be such a one as you seem in your own eyes, that is, a good deal less amiable than you are. Take care of this, if you have any regard to my quiet; for otherwise, instead of being her master, I must be only her slave.

I cannot end this letter without asking if you have received a box of books, together with letters, from Mr. Congreve and myself? It was directed to Mr. Wortley at Constantinople, by a merchant-ship that set sail last June. Mr. Congreve, in fits of the gout, remembers you. Dr. Garth makes epigrams in prose when he speaks of you. Sir Robert Rich's lady loves you, though Sir Robert admires you. Mr. Craggs commemorates you with honour ; the Duke of Buckingham with praise ; I myself with something more. When people speak most highly of you, I think them sparing ; when I try myself to speak of you, I think I am cold and stupid. I think my letters have nothing in them ; but I am sure my heart has so much, that I am vexed to find no better name for your friend and admirer, than

Your friend and admirer,

A. POPE.

XLII.

TO THE LADY RICH.

Belgrade Village, June, 17, 1717.

I HEARTILY beg your ladyship's pardon; but I really could not forbear laughing heartily at your letter, and the commissions you are pleased to honour me with.

You desire me to buy you a Greek slave, who is to be mistress of a thousand good qualities. The Greeks are subjects, and not slaves. Those who are to be bought in that manner are either such as are taken in war, or stolen by the Tartars from Russia, Circassia, or Georgia, and are such miserable, awkward, poor wretches, you would not think any of them worthy to be your housemaids. It is true that many thousands were taken in the Morea; but they have been, most of them, redeemed by the charitable contributions of the Christians, or ransomed by their own relations at Venice. The fine slaves that wait upon the great ladies, or serve the pleasures of the great men, are all bought at the age of eight or nine years old, and educated with great care, to accomplish them in singing, dancing, embroidery, &c. They are commonly Circassians, and their patron never sells them, except it is as a punishment for some very great fault. If ever they grow weary of them, they either present them to a friend, or give them their freedom. Those that are exposed to sale at the markets are always either guilty of some crime, or so entirely worthless that they are of no use at all. I am afraid you will doubt the truth of this account, which, I own, is very different from our common notions in England ; but it is no less truth for all that.

Your whole letter is full of mistakes from one end to the other. I see you have taken your ideas of Turkey from that worthy author Dumont, who has wrote with equal ignorance and confidence. ([105]) It is a particular pleasure to me here, to read the voyages to the Levant, which are generally so far removed from truth, and so full of absurdities, I am very well diverted with them. They never fail giving you an account of the women, whom it is certain they never saw, and talking very wisely of the genius of the men, into whose company they are never admitted ; and very often describe mosques, which they dare not even peep into. The Turks are very proud, and will not converse with a stranger they are not assured is considerable in his own country. I speak of the men of distinction ; for, as to the ordinary fellows, you may imagine what ideas their conversation can give of the general genius of the people.

As to the balm of Mecca, I will certainly send you some ; but it is not so easily got as you suppose it, and I cannot, in conscience, advise you to make use of it. I know not how it comes to have

---

([105]) Nevertheless, Dumont is a lively amusing writer, who had picked up many good stories illustrative of Turkish manners.—ED.

such universal applause.   All the ladies of my acquaintance at London and Vienna have begged me
to send pots of it to them.   I have had a present of
a small quantity (which I will assure you is very
valuable) of the best sort, and with great joy applied it to my face, expecting some wonderful
effect to my advantage,   The next morning the
change indeed was wonderful ; my face was swelled
to a very extraordinary size, and all over as red
as my Lady H——'s.   It remained in this lament-
able state three days, during which you may be
sure I passed my time very ill.   I believed it
would never be otherwise; and, to add to my mortification, Mr. Wortley reproached my indiscretion
without ceasing.   However, my face is since *in
statu quo ;* nay, I am told by the ladies here, that
it is much mended by the operation, which I confess I cannot perceive in my looking-glass.   Indeed,
if one were to form an opinion of this balm from
their faces, one should think very well of it.   They
all make use of it, and have the loveliest bloom in
the world.   For my part, I never intend to endure
the pain of it again ; let my complexion take its
natural course, and decay in its own due time.   I
have very little esteem for medicines of this nature ;
but do as you please, madam ; only remember before you use it, that your face will not be such as
you will care to show in the drawing-room for some
days after.

If one was to believe the women in this country,
there is a surer way of making one's self beloved than
by becoming handsome : though you know that is

our method. But they pretend to the knowledge
of secrets that, by way of enchantment, give them
the entire empire over whom they please. For me,
who am not very apt to believe in wonders, I cannot find faith for this. I disputed the point last night
with a lady, who really talks very sensibly on any
other subject : but she was downright angry with
me, in that she did not perceive she had persuaded
me of the truth of forty stories she told me of this
kind, and at last mentioned several ridiculous marriages, that there could be no other reason assigned
for. I assured her, that in England, where we were
entirely ignorant of all magic, where the climate is
not half so warm, nor the women half so handsome,
we were not without our ridiculous marriages ; and
that we did not look upon it as anything supernatural when a man played the fool for the sake of
a woman. But my arguments could not convince
her against (as she said) her certain knowledge.
To this she added, that she scrupled making use of
charms herself ; but that she could do it whenever
she pleased ; and, staring me in the face, said, (with
a very learned air,) that no enchantments would
have their effects upon me ; and that there were
some people exempt from their power, but very
few. You may imagine how I laughed at this discourse ; but all the women are of the same opinion.
They do not pretend to any commerce with the
devil ; but only that there are certain compositions adapted to inspire love. If one could send
over a shipload of them, I fancy it would be a
very quick way of raising an estate. What would

not some ladies of our acquaintance give for such merchandise.

Adieu, my dear Lady Rich ! I cannot conclude my letter with a subject that affords more delightful scenes to the imagination. I leave you to figure to yourself the extreme court that will be made to me, at my return, if my travels should furnish me with such a useful piece of learning.

I am, dear madam, yours, &c. &c.

XLIII.

TO MRS. THISTLETHWAYTE.

Pera of Constantinople, Jan. 4. 1715, 1716.

I AM infinitely obliged to you, dear Mrs. Thistlethwayte, for your entertaining letter. You are the only one of my correspondents that have judged right enough to think I would gladly be informed of the news among you. All the rest of them tell me (almost in the same words) that they suppose I know every thing. Why they are pleased to suppose in this manner, I can guess no reason, except they are persuaded, that the breed of Mahomet's pigeon still subsists in this country, and that I receive supernatural intelligence.

I wish I could return your goodness with some diverting accounts from hence. But I know not what part of the scenes here would gratify your curiosity, or whether you have any curiosity at all for things so far distant. To say the truth, I am, at

this present writing, not very much turned for the
recollection of what is diverting, my head being
wholly filled with the preparations necessary for
the increase of my family, which I expect every
day. You may easily guess at my uneasy situation. But I am, however, comforted in some degree, by the glory that accrues to me from it, and a
reflection on the contempt I should otherwise fall
under. You will not know what to make of this
speech; but, in this country, it is more despicable
to be married and not fruitful, than it is with us to
be fruitful before marriage. They have a notion,
that whenever a woman leaves off bringing forth
children, it is because she is too old for that business, whatever her face says to the contrary. This
opinion makes the ladies here so ready to make
proofs of their youth (which is as necessary, in
order to be a *received beauty*, as it is to show the
proofs of nobility, to be admitted *Knights of Malta*,)
that they do not content themselves with using the
natural means, but fly to all sorts of quackeries, to
avoid the scandal of being past child-bearing, and
often kill themselves by them. Without any ex-
aggeration, all the women of my acquaintance
have twelve or thirteen children; and the old ones
boast of having had five-and-twenty or thirty a-
piece, and are respected according to the number
they have produced. When they are with child, it
is their common expression to say, *They hope God
will be so merciful as to send them two this time;*
and when I have asked them sometimes, How they
expected to provide for such a flock as they desire?

o

they answered, That the plague will certainly kill
half of them; which, indeed, generally happens,
without much concern to the parents, who are satisfied with the vanity of having brought forth so
plentifully.

The French ambassadress is forced to comply
with this fashion as well as myself. She has not
been here much above a year, and has lain in once,
and is big again. What is most wonderful, is the
exemption they seem to enjoy from the curse en-
tailed on the sex. They see all company on
the day of their delivery, and, at the fortnight's
end, return visits, set out in their jewels and new
clothes. I wish I may find the influence of the
climate in this particular : but I fear I shall continue an Englishwoman in that affair, as well as I
do in my dread of fire and plague, which are two
things very little feared here. Most families have
had their houses burnt down once or twice, occasioned by their extraordinary way of warming themselves, which is neither by chimneys nor stoves, but
by a certain machine called a *tendour*, the height of
two feet, in the form of a table, covered with a fine
carpet or embroidery. This is made only of wood,
and they put into it a small quantity of hot ashes,
and sit with their legs under the carpet. At this
table they work, read, and very often sleep ; and, if
they chance to dream, kick down the *tendour*, and
the hot ashes commonly set the house on fire.
There were five hundred houses burnt in this manner about a fortnight ago ; and I have seen several
of the owners since, who seem not at all moved at

so common a misfortune. They put their goods into a *bark*, and see their houses burn with great philosophy, their persons being very seldom endangered, having no stairs to descend.

But, having entertained you with things I do not like, it is but just I should tell you something that pleases me. The climate is delightful in the extremest degree. I am now sitting, this present 4th of January, with the windows open, enjoying the warm shine of the sun, while you are freezing over a sad sea-coal fire; and my chamber is set out with carnations, roses, and jonquils, fresh from my garden. I am also charmed with many points of the Turkish law, to our shame be it spoken, better designed, and better executed than ours; particularly, the punishment of convicted liars (triumphant criminals in our country, God knows:) they are burnt in the forehead with a hot iron, when they are proved the authors of any notorious falsehoods. How many white foreheads should we see disfigured, how many fine gentlemen would be forced to wear their wigs as low as their eyebrows, were this law in practice with us! I should go on to tell you many other parts of justice, but I must send for my midwife. ([106])

([106]) There are no *accoucheurs* in the East, a circumstance which does credit to their taste and feelings, and sets them, in refinement, far above those nations where so odious an offence against delicacy and morals prevails. Formerly physicians were never admitted into the harem, unless when its inmates were in extreme danger; and even then could only behold them or feel their pulse through a gauze envelope. The diseases of women

XLIV.

TO THE COUNTESS OF MAR.

Pera of Constantinople, March 10, 1717.

I HAVE not written to you, dear sister, these many months; a great piece of self-denial. But I know not where to direct, or what part of the world you are in. I have received no letter from you since that short note of April last, in which you tell me that you are on the point of leaving England, and promise me a direction for the place you stay in; but I have in vain expected it till now: and now I only learn from the gazette, that you are returned; which induces me to venture this letter to your house at London. I had rather ten of my letters should be lost, than you imagine I do not write; and I think it is hard fortune if one in ten do not reach you. However, I am resolved to keep the copies, as testimonies of my inclination to give you, to the utmost of my power, all the diverting part

---

were treated by female practitioners; and it is admitted by the best informed Europeans, who generally in matters of this kind exhibit much prejudice, that the she-doctors possessed no small degree of skill and discernment. There are numerous treatises on medicine in the Turkish language, both original and translated from the European languages; but, as their religion is supposed to forbid the dissection of a corpse, anatomy and surgery necessarily remained in their infancy, until the present Sultan and Mohammed Ali introduced a more liberal style of interpreting the Koran. At present the schools of medicine at Cairo, as I have shown in my work on Egypt, are the best conducted, and by far the most flourishing in the Turkish Empire.—ED.

of my travels, while you are exempt from all the fatigues and inconveniences.

In the first place, then, I wish you joy of your niece ; for I was brought to bed of a daughter ([107]) five weeks ago. I do not mention this as one of my diverting adventures : though I must own, that it is not half so mortifying here as in England ; there being as much difference, as there is between a little cold in the head, which sometimes happens here, and the consumption cough, so common in London. Nobody keeps their house a month for lying-in ; and I am not so fond of any of our customs, as to retain them when they are not necessary. I returned my visits at three weeks' end ; and, about four days ago crossed the sea which divides this place from Constantinople, to make a new one, where I had the good fortune to pick up many curiosities.

I went to see the Sultana Hafitén, favourite of the late Emperor Mustapha, who, you know (or perhaps you do not know,) was deposed by his brother, the reigning sultan, and died a few weeks after, being poisoned, as it was generally believed. This lady was, immediately after his death, saluted with an absolute order to leave the seraglio, and choose herself a husband among the great men at the Porte. I suppose you may imagine her overjoyed at this proposal. Quite the contrary.—These women, who are called, and esteem themselves queens, look upon this liberty as the greatest dis-

---

([107]) Mary, late Countess of Bute.

grace and affront that can happen to them. She threw herself at the sultan's feet, and begged him to poniard her, rather than use his brother's widow with that contempt. She represented to him, in agonies of sorrow, that she was privileged from this misfortune, by having brought five princes into the Ottoman family; but all the boys being dead, and only one girl surviving, this excuse was not received, and she was compelled to make her choice. She chose Bekir Effendi, then secretary of state, and above fourscore years old, to convince the world that she firmly intended to keep the vow she had made, of never suffering a second husband to approach her bed; and since she must honour some subject so far as to be called his wife, she would choose him as a mark of her gratitude, since it was he that had presented her, at the age of ten years, to her last lord. But she never permitted him to pay her one visit; though it is now fifteen years she has been in his house, where she passes her time in uninterrupted mourning, with a constancy very little known in Christendom, especially in a widow of one-and-twenty, for she is now but thirty-six. She has no black eunuchs for her guard, her husband being obliged to respect her as a queen, and not to inquire at all into what is done in her apartment.

I was led into a large room with a sofa the whole length of it, adorned with white marble pillars like a *ruelle*, covered with pale blue figured velvet on a silver ground, with cushions of the same, where I was desired to repose till the sultana appeared,

who had contrived this manner of reception to avoid
rising at my entrance, though she made me an
inclination of her head when I rose up to her. ([108])
I was very glad to observe a lady that had been
distinguished by the favour of an emperor, to
whom beauties were, every day, presented from all
parts of the world. But she did not seem to me to
have ever been half so beautiful as the fair Fatima
I saw at Adrianople; though she had the remains
of a fine face, more decayed by sorrow than time.
But her dress was something so surprisingly rich,
that I cannot forbear describing it to you. She
wore a vest called *donalmá,* which differs from a
caftán by longer sleeves, and folding over at the
bottom. It was of purple cloth, straight to her
shape, and thick set on each side down to her feet,
and round the sleeves, with pearls of the best
water, of the same size as their buttons commonly
are. You must not suppose that I mean as large
as those of my Lord ———, ([109]) but about the big-

([108]) This is a very common piece of artifice in the East. The
princes of those countries do not often choose so far to honour their
guests as to rise upon their entrance; but yet will not offer them
the striking affront of remaining seated. To obviate all inconvenience they generally contrive to be found standing, as if by
mere accident; which was the case when I had the honour of
being presented to Mohammed Ali. He was talking with Boghos
Bey, and, as a mark of peculiar respect, advanced two or three
paces to meet us. Lady Mary would have made a great deal of
a circumstance of this kind.—ED.

([109]) Here we have a lacune which Lord Wharncliffe, if he
possesses the originals of her ladyship's letters, should have filled
up. He seems not to be aware that the world considers it extremely important to know what nobleman it was who dis-

ness of a pea; and to these buttons large loops of
diamonds, in the form of those gold loops so common on birthday coats. This habit was tied, at
the waist, with two large tassels of smaller pearls,
and round the arms embroidered with large diamonds. Her shift was fastened at the bottom with
a great diamond, shaped like a lozenge; her girdle
as broad as the broadest English riband, entirely
covered with diamonds. Round her neck she
wore three chains, which reached to her knees: one
of large pearl, at the bottom of which hung a fine
coloured emerald, as big as a turkey-egg; another,
consisting of two hundred emeralds, closely joined
together, of the most lively green, perfectly matched,
every one as large as a halfcrown-piece, and as thick
as three crown-pieces; and another of small emeralds, perfectly round. But her earrings eclipsed
all the rest. They were two diamonds, shaped
exactly like pears, as large as a big hazel-nut.
Round her *kalpác* she had four strings of pearl,
the whitest and most perfect in the world, at least
enough to make four necklaces, every one as large
as the Duchess of Marlborough's, and of the same
shape, fastened with two roses, consisting of a
large ruby for the middle stone, and round them
twenty drops of clean diamonds to each. Besides
this, her head-dress was covered with bodkins of
emeralds and diamonds. She wore large diamond
bracelets, and had five rings on her fingers, (except
Mr. Pitt's,) the largest I ever saw in my life. It

---

tinguished himself, in the time of his great-grandmother, by the
unusual size of his buttons.—ED.

is for jewellers to compute the value of these
things; but, according to the common estimation
of jewels in our part of the world, her whole dress
must be worth a hundred thousand pounds sterling. This I am sure of, that no European queen
has half the quantity; and the empress's jewels,
though very fine, would look very mean near hers.

She gave me a dinner of fifty dishes of meat,
which (after their fashion) were placed on the
table but one at a time, and was extremely tedious.
But the magnificence of her table answered very
well to that of her dress. The knives were of gold,
and the hafts set with diamonds. But the piece of
luxury which grieved my eyes, was the tablecloth
and napkins, which were all tiffany, embroidered
with silk and gold in the finest manner, in natural
flowers. It was with the utmost regret that I made
use of these costly napkins, which were as finely
wrought as the finest handkerchiefs that ever came
out of this country. You may be sure that they
were entirely spoiled before dinner was over. The
sherbet (which is the liquor they drink at meals)
was served in china bowls;([110]) but the covers
and salvers massy gold. After dinner, water was
brought in gold basins, and towels of the same
kind with the napkins, which I very unwillingly

([110]) The present sultan, and most of the grandees, have now
another kind of *sherbet* in their houses, known in Europe under
the unromantic name of *brandy.* Sherbet, however, is still
habitually sipped in hot weather ; and I have often joined an
old bey in hammering Turkish over a bowl of this very pleasant
beverage, reclined under a sail-awning, on the Mediterranean.—
ED.

wiped my hands upon; and coffee was served in china with gold *soucoups.*

The sultana seemed in a very good humour, and talked to me with the utmost civility, I did not omit this opportunity of learning all that I possibly could of the seraglio, which is so entirely unknown among us. She assured me, that the story of the sultan's "throwing a handkerchief" is altogether fabulous; and the manner, upon that occasion, no other than this: he sends the *kyslár agâ,* to signify to the lady the honour he intends her. She is immediately complimented upon it by the others, and led to the bath, where she is perfumed and dressed in the most magnificent and becoming manner. The emperor precedes his visit by a royal present, and then comes into her apartment: neither is there any such thing as her creeping in at the bed's foot. She said, that the first he made choice of was always afterward the first in rank, and not the mother of the eldest son, as other writers would make us believe. Sometimes the sultan diverts himself in the company of all his ladies, who stand in a circle round him. And she confessed, they were ready to die with envy and jealousy of the *happy she* that he distinguished by any appearance of preference. But this seemed to me neither better nor worse than the circles in most courts, where the glance of the monarch is watched, and every smile is waited for with impatience, and envied by those who cannot obtain it. ([111])

([111]) Her ladyship's remark is just; and, to complete it, we

She never mentioned the sultan without tears in her eyes, yet she seemed very fond of the discourse. " My past happiness," said she, " appears a dream to me. Yet I cannot forget that I was beloved by the greatest and most lovely of mankind. I was chosen from all the rest, to make all his campaigns with him ; and I would not survive him, if I was not passionately fond of the princess, my daughter. Yet all my tenderness for her was hardly enough to make me preserve my life. When I left him, I passed a whole twelvemonth without seeing the light. Time hath softened my despair ; yet I now pass some days every week in tears, devoted to the memory of my sultan."

There was no affectation in these words. It was easy to see she was in a deep melancholy, though her good humour made her willing to divert me.

She asked me to walk in her garden, and one of her slaves immediately brought her a *pelisse* of rich brocade, lined with sables. I waited on her into the garden, which had nothing in it remarkable but the fountains ; and from thence she showed me all her apartments. In her bed-chamber, her toilet was displayed, consisting of two looking-glasses, the frames covered with pearls, and her night *tal-poche* set with bodkins of jewels, and near it three vests of fine sables, every one of which is, at least,

---

may add, that, in the East, the princes make thus free and amuse themselves with their *own wives*—in Europe with the wives of others ; which makes some slight difference in favour of the East.—ED.

worth a thousand dollars (two hundred pounds English money.) I do not doubt but these rich habits were purposely placed in sight, though they seemed negligently thrown on the sofa. When I took my leave of her, I was complimented with perfumes, as at the grand vizier's, and presented with a very fine embroidered handkerchief. Her slaves were to the number of thirty, besides ten little ones, the eldest not above seven years old. These were the most beautiful girls I ever saw, all richly dressed; and I observed that the sultana took a great deal of pleasure in these lovely children, which is a vast expense; for there is not a handsome girl of that age to be bought under a hundred pounds sterling. They wore little garlands of flowers, and their own hair, braided, which was all their head-dress; but their habits were all of gold stuffs. These served her coffee, kneeling; brought water when she washed, &c. It is a great part of the work of the elder slaves to take care of these young girls, to learn them to embroider, and to serve them as carefully as if they were children of the family.

Now, do you imagine I have entertained you all this while with a relation that has, at least, received many embellishments from my hand? This, you will say, is but too like the Arabian tales: these embroidered napkins! and a jewel as large as a turkey's egg!—You forget, dear sister, those very tales were written by an author of this country, and (excepting the enchantments) are a real representation of the manners here. (^{112}) We travellers are in very hard circumstances : if we say nothing but what has been said before us, *we are dull and we have observed nothing.* If we tell any thing new, we are laughed at as *fabulous and romantic,* not allowing either for the difference of ranks, which affords difference of company, or more curiosity, or the change of customs that happen every twenty years in every country. But the truth is, people judge of travellers exactly with the same candour, good nature, and impartiality, they judge of their neighbours upon all occasions. For my part, if I live to return amongst you, I am so well acquainted with the morals of all my dear friends and acquaintances, that I am resolved to tell them nothing at all, to avoid the imputation (which their charity would certainly incline them to) of my telling too much. But I depend upon your knowing me enough to believe whatever I seriously assert for truth ; though I give you

---

(^{112}) Her ladyship is somewhat in error upon this point. The " Arabian Nights " were neither written nor collected by a Turk ; but, as Ottoman manners have a considerable resemblance to those of other Eastern nations, owing chiefly to the similarity of religion, she might, doubtless, recognise at Constantinople numerous traits of manners common to nearly all Orientals. Travellers, however, are seldom critical, and allow themselves to be struck more by resemblances than by differences. Hence the very strange approximations in matters of religion, government, and civil customs which we constantly find in works of this kind ; and hence the wonderful likeness which loose observers among the ancients found between the Egyptians and Greeks, and between the former and the Mexicans, in our own day.—ED.

leave to be surprised at an account so new to
you.

But what would you say if I told you that I have
been in a harem, where the winter apartment was
wainscoted with inlaid work of mother-of-pearl,
ivory of different colours, and olive-wood, exactly
like the little boxes you have seen brought out of
this country; ([113]) and in whose rooms, designed for
summer, the walls are all crusted with japan china,
the roofs gilt, and the floors spread with the finest
Persian carpets? Yet there is nothing more true.
Such is the palace of my lovely friend, the fair Fatima, whom I was acquainted with at Adrianople.
I went to visit her yesterday; and, if possible,
she appeared to me handsomer than before. She
met me at the door of her chamber, and, giving
me her hand with the best grace in the world,—
" You Christian ladies," said she, with a smile that
made her as beautiful as an angel, " have the
reputation of inconstancy, and I did not expect,
whatever goodness you expressed for me at Adrianople, that I should ever see you again. But I
am now convinced that I have really the happiness of pleasing you; and, if you knew how I
speak of you amongst our ladies, you would be
assured that you do me justice in making me your
friend." She placed me in the corner of the sofa,

([113]) It would have somewhat lessened her ladyship's wonder
had she been acquainted with the interior decorations of an
ancient Greek palace, in which, perhaps, the walls were still
more sumptuously adorned. See the description of a Homeric
house in the first part of my " Athens and Sparta."—ED.

and I spent the afternoon in her conversation with the greatest pleasure in the world.

The Sultana Hafitén is, what one would naturally expect to find a Turkish lady, willing to oblige, but not knowing how to go about it; and it is easy to see in her manner that she has lived excluded from the world. But Fatima has all the politeness and good breeding of a court, with an air that inspires at once respect and tenderness: and now that I understand her language, I find her wit as agreeable as her beauty. She is very curious after the manners of other countries, and has not the partiality for her own, so common in little minds. A Greek that I carried with me, who had never seen her before, (nor could have been admitted now, if she had not been in my train,) showed that surprise at her beauty and manners which is unavoidable at the first sight, and said to me in Italian, " This is no Turkish lady, she is certainly some Christian." Fatima guessed she spoke of her, and asked what she said. I would not have told her, thinking she would have been no better pleased with the compliment than one of our court beauties, to be told she had the air of a Turk: but the Greek lady told it to her; and she smiled, saying, " It is not the first time I have heard so : my mother was a Polonese, taken at the siege of Caminiec; and my father used to rally me, saying, He believed his Christian wife had found some gallant; for that I had not the air of a Turkish girl." I assured her, that, if all the Turkish ladies were like her, it was absolutely necessary to

confine them from public view, for the repose of
mankind; and proceeded to tell her what a noise
such a face as hers would make in London or
Paris. " I cannot believe you," replied she agreeably : " if beauty was so much valued in your
country, as you say, they would never have suffered you to leave it." Perhaps, dear sister, you
laugh at my vanity in repeating this compliment;
but I only do it, as I think it very well turned,
and give it you as an instance of the spirit of her
conversation. ([114])

Her house was magnificently furnished, and
very well fancied; her winter rooms being furnished with figured velvet on gold grounds, and
those for summer with fine Indian quilting, embroidered with gold. The houses of the great
Turkish ladies are kept clean with as much nicety
as those in Holland. This was situated in a high
part of the town ; and, from the window of her
summer apartment, we had the prospect of the sea,
the islands, and the Asian mountains.

My letter is insensibly grown so long, I am
ashamed of it. This is a very bad symptom. It
is well if I do not degenerate into a downright
storyteller. It may be, our proverb that "knowledge is no burthen," may be true as to one's self,
but knowing too much is very apt to make us
troublesome to other people.

I am, &c. &c.

([114]) See in Mr. Monro's " Summer Rambles in Syria," an
account of the women of Damascus ; and compare with it the
more recent information of Mr. Addison.—ED.

XLV.

TO THE LADY RICH.

Pera, March 16, 1717.

I AM extremely pleased, my dear lady, that you have at length found a commission for me that I can answer without disappointing your expectations; though I must tell you that it is not so easy as, perhaps, you think it; and that, if my curiosity had not been more diligent than any other stranger's has ever yet been, I must have answered you with an excuse, as I was forced to do when you desired me to buy you a Greek slave. I have got for you, as you desire, a Turkish love-letter, which I have put into a little box, and ordered the captain of the Smyrniote to deliver it to you with this letter. The translation of it is literally as follows : the first piece you should pull out of the purse is a little pearl, which is in Turkish called *Ingi,* and must be understood in this manner :

Ingi,	Sensin Guzelerín gingi
Pearl,	*Fairest of the young.*
Caremfil,	Caremfilsen cararen yók
	Conge gulsum timarin yók
	Benseny chok than severim
	Senin benden, haberin yók.
Clove,	*You are as slender as the clove !*
	You are an unblown rose !
	I have long loved you, and you have not known it !
Pul,	Derdime derman bul
Jonquil,	*Have pity on my passion !*

P

Kihat,   Birlerum sahat sahat
Paper,   *I faint every hour !*
Ermus,   Ver bixe bir umut
Pear,   *Give me some hope.*
Jabun,   Derdinden oldum zabun
Soap,   *I am sick with love !*
Chemur,   Ben oliyim size umur
Coal,   *May I die, and all my years be yours !*
Gul,   Ben aglarum sen gul
A rose,   *May you be pleased, and your sorrows mine !*
Hasir,   Oliim sana yazir
A straw,   *Suffer me to be your slave.*
Jo ho,   Ustune bulunmaz pahu
Cloth,   *Your price is not to be found.*
Tartsin,   Sen ghel ben chekeim senin hartsin
Cinnamon,   *But my fortune is yours.*
Giro,   Esking-ilen oldum ghira
A match,   *I burn, I burn ! my flame consumes me !*
Sirma,   Uzunu benden a yirma
Gold thread, *Don't turn away your face from me.*
Satch,   Bazmazum tatch
Hair,   *Crown of my head !*
Uzum,   Benim iki Guzum
Grape,   *My two eyes !*
Til,   Ulugorum tez ghel
Gold wire,   *I die—come quickly.*

And, by way of postscript :—

Beber,   Bize bir dogm haber
Pepper,   *Send me an answer.*

You see this letter is all in verse, and I can
assure you there is as much fancy shown in the
choice of them, as in the most studied expressions
of our letters : there being, I believe, a million of
verses designed for this use. There is no colour,
no flower, no weed, no fruit, herb, pebble, or fea-
ther that has not a verse belonging to it; and you
may quarrel, reproach, or send letters of passion,

friendship, or civility, or even of news without ever inking your fingers.

I fancy you are now wondering at my profound learning; but, alas! dear madam, I am almost fallen into the misfortune so common to the ambitous : while they are employed on distant insignificant conquests abroad, a rebellion starts up at home ;—I am in great danger of losing my English. I find it is not half so easy to me to write in it as it was a twelvemonth ago. I am forced to study for expressions, and must leave off all other languages, and try to learn my mother-tongue. Human understanding is as much limited as human power or human strength. The memory can retain but a certain number of images; and it is as impossible for one human creature to be perfect master of ten different languages, as to have in perfect subjection ten different kingdoms, or to fight against ten men at a time: I am afraid I shall at last know none as I should do. I live in a place that very well represents the tower of Babel: in Pera they speak Turkish, Greek, Hebrew, Armenian, Arabic, Persian, Russian, Sclavonian, Walachian, German, Dutch, French, English, Italian, Hungarian ; and, what is worse, there are ten of these languages spoken in my own family. My grooms are Arabs; my footmen French, English, and Germans; my nurse, an Armenian ; my housemaids, Russians: half-a-dozen other servants, Greeks: my steward, an Italian ; my janisaries, Turks. So that I live in the perpetual hearing of this medley of sounds, which produces a very ex-

able to me ; and, if it was not, I would be content
to endure some inconveniency to gratify a passion
that is become so powerful with me as curiosity.
And, indeed, the pleasure of going in a barge to
Chelsea is not comparable to that of rowing upon
the canal of the sea here, where, for twenty miles
together, down the Bosphorus, the most beautiful
variety of prospects present themselves. The Asian
side is covered with fruit-trees, villages, and the
most delightful landscapes in nature ; on the European, stands Constantinople, situated on seven
hills. The unequal heights make it seem as large
again as it is (though one of the largest cities in
the world,) showing an agreeable mixture of gardens, pine and cypress trees, palaces, mosques, and
public buildings, raised one above another, with as
much beauty and appearance of symmetry as your
ladyship ever saw in a cabinet, adorned by the
most skilful hands, where jars show themselves
above jars, mixed with canisters, babies, and candlesticks. This is a very odd comparison ; but it
gives me an exact idea of the thing.

I have taken care to see as much of the seraglio
as is to be seen. ([115]) It is on a point of land run-

([115]) It is evident that Lady Montagu did not mean to assert
that she had seen the interior of the seraglio at Constantinople.
She had certainly seen that at Adrianople, in which circumstance
the error has originated.

In Lord Wharncliffe's edition, this note by Mr. Dallaway is omitted, and in the "Introductory Anecdotes" a long
explanation is entered into, to show that Lady Mary never
visited the sultan's seraglio, either at Constantinople or Adrianople. It is well known why this point is so laboriously dis-

ning into the sea; a palace of prodigious extent,
but very irregular. The gardens take in a large
compass of ground, full of high cypress-trees, which
is all I know of them. The buildings are all of
white stone, leaded on the top, with gilded turrets
and spires, which look very magnificent; and, indeed, I believe there is no Christian king's palace
half so large. There are six large courts in it, all
built round, and set with trees, having galleries of
stone; one of these for the guard, another for the
slaves, another for the officers of the kitchen, another
for the stables, the fifth for the divan, and the sixth
for the apartment destined for audiences.   On the
ladies' side there are at least as many more, with
distinct courts belonging to their eunuchs and attendants, their kitchens, &c.

---

cussed. Her ladyship's reputation and moral character are
concerned in having it cleared up; and the evidence, as far as
it goes, certainly favours the supposition that she had not been
admitted into the interior.   But the writer of the "Anecdotes"
is mistaken in supposing that of the royal harém "she has given
no information of *any* kind, excepting what she obtained from
the Sultana Hafiten."   At least, she pretends to have *seen*
something of it: "I have taken care *to see* as much of the
seraglio as is to be seen." But how much was that? Doubtless
the outside, which every traveller, male or female, who visited
Constantinople, might see as well as Lady Montagu.   In this
letter to the Countess of Bristol she is purposely confused and
indistinct; and it is clear from its whole tenour that she meant
to mystify her correspondent, and create the *impression* that she
had been in the seraglio, but without saying it.   She disclaims,
indeed, having seen the gardens, but not the palace, and by proceeding to describe St. Sophia, which she did visit, seems willing
to class the two buildings under the same predicament in the
reader's imagination.—ED.

two candlesticks as high as a man, with wax candles as thick as three flambeaux. The pavement is spread with fine carpets, and the mosque illuminated with a vast number of lamps. The court leading to it is very spacious, with galleries of marble, of green columns, covered with twenty-eight leaded cupolas on two sides, and a fine fountain of basins in the midst of it.

This description may serve for all the mosques in Constantinople. The model is exactly the same, and they only differ in largeness and richness of materials. That of the Validé-Sultan is the largest of all, built entirely of marble, the most prodigious, and I think, the most beautiful structure I ever saw, be it spoken to the honour of our sex, for it was founded by the mother of Mahomet IV. Between friends, St. Paul's church would make a pitiful figure near it, as any of our squares would do near the *atlerdan*, ([117]) or place of horses (*at* signifying a horse in Turkish.) This was the *hippodrome* in the reign of the Greek emperors. In the midst of it is a brazen column, of three serpents twisted together, with their mouths gaping. It is impossible to learn why so odd a pillar was erected; the Greeks can tell nothing but fabulous legends when they are asked the meaning of it, and there is no sign of its having ever had any inscription. At the upper end is an obelisk of porphyry, probably brought from Egypt, the hieroglyphics all very entire, which I look upon as mere ancient puns. It

---

([117]) More commonly called " Atméydan."

is placed on four little brazen pillars, upon a pedestal of square freestone, full of figures in bas-relief
on two sides; one square representing a battle, another an assembly. The others have inscriptions
in Greek and Latin ; the last I took in my pocket-
book, and it is as follows :—

DIFFICILIS QUONDAM, DOMINIS PARERE SERENIS
JUSSUS, ET EXTINCTIS PALMAM PORTARE TYRANNIS
OMNIA THEODOSIO CEDUNT, SOBOLIQUE PERENNI.([118])

Your lord will interpret these lines. Do not fancy
they are a love-letter to him.

All the figures have their heads on ; and I cannot forbear reflecting again on the impudence of
authors, who all say they have not ; but I dare
swear the greatest part of them never saw them ;
but took the report from the Greeks, who resist,
with incredible fortitude, the conviction of their
own eyes, whenever they have invented lies to the
dishonour of their enemies. Were you to believe them, there is nothing worth seeing in Constantinople but Sancta Sophia, though there are
several larger and, in my opinion, more beautiful
mosques in that city. That of Sultan Achmet has

([118]) Two more lines were probably concealed at that time.
This inscription concludes,

" TERDENIS SIC VICTUS EGO DOMITUSQUE DIEBUS
JUDICE SUB PROCLO SUPERAS ELATUS AD AURAS,"

which is a translation from another in Greek, on the opposite
square of the base.

permission to marry, but are confined to an odd habit, which is only a piece of coarse white cloth
wrapped about them, with their legs and arms naked. Their order has few other rules except that
of performing their fantastic rites every Tuesday
and Friday, which is done in this manner : they
meet together in a large hall, where they all
stand with their eyes fixed on the ground, and
their arms across, while the *imaum*, or preacher,
reads part of the Alcoran from a pulpit placed in
the midst; and when he has done, eight or ten of
them make a melancholy concert with their pipes,
which are no unmusical instruments. Then he
reads again, and makes a short exposition on what
he has read ; after which they sing and play till
their superior (the only one of them dressed in
green clothes) rises and begins a sort of solemn dance.
They all stand about him in a regular figure ; and
while some play, the others tie their robe (which is
very wide) fast round their waist, and begin to turn
round with an amazing swiftness, and yet with great
regard to the music, moving slower or faster, as the
tune is played. This lasts above an hour, without
any of them showing the least appearance of gid-
diness, which is not to be wondered at, when it is
considered they are all used to it from their infancy; most of them being devoted to this way of life
from their birth. There turned amongst them some
little dervises, of six or seven years old, who seemed
no more disordered by that exercise than the others.
At the end of the ceremony they shout out, " There
is no other god but God, and Mahomet is his pro-

phet;" after which they kiss the superior's hand
and retire. The whole is performed with the most
solemn gravity. Nothing can be more austere than
the form of these people; they never raise their
eyes, and seem devoted to contemplation. And as
ridiculous as this is in description, there is something
touching in the air of submission and mortification
they assume.

This letter is of a horrible length; but you may
burn it when you have read enough, &c., &c.

XLVII.

TO THE COUNTESS OF BRISTOL.

I AM now preparing to leave Constantinople, and,
perhaps, you will accuse me of hypocrisy when I
tell you it is with regret; but as I am used to
the air, and have learnt the language, I am
easy here; and as much as I love travelling, I
tremble at the inconveniences attending so great
a journey with a numerous family, and a little infant hanging at the breast. However, I endeavour
upon this occasion to do as I have hitherto done in
all the odd turns of my life; turn them, if I can, to
my diversion. In order to this, I ramble every
day, wrapped up in my *ferigée* and *asmáck*, about
Constantinople, and amuse myself with seeing all
that is curious in it.

I know you will expect that this declaration
should be followed with some account of what I

selves round the rooms on the marble sofas : but
the virgins very hastily threw off their clothes, and
appeared without other ornament or covering than
their own long hair braided with pearl or ribbon.
Two of them met the bride at the door, conducted
by her mother and another grave relation.   She was
a beautiful maid of about seventeen, very richly
dressed, and shining with jewels, but was presently
reduced to the state of nature. Two others filled silver gilt pots with perfume, and began the procession, the rest following in pairs, to the number of
thirty.   The leaders sung an epithalamium, answered by the others in chorus, and the two last
led the fair bride, her eyes fixed on the ground,
with a charming affectation of modesty.([123]) In this
order they marched round the three largest rooms
of the bagnio. It is not easy to represent to you
the beauty of this sight, most of them being well
proportioned and white skinned ; all of them perfectly smooth and polished by the frequent use of
bathing. After having made their tour, the bride
was again led to every matron round the rooms,
who saluted her with a compliment and a present,
some of jewels, others of pieces of stuff, handkerchiefs, or little gallantries of that nature, which
she thanked them for, by kissing their hands.

I was very well pleased with having seen this
ceremony ; and, you may believe me, the Turkish

([123]) From this and many other expressions it is clear that
her ladyship did not believe in the existence of real modesty,
which was a thing beyond her experience.—ED.

ladies have at least as much wit and civility, nay,
liberty, as among us. It is true the same customs,
that give them so many opportunities of gratifying
their evil inclinations, (if they have any,) also put
it very fully in the power of their husbands to revenge themselves if they are discovered : and I do
not doubt but they suffer sometimes for their indis-
cretions in a very severe manner. About two
months ago, there was found at daybreak, not very
far from my house, the bleeding body of a young
woman, naked, only wrapped in a coarse sheet,
with two wounds of a knife, one in her side and
another in her breast. She was not quite cold, and
was so surprisingly beautiful, that there were very
few men in Pera that did not go to look upon her ;
but it was not possible for any body to know her,
no woman's face being known. She was supposed
to have been brought in the dead of the night from
the Constantinople side, and laid there. Very little inquiry was made about the murderer, and the
corpse was privately buried without noise. Murder
is never pursued by the king's officers as with us.
It is the business of the next relations to revenge
the dead person ; ([124]) and if they like better to compound the matter for money (as they generally
do) there is no more said of it. One would imagine this defect in their government should make
such tragedies very frequent, yet they are extremely

([124]) Here her ladyship might have discovered a genuine relic
of antiquity ; for this was both the law and the practice among
all nations of Hellenic origin.—ED.

much cheaper than in Christendom, those wretches
not being punished (even when they are publicly
detected) with the rigour they ought to be.

Now I am speaking of their law, I do not know
whether I have ever mentioned to you one custom
peculiar to their country, I mean *adoption*, very
common amongst the Turks, and yet more amongst
the Greeks and Armenians. Not having it in their
power to give their estates to a friend or distant relation, to avoid its falling into the grand signior's
treasury, when they are not likely to have any children of their own, they choose some pretty child
of either sex among the meanest people, and carry
the child and its parents before the cadi, and there
declare they receive it for their heir. The parents
at the same time renounce all future claim to it; a
writing is drawn and witnessed, and a child thus
adopted cannot be disinherited. Yet I have seen
some common beggars that have refused to part
with their children in this manner to some of the
richest amongst the Greeks, (so powerful is the in-
stinctive affection that is natural to parents,) though
the adopting fathers are generally very tender to
these *children of their souls,* as they call them. I
own this custom pleases me much better than our
absurd one of following our name. Methinks it is
much more reasonable to make happy and rich an
infant whom I educate after my own manner,
brought up (in the Turkish phrase) *upon my knees,*
and who has learned to look upon me with a filial
respect, than to give an estate to a creature without
other merit or relation to me than that of a few let-

ters. Yet this is an absurdity we see frequently practised.

Now I have mentioned the Armenians, perhaps it will be agreeable to tell you something of that nation, with which I am sure you are utterly un-acquainted. I will not trouble you with the geo-graphical account of the situation of their country, which you may see in the maps, or a relation of their ancient greatness, which you may read in the Roman history. They are now subject to the Turks; and being very industrious in trade, and increasing and multiplying, are dispersed in great numbers through all the Turkish dominions. They were, as they say, converted to the Christian religion, by St. Gregory, and are, perhaps, the devoutest Christians in the whole world. The chief precepts of their priests enjoin the strict keeping of their lents, which are at least seven months in every year, and are not to be dis-pensed with on the most emergent necessity; no occasion whatever can excuse them, if they touch anything more than mere herbs or roots, (without oil,) and plain dry bread; that is their constant diet. Mr. Wortley has one of his interpreters of this nation; and the poor fellow was brought so low by the severity of his fasts, that his life was de-spaired of. Yet neither his master's commands, nor the doctor's entreaties (who declared nothing else could save his life) were powerful enough to pre-vail with him to take two or three spoonfuls of broth. Excepting this, which may rather be called a custom than an article of faith, I see very little

court. I can only tell you, that if you please to
read Sir Paul Rycaut, you will there find a full
and true account of the viziers, the *beglerbeys*, the
civil and spiritual government, the officers of the
seraglio, &c.; things that it is very easy to procure
lists of, and therefore may be depended on; though
other stories, God knows——I say no more——
every body is at liberty to write their own remarks;
the manners of people may change, or some of
them escape the observation of travellers, but it is
not the same of the government; and, for that reason, since I can tell you nothing new, I will tell
you nothing of it.

In the same silence shall be passed over the ar-
senal and seven towers; and for mosques, I have
already described one of the noblest to you very
particularly. But I cannot forbear taking notice
to you of a mistake of Gemelli; (though I honour
him in a much higher degree than any other
voyage writer;) he says that there are no remains of
Calcedon; this is certainly a mistake: I was there
yesterday, and went across the canal in my galley,
the sea being very narrow between that city and
Constantinople. It is still a large town, and has
several mosques in it. The Christians still call it
Calcedonia, and the Turks give it a name I forget,
but which is only a corruption of the same word.[125]
I suppose this is an error of his guide, which his
short stay hindered him from rectifying; for I have,

---

[125] Cádykúy, or the Town of Judges, from the great Christian council held there.

in other matters, a very just esteem for his veracity. Nothing can be pleasanter than the canal;
and the Turks are so well acquainted with its beauties, that all their pleasure-seats are built on its
banks, where they have, at the same time, the most
beautiful prospects in Europe and Asia; there are
near one another some hundreds of magnificent palaces.

Human grandeur being here yet more unstable
than anywhere else, it is common for the heirs of
a great three-tailed pasha not to be rich enough to
keep in repair the house he built; thus, in a few
years, they all fall to ruin. I was yesterday to
see that of the late grand vizier, who was killed at
Peterwaradin. It was built to receive his royal
bride, daughter of the present sultan, but he did
not live to see her there. I have a great mind to
describe it to you; but I check that inclination,
knowing very well that I cannot give you, with my
best description, such an idea of it as I ought. It
is situated on one of the most delightful parts of the
canal, with a find wood on the side of a hill behind
it. The extent of it is prodigious; the guardian
assured me there are eight hundred rooms in it; I will
not, however, answer for that number, since I did
not count them: but it is certain the number is
very large, and the whole adorned with a profusion
of marble, gilding, and the most exquisite painting of fruit and flowers. The windows are all
sashed with the finest crystalline glass brought from
England; and here is all the expensive magnificence that you can suppose in a palace founded by

rather be a rich *effendi*, with all his ignorance, than Sir Isaac Newton, with all his knowledge. ([125])

I am, sir, &c. &c.

XLIX.

TO THE ABBOT ——.

Tunis, July 31, 1718.

I LEFT Constantinople the sixth of the last month, and this is the first post from whence I could send a letter, though I have often wished for the opportunity, that I might impart some of the pleasure I found in this voyage through the most agreeable part of the world, where every scene presents me some poetical idea.

> Warmed with poetic transport I survey
> Th' immortal islands, and the well-known sea.
> For here so oft the muse her harp has strung,
> That not a mountain rears its head unsung.

I beg your pardon for this sally, and will, if I can, continue the rest of my account in plain prose.

([126]) Let who will doubt the sincerity of this declaration, I certainly do not. Lady Mary, by the help of her Turkish tutors, had now discovered what is most valuable in life, which she found to be—not knowledge, with reserved and modest manners, but riches, ignorance, and an immoderate appetite for sensual indulgence. This, the classical reader will remember is the creed of Callicles in Plato's Gorgias ; and in the same dialogue will be found the opinion of a profound judge of human nature on the subject. It is different from that of Lady Montagu.— ED.

The second day after we set sail we passed Galli-
polis, a fair city, situated in the bay of Chersonesus,
and much respected by the Turks, being the first
town they took in Europe.   At five the next morning we anchored in the Hellespont, between the
castles of Sestos and Abydos, now called the Dar-
danelli. These are now two little ancient castles, but
of no strength, being commanded by a rising
ground behind them, which I confess I should
never have taken notice of, if I had not heard it observed by our captain and officers, my imagination
being wholly employed by the tragic story that you
are well acquainted with :

> The swimming lover, and the nightly bride,
> How Hero loved, and how Leander died.

Verse again !—I am certainly infected by the poetical air I have passed through.   That of Abydos is
undoubtedly very amorous, since that soft passion
betrayed the castle into the hands of the Turks who
besieged it in the reign of Orchanes.   The governor's daughter imagining to have seen her future
husband in a dream, (though I do not find she had
either slept upon bridecake, or kept St. Agnes's
fast,) fancied she saw the dear figure in the form of
one of her besiegers ; and, being willing to obey
her destiny, tossed a note to him over the wall,
with the offer of her person and the delivery of the
castle. He showed it to his general, who consented
to try the sincerity of her intentions, and withdrew
his army, ordering the young man to return with a
select body of men at midnight.   She admitted

on their heads a large piece of muslin, which falls in large folds on their shoulders. One of my countrymen, Mr. Sandys,([128]) (whose book I doubt not you have read, as one of the best of its kind,) speaking of these ruins, supposes them to have been the foundation of a city begun by Constantine, before his building Byzantium; but I see no good reason for that imagination, and am apt to believe them much more ancient.

We saw very plainly from this promontory the river Simois rolling from mount Ida, and running through a very spacious valley. It is now a considerable river, and is called Simores; it is joined in the vale by the Scamander, which appeared a small stream half choked with mud, but is perhaps large in the winter. This was Xanthus among the gods, as Homer tells us; and it is by that heavenly name the nymph Oenone invokes it in her epistle to Paris. The Trojan virgins([129]) used to offer their first favours to it, by the name of Scamander, till the adventure which Monsieur de la Fontaine has told so agreeably abolished that heathenish ceremony. When the stream is mingled with the Simois, they run together to the sea.

All that is now left of Troy is the ground on which it stood; for, I am firmly persuaded, whatever pieces of antiquity may be found round it are

---

([128]) George Sandys, one of the most valuable travellers into the Levant, whose work had reached four editions in the reign of Charles the First.

([129]) For this curious story Monsieur Bayle may be consulted in his Dictionary, article "Scamander."

much more modern, and I think Strabo says the same thing. However, there is some pleasure in seeing the valley where I imagined the famous duel of Menelaus and Paris had been fought, and where the greatest city in the world was situated. It is certainly the noblest situation that can be found for the head of a great empire, much to be preferred to that of Constantinople, the harbour here being always convenient for ships from all parts of the world, and that of Constantinople inaccessible almost six months in the year, while the north wind reigns.

North of the promontory of Sigæum we saw that of Rhæteum, famed for the sepulchre of Ajax. While I viewed these celebrated fields and rivers, I admired the exact geography of Homer, whom I had in my hand. Almost every epithet he gives to a mountain or plain is still just for it; and I spent several hours here in as agreeable cogitations as ever Don Quixote had on mount Montesinos. We sailed next night to the shore, where it is vulgarly reported Troy stood; and I took the pains of rising at two in the morning, to view coolly those ruins which are commonly shown to strangers, and which the Turks call *Eski Stamboul*, ([130]) i. e. Old Constantinople. For that reason, as well as some others, I conjecture them to be the remains of that city begun by Constantine. I hired an ass, (the only voiture to be had there,) that I might go some

---

([130]) Alexander Troas, which the early travellers have erroneously considered as the true site of ancient Troy.

miles into the country, and take a tour round the
ancient walls, which are of a vast extent. We found
the remains of a castle on a hill, and of another in
a valley, several broken pillars, and two pedestals,
from which I took these Latin inscriptions.

1.

DIVI. AUG. COL.
ET COL. IUL. PHILIPPENSIS
EORUNDEM PRINCIPUM
COL. IUL. PARIANAE. TRIBUN.
MILIT. COH. XXXII. VOLUNTAR.
TRIB. MILIT. LEG. XIII. GEM.
PRAEFECTO EQUIT. ALAE. I.
SCUBULORUM
VIC. VIII.

2.

DIVI. IULI. FLAMINI
C. ANTONIO. M. F.
VOLT. RUFO. FLAMIN.
DIV. AUG. COL. CL. APRENS.
ET. COL. IUL. PHILIPPENSIS
EORUNDEM ET PRINCIP. ITEM
CQL. IUL. PARIANAE TRIB.
MILIT. COH. XXXII. VOLUNTARIOR.
TRIB. MILIT. XIII.
GEM. PRAEF. EQUIT. ALAE. I.
SCUBULORUM
VIC. VII.

I do not doubt but the remains of a temple near
this place are the ruins of one dedicated to Augus-
tus; and I know not why Mr. Sandys calls it a
Christian temple, since the Romans certainly built
hereabouts. Here are many tombs of fine marble,

and vast pieces of granite, which are daily lessened
by the prodigious balls that the Turks make from
them for their cannon. We passed that evening
the isle of Tenedos, once under the patronage of
Apollo, as he gave it in himself in the particulars
of his estate when he courted Daphne. It is but
ten miles in circuit, but in those days very rich and
well peopled, still famous for its excellent wine. I
say nothing of Tennes, from whom it was called;
but naming Mitylene, where we passed next, I cannot forbear mentioning Lesbos, where Sappho sung,
and Pittacus reigned, famous for the birth of
Alcæus, Theophrastus, and Arion, those masters in
poetry, philosophy, and music. This was one of
the last islands that remained in the Christian dominion after the conquest of Constantinople by the
Turks. But need I talk to you of Cantacuseni, &c.
princes that you are as well acquainted with as I
am ? It was with regret I saw us sail from this
island into the Ægæan sea, now the Archipelago,
leaving Scio (the ancient Chios) on the left, which
is the richest and most populous of these islands,
fruitful in cotton, corn, and silk, planted with groves
of orange and lemon trees, and the Arvisian mountain, still celebrated for the nectar that Virgil men-
tions. Here is the best manufacture of silks in all
Turkey. The town is well built, the women famous
for their beauty, and show their faces as in Christendom. There are many rich families, though
they confine their magnificence to the inside of
their houses, to avoid the jealousy of the Turks,
who have a pasha here : however, they enjoy a rea-

sonable liberty, and indulge the genius of their
country;

> And eat, and sing, and dance away their time,
> Fresh as their groves, and happy as their clime.

Their chains hang lightly on them, though it is not
long since they were imposed, not being under the
Turk till 1566. But, perhaps, it is as easy to obey
the grand signior as the state of Genoa, to whom
they were sold by the Greek emperor. But I forget myself in these historical touches, which are
very impertinent when I write to you. Passing
the strait between the islands of Andros and Achaia,
now Libadia, we saw the promontory of Sunium,
now called cape Colonna, where are yet standing the
vast pillars of a temple of Minerva. This venerable
sight made me think, with double regret, on a beautiful temple of Theseus, which I am assured was
almost entire at Athens till the last campaign in
the Morea, that the Turks filled it with powder, and
it was accidently blown up. You may believe I
had a great mind to land on the famed Peloponne-
sus, though it were only to look on the rivers of
Æsopus, Peneus, Inachus, and Eurotas, the fields
of Arcadia, and other scenes of ancient mythology.
But instead of demigods and heroes, I was credibly
informed it is now overrun by robbers, and that I
should run a great risk of falling into their hands
by undertaking such a journey through a desert
country, for which, however, I have so much respect,
that I have much ado to hinder myself from trou-
bling you with its whole history, from the founda-

tion of Mycenæ and Corinth, to the last campaign
there; but I check the inclination, as I did that of
landing. We sailed quietly by Cape Angelo, once
Malea, where I saw no remains of the famous temple of Apollo. We came that evening in sight of
Candia: it is very mountainous; we easily distinguished that of Ida.—We have Virgil's authority
that here were a hundred cities—

—— Centum urbes habitant magnas ——

The chief of them—the scene of monstrous passions.
——Metellus first conquered this birthplace of
his Jupiter; it fell afterwards into the hands of——
I am running on to the very siege of Candia; and
I am so angry with myself, that I will pass by all
the other islands with this general reflection, that it
is impossible to imagine anything more agreeable
than this journey would have been two or three
thousand years since, when, after drinking a dish
of tea with Sappho, I might have gone the same
evening to visit the temple of Homer in Chios, and
passed this voyage in taking plans of magnificent
temples, delineating the miracles of statuaries, and
conversing with the most polite and most gay of
mankind.   Alas! art is extinct here; the wonders
of nature alone remain; and it was with vast pleasure I observed those of mount Ætna, whose flame
appears very bright in the night many leagues off
at sea, and fills the head with a thousand conjec-
tures.   However, I honour philosophy too much,
to imagine it could turn that of Empedocles; and
Lucian shall never make me believe such a scandal
of a man, whom Lucretius says,

———— Vix humana videtur stirpe creatus ————

We passed Trinacria without hearing any of the
sirens that Homer describes ; and, being thrown on
neither Scylla nor Charybdis, came safe to Malta,
first called Melita from the abundance of honey. It
is a whole rock covered with very little earth. The
grand master lives here in the state of a sovereign
prince; but his strength at sea now is very small.
The fortifications are reckoned the best in the world,
all cut in the solid rock with infinite expense and
labour.————Off this island we were tossed by a
severe storm, and were very glad, after eight days,
to be able to put into Porto Farine on the African
shore, where our ship now rides. At Tunis we were
met by the English consul who resides there. I
readily accepted of the offer of his house for some
days, being very curious to see this part of the
world, and particularly the ruins of Carthage. I
set out in his chaise at nine at night, the moon being
at full. I saw the prospect of the conntry almost
as well as I could have done by daylight; and the
heat of the sun is now so intolerable, it is impossible
to travel at any other time. The soil is for the
most part sandy, but everywhere fruitful of date,
olive, and fig-trees, which grow without art, yet afford the most delicious fruit in the world. Their
vineyards and melon-fields are enclosed by hedges
of that plant we call Indian-fig, which is an admirable fence, no wild beast being able to pass it. It
grows a great height, very thick, and the spikes or
thorns are as long and sharp as bodkins ; it bears a

fruit much eaten by the peasants, and which has no ill taste.

It being now the season of the Turkish *ramazan*, or Lent, and all here professing, at least, the Mahometan religion, they fast till the going down of the sun, and spend the night in feasting. We saw under the trees companies of the country people, eating, singing, and dancing to their wild music. They are not quite black, but all mulattoes, and the most frightful creatures that can appear in a human figure. They are almost naked, only wearing a piece of coarse serge wrapped about them. But the women have their arms, to their very shoulders, and their necks and faces, adorned with flowers, stars, and various sorts of figures impressed by gunpowder: a considerable addition to their natural deformity; which is, however, esteemed very ornamental among them; and I believe they suffer a good deal of pain by it.

About six miles from Tunis we saw the remains of that noble aqueduct, which carried the water to Carthage over several high mountains, the length of forty miles. There are still many arches entire. We spent two hours viewing it with great attention, and Mr. Wortley assured me that of Rome is very much inferior to it. The stones are of a prodigious size, and yet all polished, and so exactly fitted to each other, very little cement has been made use of to join them. Yet they may probably stand a thousand years longer, if art is not made use of to pull them down. Soon after daybreak I arrived at Tunis, a town fairly built of very white stone, but

quite without gardens, which, they say, were all destroyed when the Turks first took it, none having been planted since. The dry sand gives a very disagreeable prospect to the eye; and the want of shade contributing to the natural heat of the climate, renders it so excessive, that I have much ado to support it. It is true here is every noon the refreshment of the sea-breeze, without which it would be impossible to live; but no fresh water but what is preserved in the cisterns of the rains that fall in the month of September. The women of the town go veiled from head to foot under a black crape; and, being mixed with a breed of renegadoes, are said to be many of them fair and handsome. This city was beseiged in 1270, by Louis king of France, who died under the walls of it of a pestilential fever. After his death, Philip, his son, and our Prince Edward, son of Henry III. raised the siege on honourable terms. It remained under its natural African kings, till betrayed into the hands of Barbarossa, admiral of Solyman the Magnificent. The Emperor Charles V. expelled Barbarossa, but it was recovered by the Turk, under the conduct of Sinan Pasha, in the reign of Selim II. From that time till now it has remained tributary to the grand signior, governed by a *bey*, who suffers the name of subject to the Turk, but has renounced the subjection, being absolute, and very seldom paying any tribute. The great city of Bagdad is at this time in the same circumstances; and the grand signior connives at the loss of these domions, for fear of losing even the titles of them.

I went very early yesterday morning (after one
night's repose) to see the ruins of Carthage.——I
was, however, half broiled in the sun, and overjoyed
to be led into one of the subterranean apartments,
which they called "The stables of the elephants,"
but which I cannot believe were ever designed for
that use. I found in them many broken pieces of
columns of fine marble, and some of porphyry. I
cannot think any body would take the insignificant
pains of carrying them thither, and I cannot imagine such fine pillars were designed for the use of
stables. I am apt to believe they were summer
apartments under their palaces, which the heat of
the climate rendered necessary: they are now used
as granaries by the country people. While I sat
here, from the town of *Tents,* not far off, many of
the women flocked in to see me, and we were
equally entertained with viewing one another.
Their posture in sitting, the colour of their skin,
their lank black hair falling on each side their faces,
their features, and the shape of their limbs, differ
so little from their country people, the baboons, it
is hard to fancy them a distant race; I could not
help thinking there had been some ancient alliances
between them.

When I was a little refreshed by rest, and some
milk and exquisite fruit they brought me, I went
up the little hill where once stood the castle of
Byrsa, and from thence I had a distinct view of the
situation of the famous city of Carthage, which
stood on an isthmus, the sea coming on each side
of it. It is now a marshy ground on one side,

where there are salt ponds.   Strabo calls Carthage
forty miles in circumference.   There are now no
remains of it, but what I have described ; and the
history of it is too well known to want my abridg-
ment of it.   You see, sir, that I think you esteem
obedience better than compliments.   I have answered your letter, by giving you the accounts you
desired, and have reserved my thanks to the conclusion.   I intend to leave this place to-morrow,
and continue my journey through Italy and France.
In one of those places I hope to tell you, by word
of mouth, that I am,

Your humble servant, &c. &c.

L.

TO THE COUNTESS OF MAR.

Genoa, Aug. 28, 1718.

I BEG your pardon, my dear sister, that I did not
write to you from Tunis, the only opportunity I
have had since I left Constantinople. But the heat
there was so excessive, and the light so bad for the
sight, I was half blind by writing one letter to the
Abbot ——, and durst not go to write many others
I had designed ; nor, indeed, could I have entertained you very well out of that barbarous country.
I am now surrounded with subjects of pleasure,
and so much charmed with the beauties of Italy,
that I should think it a kind of ingratitude not to
offer a little praise in return for the diversion I have

had here. I am in the house of Mrs. d'Avenant,
at St. Pierre d'Arena, and should be very unjust
not to allow her a share of that praise I speak of,
since her good humour and good company have
very much contributed to render this place agreeable to me.

Genoa is situated in a very fine bay ; and being
built on a rising hill, intermixed with gardens, and
beautified with the most excellent architecture,
gives a very fine prospect off at sea ; though it lost
much of its beauty in my eyes, having become accustomed to that of Constantinople. The Genoese were
once masters of several islands in the Archipelago,
and all that part of Constantinople which is now
called Galata. Their betraying the Christian
cause, by facilitating the taking of Constantinople
by the Turks, deserved what has since happened to
them, even the loss of all their conquests on that
side to those infidels. They are at present far from
rich, and are despised by the French, since their
doge was forced by the late king to go in person to
Paris, to ask pardon for such a trifle as the arms of
France over the house of the envoy being spattered
with dung in the night. This, I suppose, was done
by some of the Spanish faction, which still makes
up the majority here, though they dare not openly
declare it. The ladies affect the French habit, and
are more genteel than those they imitate. I do not
doubt but the custom of cecisbeos has very much
improved their airs. I know not whether you ever
heard of those animals. Upon my word, nothing
but my own eyes could have convinced me there

were any such upon earth. The fashion began
here, and is now received all over Italy, where the
husbands are not such terrible creatures as we represent them. There are none among them such
brutes as to pretend to find fault with a custom so
well established, and so politically founded, since
I am assured that it was an expedient first found
out by the senate, to put an end to those family
hatreds which tore their state to pieces, and to
find employment for those young men who were
forced to cut one another's throats *pour passer le
temps;* and it has succeeded so well, that, since the
institution of cecisbei, there has been nothing but
peace and good humour among them. These are
gentlemen who devote themselves to the service of
a particular lady : (I mean a married one, for the
virgins are all invisible, and confined to convents :)
they are obliged to wait on her to all public places,
such as the plays, operas, and assemblies (which
are here called *conversations,*) where they wait behind her chair, take care of her fan and gloves if
she play, have the privilege of whispers, &c. When
she goes out, they serve her instead of lacqueys,
gravely trotting by her chair. It is their business
to prepare for her a present against any day of public appearance, not forgetting that of her own
name : ([131]) in short, they are to spend all their
time and money in her service, who rewards them
accordingly (for opportunity they want none ;) but
the husband is not to have the impudence to sup-

([131]) This is, the day of the saint after whom she is called.

pose this any other than pure Platonic friendship.
It is true, they endeavour to give her a cecisbeo of
their own choosing ; but when the lady happens
not to be of the same taste, as that often happens,
she never fails to bring it about to have one of her
own fancy.   In former times, one beauty used to
have eight or ten of these humble admirers ; but
those days of plenty and humility are no more :
men grow more scarce and saucy; and every lady
is forced to content herself with one at a time.

You may see in this place the *glorious liberty* of
a republic, or, more properly an aristocracy, the
common people being here as errant slaves as the
French : but the old nobles pay little respect to
the doge, who is but two years in his office, and
whose wife, at that very time, assumes no rank
above another noble lady.   It is true, the family of
Andrea Doria (that great man, who restored them
that liberty they enjoy) have some particular privileges :   when the senate found it necessary to
put a stop to the luxury of dress, forbidding the
wearing of jewels and brocades, they left them at
liberty to make what expense they pleased.   I look
with great pleasure on the statue of that hero, which
is in the court belonging to the house of Duke
Doria.   This puts me in mind of their palaces,
which I can never describe as I ought.   Is it not
enough that I say they are, most of them, the design of Palladio ?   The street called Strada Nova is
perhaps the most beautiful line of building in the
world.   I must particularly mention the vast palaces of Durazzo ; those of the two Balbi, joined

together by a magnificent colonade : that of the
Imperiale at this village of St. Pierre d'Arena ; and
another of the Doria. The perfection of architecture, and the utmost profusion of rich furniture, are
to be seen here disposed with the most elegant taste
and lavish magnificence. But I am charmed with
nothing so much as the collection of pictures by
the pencils of Raphael, Paulo Veronese, Titian,
Caracci, Michael Angelo, Guido, and Corregio,
which two I mention last as my particular favourites. I own I can find no pleasure in objects of
horror; and, in my opinion, the more naturally a
crucifix is represented, the more disagreeable it is.
These, my beloved painters, show nature, and show
it in the most charming light. I was particularly
pleased with a Lucretia in the house of Balbi : the
expressive beauty of that face and bosom, gives
all the passion of pity and admiration that could
be raised in the soul by the finest poem on that
subject. A Cleopatra of the same hand deserves
to be mentioned ; and I should say more of her, if
Lucretia had not first engaged my eyes. Here are
also some inestimable ancient bustos. The church
of St. Lawrence is built of black and white marble,
where is kept that famous plate of a single emerald, which is not now permitted to be handled,
since a plot, which they say was discovered, to
throw it on the pavement and break it—a child-
ish piece of malice, which they ascribe to the King
of Sicily, to be revenged for their refusing to sell it
to him. The church of the Annunciation is finely

lined with marble, the pillars are of red and white
marble ; that of St. Ambrose has been very much
adorned by the Jesuits ; but I confess, all the
churches appeared so mean to me, after that of
Sancta Sophia, I can hardly do them the honour
of writing down their names.—But I hope you
will own I have made good use of my time, in seeing so much, since it is not many days that we
have been out of the quarantine, from which nobody is exempted coming from the Levant.   Ours,
indeed, was very much shortened, and very agreeably passed in M. d'Avenant's company, in the
village of St. Pierre d'Arena, about a mile from
Genoa, in a house built by Palladio, so well designed, and so nobly proportioned, it was a pleasure to walk in it.   We were visited here only by
a few English in the company of a noble Genoese,
commissioned to see we did not touch one another.
I shall stay here some days longer, and could almost wish it were for all my life ; but mine, I fear,
is not destined to so much tranquillity.

I am &c. &c.

LI.

TO THE COUNTESS OF BRISTOL.

Turin, Sept. 12, 1718.

I came in two days from Genoa, through fine roads,
to this place.   I have already seen what is shown
to strangers in the town, which, indeed, is not

s

worth a very particular description : and I have
not respect enough for the holy handkerchief to
speak long of it. The churches are handsome, and
so is the king's palace; but I have lately seen
such perfection of architecture, I did not give much
of my attention to these pieces. The town itself is
fairly built, situated in a fine plain on the banks of
the Po. At a little distance from it, we saw the
palaces of La Venerie and La Valentin, both very
agreeable retreats. We were lodged in the Piazza
Royale, which is one of the noblest squares I ever
saw, with a fine portico of white stone quite round
it. We were immediately visited by the Chevalier
——, whom you knew in England; who, with great
civility, begged to introduce us at court, which is
now kept at Rivoli, about a league from Turin. I
went thither yesterday, and had the honour of waiting on the queen, being presented to her by her
first lady of honour. I found her majesty in a
magnificent apartment, with a train of handsome
ladies, all dressed in gowns, among whom it was
easy to distinguish the fair princess of Carignan.
The queen entertained me with a world of sweetness and affability, and seemed mistress of a great
share of good sense. She did not forget to put me
in mind of her English blood, and added, that she
always felt in herself a particular inclination to love
the English. I returned her civility, by giving her
the title of majesty as often as I could, which, perhaps, she will not have the comfort of hearing many
months longer. The king has a great deal of vivacity in his eyes; and the young Prince of Pied-

mont is a very handsome young man; but the
great devotion which this court is at present fallen
into does not permit any of those entertainments
proper for his age.   Processions and masses are all
the magnificence in fashion here; and gallantry is
so criminal, that the poor Count of ——, who was
our acquaintance at London, is very seriously dis-
graced, for some small overtures he presumed to
make to a maid of honour.   I intend to set out to-
morrow, and to pass those dreadful Alps, so much
talked of.   If I come to the bottom you shall hear
of me.

I am, &c. &c.

LII.

TO MRS. THISTLETHWAYTE.

Lyons, Sept. 25, 1718.

I RECEIVED, at my arrival here, both your obliging
letters, and also letters from many of my other
friends, designed to Constantinople, and sent me
from Marseilles hither ; our merchant there knowing we were upon our return.   I am surprised to hear
my sister Mar has left England.   I suppose what I
wrote to her from Turin will be lost, and where to
direct I know not, having no account of her affairs
from her own hand.   For my own part, I am confined to my chamber, having kept my bed, till yesterday, ever since the 17th, that I came to this town;
where I have had so terrible a fever, I believed for

s 2

some time that all my journeys were ended here; and I do not at all wonder that such fatigues as I have passed should have such an effect. This first day's journey, from Turin to Novalesse, is through a very fine country, beautifully planted, and enriched by art and nature. The next day we began to ascend mount Cenis, being carried in little seats of twisted osiers, fixed upon poles, upon men's shoulders; our chaises taken to pieces, and laid upon mules.

The prodigious prospect of mountains covered with eternal snow, of clouds hanging far below our feet, and of vast cascades tumbling down the rocks with a confused roaring, would have been entertaining to me, if I had suffered less from the extreme cold that reigns here: but the misty rains, which fall perpetually, penetrated even the thick fur I was wrapped in; and I was half dead with cold before we got to the foot of the mountain, which was not till two hours after dark. This hill has a spacious plain on the top of it, and a fine lake there; but the decent is so steep and slippery, it is surprising to see these chairman go so steadily as they do. Yet I was not half so much afraid of breaking my neck as I was of falling sick; and the event has shown that I placed my fears right.

The other mountains are now all passable for a chaise, and very fruitful in vines and pastures: among them is a breed of the finest goats in the world. Acquebellet is the last; and soon after we entered Pont Beauvoisin, the frontier town of France, whose bridge parts this kingdom and the dominions of Savoy. The same night we arrived late at this town, where I have had nothing to do but to take care of my health. I think myself already out of danger, and am determined that the sore throat, which still remains, shall not confine me long. I am impatient to see the curiosities of this famous city, and more impatient to continue my journey to Paris, from whence I hope to write you a more diverting letter than it is possible for me to do now, with a mind weakened by sickness, a head muddled with spleen, from a sorry inn, and a chamber crammed with mortifying objects of apothecaries' vials and bottles.

I am, &c. &c.

LIII.

TO MR. POPE.

Lyons, Sept. 28, 1718.

I RECEIVED yours here, and should thank you for the pleasure you seem to enjoy from my return; but I can hardly forbear being angry at you for rejoicing at what displeases me so much. You will think this but an odd compliment on my side. I will assure you it is not from insensibility of the joy of seeing my friends; but when I consider that I must at the same time see and hear a thousand disagreeable impertinents, that I must receive and, pay visits, make curtsies, and, assist at tea-tables, where I shall be half killed with questions; and

on the other part, that I am a creature that cannot
serve any body but with insignificant good wishes;
and that my presence is not a necessary good to
any one member of my native country, I think
I might much better have staid where ease and
quiet made up the happiness of my indolent
life. I should certainly be melancholy if I pursued this theme one line further. I will rather fill
the remainder of this paper with the inscriptions on
the tables of brass that are placed on each side of
the town-house.

I. TABLE.

Mærorum. nostr. : : : sii : : : equidem. primam.
omnium. illam. cogitationem. hominum. quam.
maxime. primam. occursuram. mihi. provideo. de-
precor. ne. quasi. novam. istam. rem. introduci. ex-
horrescatis. sed. illa. potius. cogitetis. quam. multa.
in. hac. civitate. novata. sint. et. quidem. statim. ab.
origine. urbis. nostræ. in. quod. formas. statusque.
res. p. nostra. diducta. sit.

Quondam. reges. hanc. tenuere. urbem. ne. ta-
men. domesticis. successoribus. eam. tradere. conti-
git. supervenere. alieni. et. quidam. externi. ut.
Numa. Romulo. successerit. ex. Sabinis. veniens.
vicinus. quidem. sed. tunc. externus. ut. Anco.
Marcio. Priscus. Tarquinius. propter. temeratum.
sanguinem. quod. patre. de. marato. Corinthio. natus. erat. et. Tarquiniensi. matre. generosa. sed.
inopi. ut. quæ. tali. marito. necesse. habuerit. suc-
cumbere. cum. domi. repelleretur. a. gerendis. ho-

noribus. postquam. Romam. migravit. regnum.
adeptus. est. huic. quoque. et. filio. nepotive. ejus.
nam. et. hoc. inter. auctores. discrepat. incretus.
Servius. Tullius. si. nostros. sequimur. captiva.
natus. Ocresia. si. Tuscos. coeli. quondam. Viven-
næ. sodalis. fidelissimus. omnisque. ejus. casus.
comes. postquam. varia. fortuna. exactus. cum.
omnibus. reliquis. coeliani. exercitus. Etruria.
excessit. montem. Coelium. occupavit. et. a. duce.
suo. coelio. ita. appellitatus. mutatoque. nomine.
nam. Tusce. Mastarna. ei. nomen. erat. ita. appellatus. est. ut. dixi. et. regnum. summa. cum. reip.
utilitate. obtinuit. deinde. postquam. Tarquini.
Superbi. mores. invisi. civitati. nostræ. esse. coepe-
runt. qua. ipsius. qua. filiorum. ejus. nempe. per-
tæsum. est. mentes. regni. et. ad. consules. annuos.
magistratus. administratio. reip. translata. est.

Quid. nunc. commemorem. dictaturæ. hoc. ipso.
consulari. imperium. valentius. repertum. apud.
majores. nostros. quo. in. asperioribus. bellis. aut.
in. civili. motu. difficiliori. uterentur. aut. in. aux-
ilium. plebis. creatos. tribunos. plebei. quid. a.
consulibus. ad. decemviros. translatum. imperium.
solutoque. postea. decemvirali. regno. ad. consules.
rursus. reditum. quod. im. : : : : : v. ris. distribu-
tum. consulare. imperium. tribunosque. militum.
consulari. imperio. appellatus. qui. seni. et. octoni.
crearentur. quid. communicatos. postremo. cum.
plebe. honores. non. imperi. solum. sed. sacerdo-
torum. quoque. jamsi. narrem. bella. a. quibus.
coeperint. majores. nostri. et. quo. processerimus.
vereor. ne. nimio. insolentior. esse. videar. et. quæ-

sisse. jactationem. gloriæ. prolati. imperi. ultra. oceanum. sed. illo. C. Porius. revertar. civitatem.

II. TABLE.

: : : : : : : : : : : : : sane : : : : : : : : : : : :
: : : : : : novo : : : divus : Aug : : : no : lus.
et. patruus. Ti. Cæsar. omnem. florem. ubique. coloniarum. ac. municipiorum. bonorum. scilicet. virorum. et. locupletium. in. hac. curia. esse. voluit. quid. ergo. non. Italicus. senator. provinciali. potior. est. jam. vobis. cum. hanc. partem. censuræ. meæ. approbare. coepero. quid. de. ea. re. sentiam. rebus. ostendam. sed. ne. provinciales. quidem. si. modo. ornare. curiam. poterint. rejiciendos. puto.

Ornatissima. ecce. colonia. valentissimaque. Riennensium. quam. longo. jam. tempore. senatores. huic. curiæ. confert. ex. qua. colonia. inter. paucos. equestris. ordinis. ornamentum. L. Restinum. familiarissime. diligo. et. hodieque. in. rebus. meis. detineo. cujus. liberi. fruantur. quæso. primo. sacerdotiorum. gradu. post. modo. cum. annis. promoturi. dignitatis. suæ. incrementa. ut. dirum. nomen. latronis. taceam. et. odi. illud. palestricum. prodiguum. quod. ante. in. domum. consulatum. intulit. quam. colonia. sua. solidum. civitatis. Romanæ. beneficium. consecuta. est. idem. de. fratre. ejus. possum. dicere. miserabili. quidem. indignissimoque. hoc. casu. ut. vobis. utilis. senator. esse. non. possit.

Tempus. est. jam. Ti. Cæsar. Germanice. detegere. te. Patribus. Conscriptis. quo. tendat. oratio.

tua. jam. enim. ad. extremos. fines. Galliæ. Narbonensis. venisti.

Tot. ecce. insignes. juvenes. quot. intueor. non.
magis. sunt. poenitendi. senatorib. quam. poenitet.
Persicum. nobilissimum. virum. amicum. meum.
inter. imagines. majorum. suorum. Allorogici.
nomen. legere. quod. si. hæc. ita. esse. consenti. is.
quid. ultra. desideratis. quam. ut. vobis. digito.
demonstrem. solum. ipsum. ultra. fines. provinciæ.
Narbonensis. jam. vobis. senatores. mittere. quando. ex. Lugduno. habere. nos. nostri. ordinis. viros.
non. poenitet. timide. quidem. P. C. egressus. ad-
suetos. familiaresque. vobis. provinciarum. termi-
nos. sum. sed. destricte. jam. Comatæ. Galliæ.
causa. agenda. est. in. qua. si. quis. hoc. intue-
tur. quod. bello. per. decem. annos. exercuerunt.
Divom. Julium. idem. opponat. centum. annorum.
immobilem. fidem. obsequiumque. multis. tripidis.
rebus. nostris. plusquam. expertum. illi. patri. meo.
Druso. Germaniam. subigenti. tutam. quiete. sua.
securamque. a. tergo. pacem. præstiterunt. et. quidem. cum. ad. census. novo. tum. opere. et. in.
adsueto. Galliis. ad. bellum. avocatus. esset. quod.
opus. quam. arduum. sit. nobis. nunc. cum. maxime. quamvis. nihil. ultra. quam. ut. publice. notæ.
sint. facultates. nostræ. exquiratur. nimis. magno.
experimento. cognoscimus.

I was also shown, without the gate of St. Justi-
nus, some remains of a Roman aqueduct; and behind the monastery of St. Mary there are the ruins
of the imperial palace where the Emperor Claudius

was born, and where Severus lived. The great
cathedral of St. John is a good Gothic building,
and its clock much admired by the Germans. In
one of the most conspicuous parts of the town is
the late king's statue set up, trampling upon mankind. I cannot forbear saying one word here of
the French statues (for I never intend to mention
any more of them) with their gilded full-bottomed
wigs. If their king had intended to express in one
image, *ignorance, ill-taste,* and *vanity,* his sculptors
could have made no other figure so proper for that
purpose as this statue, which represents the odd
mixture of an old beau, who had a mind to be a
hero, with a bushel of curled hair on his head, and
a gilt truncheon in his hand. The French have
been so voluminous on the history of this town, I
need say nothing of it. The houses are tolerably
well built, and the Belle Cour well planted, from
whence is seen the celebrated joining of the Saone
and Rhone,

> " Ubi Rhodanus ingens amne præapido fluit,
>   Ararque dubitans quo suos fluctus agat."

I have had time to see every thing with great leisure, having been confined several days to this
town by a swelling in my throat, the remains of a
fever, occasioned by a cold I got in the damps of the
Alps. The doctors here threaten me with all sorts
of distempers, if I dare to leave them ; but I, that
know the obstinacy of it, think it just as possible
to continue my way to Paris with it, as to go about
the streets of Lyons; and am determined to pursue

my journey to-morrow, in spite of doctors, apothecaries, and sore throats.

When you see Lady Rich, tell her I have received her letter, and will answer it from Paris,
believing that the place that she would most willingly hear of.

I am, &c. &c.

LIV.

TO THE LADY RICH.

Paris, Oct. 10, 1718.

I CANNOT give my dear Lady Rich a better proof
of the pleasure I have in writing to her, than
choosing to do it in this seat of various amusements, where I am *accabléed* with visits, and those
so full of vivacity and compliments, that it is
full employment enough to hearken, whether one
answers or not. The French ambassadress at
Constantinople has a very considerable and numerous family here, who all come to see me, and are
never weary of making inquiries. The air of Paris
has already had a good effect upon me; for I was
never in better health, though I have been extremely ill all the road from Lyons to this place.
You may judge how agreeable the journey has
been to me; which did not want that addition to
make me dislike it. I think nothing so terrible as
objects of misery, except one had the godlike attribute of being capable to redress them; and all

the country villages of France show nothing else.
While the post-horses are changed, the whole
town comes out to beg, with such miserable starved
faces, and thin tattered clothes, they need no other
eloquence to persuade one of the wretchedness of
their condition. This is all the French magnificence till you come to Fontainbleau, when you
are showed one thousand five hundred rooms in
the king's hunting-palace. The apartments of the
royal family are very large, and richly gilt; but I
saw nothing in the architecture or painting worth
remembering. The long gallery, built by Henry
IV., has prospects of all the king's houses. Its
walls are designed after the taste of those times,
but appear now very mean. The park is, indeed,
finely wooded and watered, the trees well grown
and planted, and in the fish-ponds are kept tame
carp, said to be, some of them, eighty years of age.
The late king passed some months every year at
this seat : and all the rocks round it, by the pious
sentences inscribed on them, show the devotion in
fashion at his court, which I believe died with
him ; at least, I see no exterior marks of it at
Paris, where all people's thoughts seem to be on
present diversion.

The fair of St. Lawrence is now in season. You
may be sure I have been carried thither, and think
it much better disposed than ours of Bartholomew.
The shops being all set in rows so regularly and
well lighted, they made up a very agreeable spectacle. But I was not at all satisfied with the
grossierté of their harlequin, no more than with

their music at the opera, which was abominably
grating, after being used to that of Italy. Their
house is a booth, compared to that of the Haymarket, and the play-house not so neat as that of
Lincoln's-inn-fields; but then it must be owned,
to their praise, their tragedians are much beyond
any of ours. I should hardly allow Mrs. O——d
a better place than to be confidante to La——. I
have seen the tragedy of Bajazet so well represented, that I think our best actors can be only
said to speak, but these to feel, and it is certainly
infinitely more moving to see a man appear unhappy, than to hear him say that he is so, with a
jolly face, and a stupid smirk in his countenance.
—*A-propos* of countenances, I must tell you something of the French ladies; I have seen all the
beauties, and such —— (I cannot help making use
of the coarse word) nauseous creatures! so fantasti-
cally absurd in their dress! so monstrously unnatural in their paints; their hair cut short, and
curled round their faces, and so loaded with powder
that it makes it look like white wool! and on their
cheeks to their chins, unmercifully laid on a shining red japan, that glistens in a most flaming
manner, so that they seem to have no resemblance
to human faces. I am apt to believe that they
took the first hint of their dress from a fair sheep
newly ruddled. It is with pleasure I recollect
my dear pretty countrywomen : and if I was
writing to any body else, I should say that these
grotesque daubers give me still a higher esteem of
the natural charms of dear Lady Rich's auburn

hair, and the lively colours of her unsullied complexion.

I am, &c. &c.

P. S. I have met the Abbé here, who desires me to make his compliments to you.

LV.

TO MR. T——.

Paris, Oct. 16, 1718.

You see I am just to my word, in writing to you from Paris, where I was very much surprised to meet my sister; I need not add, very much pleased. She as little expected to see me as I her; (having not received my late letters;) and this meeting would shine under the hand of De Scuderie; but I shall not imitate his style so far as to tell you how often we embraced; how she inquired by what odd chance I returned from Constantinople? And I answered her by asking what adventure brought her to Paris? To shorten the story, all questions and answers, and exclamations and compliments being over, we agreed upon running about together, and have seen Versailles, Trianon, Marli, and St. Cloud. We had an order for the water to play for our diversion, and I was followed thither by all the English at Paris. I own Versailles appeared to me rather vast than beautiful; and after having seen the exact proportions of the

Italian buildings, I thought the irregularity of it shocking.

The king's cabinet of antiques and medals is, indeed, very richly furnished. Among that collection none pleased me so well as the apotheosis of Germanicus, on a large agate, which is one of the most delicate pieces of the kind that I remember to have seen. I observed some ancient statues of great value. But the nauseous flattery, and tawdry pencil of Le Brun, are equally disgusting in the gallery. I will not pretend to describe to you the great apartment, the vast variety of fountains, the theatre, the grove of Æsop's fables, &c., all which you may read very amply particularized in some of the French authors that have been paid for these descriptions. Trianon, in its littleness, pleased me better than Versailles : Marli better than either of them ; and St. Cloud best of all ; having the advantage of the Seine running at the bottom of the gardens, the great cascade, &c. You may find information in the aforesaid books, if you have any curiosity to know the exact number of the statues, and how many feet they cast up the water.

We saw the king's pictures in the magnificent house of the Duke d'Antin, who has the care of preserving them till his majesty is of age. There are not many, but of the best hands. I looked with great pleasure on the archangel of Raphael, where the sentiments of superior beings are as well expressed as in Milton. You will not forgive me if I say nothing of the Tuileries, much finer than our

Mall; and the Cour, more agreeable than our Hyde-park, the high trees giving shade in the hottest season. At the Louvre I had the opportunity of seeing the king, accompanied by the duke regent. He is tall and well shaped, but has not the air of holding the crown so many years as his grandfather. And now I am speaking of the court, I must say I saw nothing in France that delighted me so much as to see an Englishman (at least a Briton) absolute at Paris; I mean Mr. Law,([132]) who treats their dukes and peers extremely *de haut en bas,* and is treated by them with the utmost submission and respect.— Poor souls!—this reflection on their abject slavery puts me in mind of the *place des victoires;* but I will not take up your time and my own with such descriptions, which are too numerous.

In general I think Paris has the advantage of London, in the neat pavement of the streets, and the regular lighting of them at nights, and in the proportion of the streets, the houses being all built of stone, and most of those belonging to people of quality, being beautified by gardens. But we certainly may boast of a town very near twice as large; and when I have said that, I know nothing else we surpass it in. I shall not continue here long; if you have any thing to command me during my short stay, write soon, and I shall take pleasure in obeying you.

I am, &c. &c.

([132]) Mr. Law was the projector of the Mississippi scheme and the colonization of Louisiana, similar in its plan and event to our South Sea bubble.

LVI.

TO THE ABBOT ———.

Dover, Oct. 31, 1718.

I AM willing to take your word for it, that I shall really oblige you, by letting you know, as soon as possible, my safe passage over the water. I arrived this morning at Dover, after being tossed a whole night in the packet-boat, in so violent a manner, that the master, considering the weakness of his vessel, thought it proper to remove the mail, and give us notice of the danger. We called a little fishing-boat, which could hardly make up to us; while all the people on board us were crying to heaven. It is hard to imagine one's self in a scene of greater horror than on such an occasion; and yet, shall I own it to you? though I was not at all willing to be drowned, I could not forbear being entertained at the double distress of a fellow-passenger. She was an English lady that I had met at Calais, who desired me to let her go over with me in my cabin. She had bought a fine point-head, which she was contriving to conceal from the custom-house officers. When the wind grew high, and our little vessel cracked, she fell very heartily to her prayers, and thought wholly of her soul. When it seemed to abate, she returned to the worldly care of her head-dress, and addressed herself to me——— "Dear madam, will you take care of this point? if it should be lost!—Ah, Lord, we shall all be lost!—

T

Lord have mercy on my soul!—Pray, madam, take care of this head-dress." This easy transition from her soul to her head-dress, and the alternate agonies that both gave her, made it hard to determine which she thought of greatest value. But, however, the scene was not so diverting, but I was glad to get rid of it, and be thrown into the little boat, though with some hazard of breaking my neck. It brought me safe hither; and I cannot help looking with partial eyes on my native land. That partiality was certainly given us by nature, to prevent rambling, the effect of an ambitious thirst after knowledge, which we are not formed to enjoy. All we get by it is a fruitless desire of mixing the different pleasures and conveniences which are given to the different parts of the world, and cannot meet in any one of them. After having read all that is to be found in the languages I am mistress of, and having decayed my sight by midnight studies, I envy the easy peace of mind of a ruddy milk-maid, who undisturbed by doubt, hears the sermon with humility, every Sunday, not having confounded the sentiments of natural duty in her head by the vain inquiries of the schools who may be more learned, yet after all, must remain as ignorant. And, after having seen part of Asia and Africa, and almost made the tour of Europe, I think the honest English squire more happy, who verily believes the Greek wines less delicious than March beer; that the African fruits have not so fine a flavour as golden-pippins; that he beca-figuas of Italy are not so well tasted as a rump of beef; and that, in short, there is no per-

fect enjoyment of this life out of Old England. I
pray God I may think so for the rest of my life;
and since I must be contented with our scanty al-
lowance of day-light, that I may forget the enliven-
ing sun of Constantinople.

I am, &c. &c.

LVII.

TO LADY MONTAGU.

MADAM,

MY LORD says, in reading your most ingenious descriptions, he observed that your ladyship had the
art of making common circumstances agreeable;
as the lady's care of her lace in the storm, &c.
You have also made learned things instructive, as
the copy of the Greek inscription, the which my
lord desires that your ladyship will be pleased to
send him again by the bearer, that he may better
understand it than by one he has: care will be
taken to return it safe again. Though this is my
lord's letter, yet I must beg leave to add to it that
I am, with unfeigned esteem,

Your ladyship's
Most obedient humble servant,
MARY PEMBROKE.([133])

([133]) Mary Howe, sister of Scrope, Lord Viscount Howe,
lady of the bedchamber to Queen Caroline, was the third wife
of Thomas Earl of Pembroke.—ED.

LVIII.

TO LADY MONTAGU.

MADAM.

MY Lord Pembroke agrees with your ladyship, that it is a great surprise to him to know you are the person that copied the inscription, but at the same time desires I will assure you that it is the most agreeable one he ever met with; and if you will give him leave, with the utmost pleasure, will wait on you this evening, between six and seven o'clock; and though I know nothing of inscriptions, yet I cannot deny myself the satisfaction of going with him to the most agreeable conversation in the world, there being no one more sensible of your merit,

Than your ladyship's
Most obedient humble servant,
MARY PEMBROKE.

LIX.

MR. POPE TO LADY MONTAGU.

MADAM,   September 1.

I HAVE been (what I never was till now) in debt to you for a letter some weeks. I was informed you were at sea, and that it was to no purpose to write till some news had been heard of your arriving somewhere or other. Besides I have had a second dangerous illness, from which I was more diligent to be recovered than from the first, having now some hopes of seeing you again. If you make any tour in Italy, I shall not easily forgive you for not acquainting me soon enough to have met you there. I am very certain I can never be polite unless I travel with you: and it is never to be repaired, the loss that Homer has sustained for want of my translating him in Asia. You will come hither full of criticisms against a man who wanted nothing to be in the right but to have kept you company; you have no way of making me amends, but by continuing an Asiatic when you return to me, whatever English airs you may put on to other people.

I prodigiously long for your sonnets, your remarks, your oriental learning;—but I long for nothing so much as your oriental self. You must of necessity be *advanced* so far *back* into true nature and simplicity of manners, by these three years residence in the East, that I shall look upon you as so many years younger than you were, so much nearer innocence (that is truth) and infancy (that is openness.) I expect to see your soul as much thinner dressed as your body; and that you have left off as unwieldly and cumbersome, a great many European habits. Without offence to your modesty be it spoken, I have a burning desire to see your soul stark naked, for I am confident it is the prettiest kind of white soul in the universe. But I forget whom I am talking to; you may pos-

sibly by this time believe, according to the prophet,
that you have none; if so, show me that which
comes next to a soul; you may easily put it upon
a poor ignorant Christian for a soul, and please him
as well with it;—I mean your heart;—Mahomet, I
think, allows you hearts; which (together with fine
eyes and other agreeable equivalents) are worth all
the souls on this side the world. But if I must be
content with seeing your body only, God send it to
come quickly : I honour it more than the diamond
casket that held Homer's Iliads; for in the very
twinkle of one eye of it there is more wit, and in the
very dimple of one cheek of it there is more meaning,
than all the souls that ever were casually put into
women since men had the making of them.

I have a mind to fill the rest of this paper with
an accident that happened just under my eyes, and
has made a great impression upon me. I have
just passed part of this summer at an old romantic
seat of my Lord Harcourt's, which he lent me. It
overlooks a common field, where, under the shade
of a haycock, sat two lovers, as constant as ever
were found in romance, beneath a spreading beech.
The name of the one (let it sound as it will) was
John Hewet, of the other Sarah Drew. John was
a well-set man of about five-and-twenty, Sarah a
brown woman of eighteen. John had for several
months borne the labour of the day in the same
field with Sarah ; when she milked, it was his morning and evening charge to bring the cows to her
pail. Their love was the talk, but not the scandal
of the whole neighbourhood ; for all they aimed at

was the blameless possession of each other in marriage. It was but this very morning that he had
obtained her parents' consent, and it was but till
the next week that they were to wait to be happy.
Perhaps this very day, in the intervals of their work,
they were talking of their wedding clothes; and
John was now matching several kinds of poppies
and field-flowers to her complexion, to make her a
present of knots for the day. While they were
thus employed, (it was on the last of July,) a
terrible storm of thunder and lightning arose, and
drove the labourers to what shelter the trees or
hedges afforded. Sarah, frighted and out of breath,
sunk on a haycock, and John (who never separated
from her) sat by her side, having raked two or three
heaps together to secure her. Immediately there
was heard so loud a crack as if heaven had burst
asunder. The labourers, all solicitous for each
other's safety, called to one another: those that
were nearest our lovers, hearing no answer, stepped
to the place where they lay : they first saw a little
smoke, and after, this faithful pair;—John, with one
arm about his Sarah's neck, and the other held over
her face, as if to screen her from the lightning.
They were struck dead, and already grown stiff and
cold in this tender posture. There was no mark or
discolouring on their bodies, only that Sarah's eye-
brow was a little singed, and a small spot between
her breasts. They were buried the next day in one
grave, in the parish of Stanton Harcourt, in Oxford-
shire; where my Lord Harcourt, at my request,
has erected a monument over them. Of the follow-

ing epitaphs which I made, the critics have chosen
the godly one: I like neither, but wish you had been
in England to have done this office better; I think
it was what you could not have refused me on so
moving an occasion.

When Eastern lovers feed the funeral fire,
On the same pile their faithful fair expire;
Here pitying Heav'n that virtue mutual found,
And blasted both that it might neither wound.
Hearts so sincere th' Almighty saw well pleased,
Sent his own lightning, and the victims seized.

1.

Think not, by rigorous judgment seized,
    A pair so faithful could expire;
Victims so pure Heav'n saw well pleased,
    And snatch'd them in celestial fire.

2.

Live well, and fear no sudden fate:
    When God calls virtue to the grave,
Alike 'tis justice, soon or late,
    Mercy alike to kill or save.
Virtue unmoved can hear the call,
And face the flash that melts the ball.

Upon the whole, I cannot think these people unhappy. The greatest happiness, next to living as
they would have done, was to die as they did. The
greatest honour people of this low degree could
have was to be remembered on a little monument;
unless you will give them another,—that of being
honoured with a tear from the finest eyes in the world.
I know you have tenderness; you must have it; it
is the very emanation of good sense and virtue; the

finest minds, like the finest metals, dissolve the easiest.

But when you are reflecting upon objects of pity, pray do not forget one who had no sooner found out an object of the highest esteem, than he was separated from it; and who is so very unhappy as not to be susceptible of consolation from others, by being so miserably in the right as to think other women what they really are. Such a one cannot but be desperately fond of any creature that is quite different from these. If the Circassian be utterly void of such honour as these have, and such virtue as these boast of, I am content. I have detested the sound of *honest woman,* and *loving spouse,* ever since I heard the pretty name of *Odalische.* Dear madam, I am for ever

Yours, &c.

My most humble services to Mr. Wortley. Pray let me hear from you soon, though I shall very soon write again. I am confident half our letters are lost.

LXI.

TO MR. POPE.

Dover, Nov. 1, 1718.

I HAVE this minute received a letter of yours, sent me from Paris. I believe and hope I shall very soon see both you and Mr. Congreve; but as I am here in an inn, where we stay to regulate our march to London, bag and baggage, I shall employ some of my leisure time in answering that part of yours that seems to require an answer.

I must applaud your good-nature, in supposing, that your pastoral lovers (vulgarly called haymakers) would have lived in everlasting joy and harmony, if the lightning had not interrupted their scheme of happiness. I see no reason to imagine that John Hewet and Sarah Drew were either wiser or more virtuous than their neighbours. That a well-set man of twenty-five should have a fancy to marry a brown woman of eighteen, is nothing marvellous; and I cannot help thinking, that had they married, their lives would have passed in the common track with their fellow parishoners. His endeavouring to shield her from the storm was a natural action, and what he would have certainly done for his horse, if he had been in the same situation. Neither am I of opinion, that their sudden death was a reward of their mutual virtue. You know the Jews were reproved for thinking a village destroyed by fire more wicked than those that had escaped the thunder. Time and chance happen to all men. Since you desire me to try my skill in an epitaph, I think the following lines perhaps more just, though not so poetical as yours.

> Here lie John Hewet and Sarah Drew;
> Perhaps you'll say, what's that to you?
> Believe me, friend, much may be said
> Of this poor couple that are dead.

On Sunday next they should have married;
But see how oddly things are carried!
On Thursday last it rained and lighten'd;
These tender lovers, sadly frighten'd,
Sheltered beneath the cocking hay,
In hopes to pass the time away;
But the bold thunder found them out,
(Commissioned for that end no doubt,)
And seizing on their trembling breath,
Consign'd them to the shades of death.
Who knows if 'twas not kindly done?
For had they seen the next year's sun,
A beaten wife and cuckold swain
Had jointly cursed the marriage chain;
Now they are happy in their doom,
For Pope has wrote upon their tomb.

I confess these sentiments are not altogether so heroic as yours; but I hope you will forgive them in favour of the two last lines. You see how much I esteem the honour you have done them; though I am not very impatient to have the same, and had rather continue to be your stupid *living* humble servant, than be *celebrated* by all the pens in Europe.

I would write to Congreve, but suppose you will read this to him, if he inquires after me.

THE END.

Joseph Rickerby, Printer, Sherbourn Lane.